Race and Class in American Society
Black, Chicano, Anglo

RACE AND CLASS IN AMERICAN SOCIETY

Black, Chicano, Anglo

by H. Edward Ransford

Schenkman Publishing Company, Inc.
Cambridge, Massachusetts

Copyright© 1977
Schenkman Publishing Company
3 Mt. Auburn Place
Cambridge, Massachusetts 02138

Library of Congress Catalog Card Number: 74-8474
Ransford, Edward
    Race and Class in American Society
Cambridge, Mass.   Schenkman Pub Co Inc

ISBN 87073-039-8 pbk
     87073-041-X cl

Printed in the United States of America

TABLE OF CONTENTS

Chapter One   Introduction   1

PART I   Concepts, Theory and
                   Demographic Profiles

Chapter Two   *Origins and Development*   7
                   of Racial Stratification
                   . . . From Origins to Stable
                   Systems of Stratification
                   . . . Paternalistic Racial
                   Stratification
                   . . . From Paternalistic to
                   Competitive Race Relations
                   . . . Internal Colonialism
                   . . . Racial Stratification
                   under Competitive Systems
                   . . . Class within a Caste
                   . . . Application of Paternalistic-
                   Competitive Model to Blacks,
                   Chicanos, and Native Americans
                   . . . Concluding note

Chapter Three   *The Interaction Between Race*   31
                   and Class in Contemporary
                   America
                   . . . Two Hierarchies
                   . . . Racial Ethnic Stratification
                   . . . Comparisons and Differences
                   Between the Social Class Order
                   and the Race-Ethnic Order
                   . . . The Lack of Research on Race-
                   Class Interaction

Chapter Four   *Three Models*   45
                    . . . An open Marketplace of Status
                    Configurations
                    . . The Minority Subcommunity
                    Perspective
                    . . . Ethclass
                    . . . Summary
                    . . . The Three Models and Prediction
Chapter Five   *Demographic Trends: The Rise of*   65
                    Black and Chicano Upper-Working
                    and Middle Classes
                    . . . Black Americans
                    . . . The Illusion of Collective
                    Progress
                    . . . Socioeconomic Characteristics
                    of Spanish Surname Persons in
                    California, Texas, Los Angeles
                    Metropolitan Area, and East
                    Los Angeles
                    . . . Summary and Discussion
Chapter Six   *Militance and the Perception*   89
                    of Discrimination: Comparisons
                    Between Blacks and Chicanos of
                    Different Classes
                    . . . The Black Middle Class:
                    Materialistic Bourgeoise Consumers
                    or Militant Activists?
                    . . . Social Class, Perceived Dis-
                    crimination and Protest Potential
                    among Mexican Americans
                    . . . Reactions to Police Force in a
                    Period Shortly After The East Los
                    Angeles Riot
                    . . . Mexican American Farmworkers
Chapter Seven   *Values, Power, Solidarity, and In-*   123
                    teraction: Empirical Explorations in
                    Race and Class
                    . . . Three Empirical Patterns

. . . Exploration No. 1 — Subjective
Powerlessness
. . . Exploration No. 2 — Values
. . . Exploration No. 3 — Stratum Solidarity
. . . Exploration No. 4 — Race Versus Class
in Friendship Choice

Chapter Eight   *Current Issues and Policy: Selected*   157
                  Review of Recent Race-Class Studies
                  . . . Race, Class, and Self Image Among
                  Black Young People
                  . . . Race, Class, and the Alleged Weak
                  Father Figure
                  . . . The Pile-up of Race Class Barriers
                  and Policy Research on Educational
                  Institutions

Chapter Nine   *The White Working Class*   179
                  . . . "Blue Collar Anger," A Recent
                  Study of the White Working Class
                  . . . White Ethnicity and the Blue Collar
                  Situation

Selected Bibliography   195

Chapter 1

INTRODUCTION

A major goal of this book is to explore the interrelationships between the social class hierarchy in the United States and a racial hierarchy consisting of the white majority and the conquered minorities — blacks, Mexican Americans, and American Indians. The motivation to write this book stemmed from what I perceived to be major shortcomings in the sociology of racial stratification:

(1) Despite apparent continued poverty and oppression in the ghettos and barrios, in the last twenty years, a fairly sizeable proportion of blacks and Mexican Americans have moved into skilled and white-collar positions. Even so, much of the social science literature continues to treat blacks and Chicanos as uniformly poor and unskilled. Little is known about the outlooks, values, and unique battles against discrimination fought by Chicanos and blacks in skilled and white-collar positions. Moreover, there are few explanatory models to deal with these mobile populations. Often the literature falls back on the old assumption that the middle class segment of any minority group detaches itself from ethnic identification and becomes an undifferentiated part of the white middle class. However, with the ethnic identity movements of the last decade (represented by such slogans as "Black is Beautiful," "Black Power," "La Raza" and "Brown Power") the acculturation-assimilation assumption seems totally unjustified. Currently, many middle-class blacks and Mexican Americans are expressing a strong sense of ethnic identification. Some evidence suggests that younger blacks and Chicanos recently graduated from or presently enrolled in colleges and universities have an extremely intense ethnic consciousness and a strong commitment to collective progress for their groups. Sociologists simply have not developed an explanatory model to handle the simultaneous trends of upward mobility and increased ethnic identification among America's conquered racial minorities.

(2) A second problem area to be addressed is the tendency to view the stratification of minority populations only in the contexts of encap-

1

sulated ghettos or barrios. Skilled and white-collar minority persons are seen as relatively high in position, but only within their own ethnic or racial categories. Thus, middle-class blacks are viewed as persons of relatively high class *within a caste*. The assumption seems to be that no matter how high the socioeconomic achievement of a black, his "blackness" is a more important factor in social differentiation than his occupation or his income. Although this class-within-a-caste model was extremely important for explaining race relations in the rural South in the 1940s, it is not sufficient to explain contemporary race relations.

This book will attempt to break out of this traditional caste perspective and to note the effects of upward mobility on the rising skilled black and Chicano populations in the larger society. Many of these persons are employed in the predominantly "Anglo" occupational structure as foremen, machinists, parole officers, and teachers, rather than in separate ghetto structures. They are interacting in a more open status marketplace than a caste perspective would suggest.

The existence of this new mobility raises important questions about the relationships of these minority groups with the white power structure. To what extent does class achievement override racial restrictions? If a black person moves into a professional position does his increased power erode racial barriers or do many restrictions remain? As blacks move into positions of authority and power in formal organizations, to what extent are traditional role relationships with whites affected? How do whites react to the upward mobility of blacks and Chicanos?

(3) A third problem on which this book will focus is that many of the theories and generalizations in racial stratification are extremely out-of-date. Many generalizations have been made in the past about the black middle class, theories which have not been reexamined in recent years. Classic accounts (some published as late as the mid-1960s) assume that this class is striving to be white and politically conservative, strongly rejecting the lower class blacks. It is time that we reviewed such generalizations with current data that take into account the civil rights movement, ghetto rebellions, and the rise of Black Power ideology. How have different class groups within the black community reacted to, participated in, or otherwise been affected by recent black movements?

(4) There is also a need for developing new concepts to explain social organization at the lower end of the race and class hierarchies. Too often there is a tendency to view oppression in ghettos and barrios through a single prism of race or class. We speak of the culture of poverty (a class explanation of social barriers) *or* racial discrimination (a racial explanation) but fail to search for the more complex barriers that may be caused by the interaction of race and class.

(5) When minority and majority populations have been viewed hierarchically, there has been too much emphasis upon inequalities of social honor and status, and not enough emphasis on power inequality. There have been many racial stratification studies based on social distance schemes in which Anglos have been asked the degree of intimacy they would grant to various racial minorities (e.g., Would you find it distasteful to have a Negro move next door? marry your daughter?). This almost exclusive concern for social honor and social distance has reflected predominantly white concerns and has not dealt with the basic equation that is of primary concern to disprivileged minorities: which persons have control over their own lives and instititions and which persons are relatively powerless? Throughout this book there is an attempt to put power inequality "up front" as the prime mover of a racial stratification system.

One book cannot fully explore, correct, and develop new formulations to solve these five problems. But it can scratch the surface. This book is a beginning toward a revised conceptualization, theory, and empirical exploration of race and class in interaction. A complete account of the interactions between race and class would involve the inclusion of a great many strata: the white poor in Appalachia, the white aged poor, and white ethnic groups as well as the black, Chicano, and Indian lower and middle classes. To cover all these populations would be an impossible task in a volume of this size. Instead, this book focuses on the growing class heterogeneity within the black and Chicano populations. But this is not to say that class diversity within the white majority is completely ignored, since many of the empirical explorations and theoretical models presented involve the *joint* consideration of race and class — for example, comparisons between lower and middle-class whites, blacks, and Chicanos. Further, the effect of the rise of black and Chicano middle classes on the attitudes, behavior, and prejudices of the white majority will be examined.

Some brief comments on the overall organization and content of this book are in order. The first half of the book deals with concepts, theory, and (in the case of blacks and Chicanos) demographic profiles. Chapter 2 presents origins of racial stratification and the application of van den Berghe's paternalistic-competitive model to the historical facts of black, Mexican, and Indian subordination in the U.S. Chapters 3 and 4 pertain to current issues and models for the ways in which race and class interact in contemporary America. Chapter 5 reviews current (1970-1972) census data in order to note the size and growth of the Chicano and black working and middle-class strata.

The second half of the book deals with some original empirical explorations as well as reviews of current research in race and class. Chapter 6 is an exploration of class and perceived inequality and militant outlooks among blacks and Chicanos involving some original analyses as well as a selective review of studies on the topic. Using current survey data, Chapter 7 explores the relations of race and class to values, perceived power, stratum solidarity, and friendship choices. Chapter 8 is a highly selective review of recent empirical race-class studies that have strong current relevance to or policy implications for contemporary social organization — studies of minority self images, the matriarchy, minority IQ test scores, and "tracking." Chapter 9 deals with the reactions of white working-class persons to student and black protests, with some hypotheses tested in a recent Los Angeles survey.

PART I

CONCEPTS, THEORY, AND DEMOGRAPHIC PROFILES

Chapter 2

ORIGINS AND DEVELOPMENT OF RACIAL STRATIFICATION

In most multiracial societies, racial groups are found in a hierarchy of power, wealth, and prestige. The most important of these three variables is differential power. In this case, power means the ability of one race to impose its will upon another.[1] The dominant stratum in the power hierarchy has the most immediate access to the means of force (such as monopoly on the use of weapons), to the technology, and to the control of economic institutions and the mass media. When we speak of racial stratification, it is important to note that we are referring to a *system* of power inequality. The hierarchy normally represents unequal power *institutionalized* in such a way that the mechanisms of domination and control of the most powerful stratum over minority communities survive over time. Like all stratification systems, racial inequality usually endures beyond the lifetimes of single individuals.

What are the origins of racial stratification systems? A number of recent works have attempted to ferret out the key variables in the development of racial hierarchies. Donald Noel argues that there are three crucial components of racial stratification: ethnocentrism, competition, and differential power.[2] When two distinct ethnic populations come into contact with each other, inequalities or stratified relations are only likely to occur when all three of these variables are operating simultaneously. Ethnocentrism, a term referring to a tendency for members of a social entity to view their values, institutions, and belief systems as more natural or superior to those of others, is a prospensity factor, but ethnocentrism alone is not enough to set in motion a system of stratification. Thus, although Population One may regard the beliefs, accumulation of knowledge, and social institutions of Population Two as hopelessly backward, this fact in itself may not lead to a system of inequality. In addition, Noel argues there must be a strong desire for Population One to seize and exploit the resources of Population Two. Typically, this is land or other natural resources. In the conquest of the American Indians, for example, the white con-

7

querors were strongly led by one goal: to seize the choice fertile land held by the Indians. A variant of economic competition is that Ethnic Group One may define a goal as desirable while Ethnic Group Two is indifferent to the same goal. In such a case, Group One may attempt to exploit the labor of Group Two to maximize goal attainment.

Yet, ethnic stratification will not be generated until Noel's third condition, that of differential power, occurs. "Without differential power it would simply be impossible for one group to achieve dominance and impose subordination to its will and ideals upon the other(s)." [3] Superior organization, technology, and gun power were crucial facts in European colonization, American slavery, and the forcing of Indians onto barren reservations.

Diagrammatically the Noel thesis can be summarized thusly:

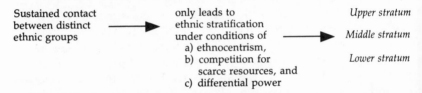

Sustained contact between distinct ethnic groups → only leads to ethnic stratification under conditions of a) ethnocentrism, b) competition for scarce resources, and c) differential power → *Upper stratum* *Middle stratum* *Lower stratum*

If one of these three conditions is missing then something other than racial or ethnic stratification develops. If ethnocentrism is absent, the two populations would be likely to merge (because of cultural similarity) with competition and stratification developing along class rather than ethnic lines. Similarly, if ethnocentrism and competition are present, but a power differential is missing, a kind of structural pluralism may emerge with the two closed societies competing for scarce resources but unable to dominate each other.

We have stated that ethnic stratification refers to an enduring system of power inequality. Accordingly, the next question is: How are these three factors — belief in cultural superiority, desire for scarce resources, and superior power — translated into an enduring system?

FROM ORIGINS TO STABLE SYSTEMS OF STRATIFICATION

Systems can rarely be held together very long by force and coercion. Once having gained control, a more powerful stratum either strengthens and institutionalizes its position or it will be subject to the constant threat of rebellion. Racial strata are no exception to this rule. A system of mutually understood inequality legitimizes the gains of the dominant stratum. Most immediately, the natural resources and labor of the conquered stratum can be exploited on a regular and predictable basis. Most important, shared norms of interaction develop so that roles and statuses become complementary, members of each stratum having a clear definition of expected behavior. New generations of the less powerful stratum do not have to be conquered again but are socialized into an ongoing system of superiority and deference.

Paternalistic Racial Stratification

Early systems of racial stratification (from roughly the mid-1500s to the mid-1800s) had an amazing similarity in form across different countries and in various instances of oppressor and oppressed. This similarity developed despite very different patterns of conquest. For example, in the case of European colonialism, a relatively small number of white (Dutch, Spanish, Portuguese, English) conquerors subjected large indigenous populations of another color (e.g., Africans or Aztec Indians). The result was a small white ruling class, representing European states, exerting control over a large indigenous population. In contrast, the subjugation of blacks in the United States (often called internal colonialism) resulted from a relatively powerless racial group being forced to enter a foreign society as slave labor, with a white ruling class having already established dominance over the majority of the population. Despite these differences in numerical ratio of whites to non-whites and the ways in which the non-whites were brought under the control of the dominant society, the *systems* of inequality showed great consistency. Thus van den Berghe speaks of a common paternalistic form to describe the early systems in South Africa, the United States, Brazil, and Mexico.[4] Of the many characteristics of a paternalistic system, there are four that are most conspicuous.

1) Under paternalism, stratification approaches its most rigid, closed form — that of caste. The caste line (or color bar) results in a huge gap in power, wealth, health, status, and life-chances between the castes.

The color bar is conceptualized as horizontal; there is no overlap in class achievement or statuses between races. Thus, even when individuals in the lower caste are respected for their wisdom or accomplishments, they are all still regarded as lower in social status than any member of the upper caste. Because caste is racially defined, there is no opportunity for members of the lower caste to rise into the upper caste or for members of the upper caste to fall into the lower caste. Crucial to the idea of caste is the total control that the powerful racial group exerts over the powerless.

Unlike many modern systems of racial stratification in which the status and treatment of minority persons change from situation to situation, a caste system implies that every part of the system observes the same rules. The subordinate racial population stays "in its place" because there is no other socially legitimate alternative. Protests and rising expectations of change become increasingly dimmer lights as the caste system takes firmer hold. To perpetuate the caste, three other characteristics are commonly found: endogamy (within-race marriage), rules of etiquette specifying appropriate deference when members of the subordinate race interact with members of the dominant race, and a supporting ideology justifying the subordination of the lower caste (e.g., on grounds that they are biologically inferior). In sum, a racial caste stratification system implies that there is one single dominant hierarchy and although obvious status differences within each caste do exist, they are always superseded by racial differences in affecting interaction.

The visibility of racial characteristics adds to the ease of maintaining such a pattern of a racial basis; in fact, where it is lacking, casual observations suggest that some visible distinction will be supplied, ranging from brands to distinctive coiffures or clothing. Skin color is ideal for these purposes, since it is virtually impossible to conceal or change.

2) Important to the conceptions of paternalistic relations is the idea that racial stratification is naturally linked to the economic system of its time. Van den Berghe notes that a pre-industrial, agricultural plantation economy is conducive to a particular kind of caste stratification — one in which large numbers of unskilled workers are completely controlled by their masters in face-to-face, intimate relations. So close is this interaction that van den Berghe labels it symbiotic.

3) The plantation system encourages another characteristic of paternalism: very little segregation or spatial separation between dominant and subordinate groups, unlike the American Indian reservations or the modern urban ghettos and barrios in which blacks and

Chicanos live. Contact on the plantation is intimate but of unequal status. A classic example of this intimate but unequal relationship is the institutionalized concubinage between men of the ruling group and women of the subordinate racial group. In commenting on relations between white (Portuguese) masters and Negro slaves of the Brazilian *fazendas* (sugar cane plantations), van den Berghe notes, "when a white boy reached sexual maturity he was sexually initiated with one of his father's slaves and continued to engage in promiscuous concubinage with female slaves throughout his sexually active lifetime."[5] Interracial concubinage with female slaves was completely accepted for white men. According to the dual standard of sexual morality, marriage was not considered an impediment to the maintenance of a slave harem in Brazil.

Similarly, Gilberto Freyre describes Brazilian planters:

> Slothful but filled to overflowing with sexual concerns, the life of the sugar planter tended to become a life that was lived in a hammock. A stationary hammock, with the master taking his ease, sleeping, dozing. Or a hammock on the move, with the master on a journey or a promenade between the heavy draperies or curtains. Or again, a squeaking hammock, with the master copulating in it.[6]

4) Finally, in paternalistic system there are highly developed sterotypes about the lower racial caste. "Child-like," "irresponsible," "intellecutally inferior," and "lovable, when they stay in their places," are common descriptions. To explain the origin and persistence of such stereotypes one must go beyond the tendency of the dominant Europeans to view the conquered people as backward, child-like heathens (i.e., simple ethnocentrism). Rather, a paternalistic *system* institutionalizes the parent-child relationship with many informal rules (caste etiquette) requiring a lower caste person to take on a humble, inferior posture whenever in the presence of an upper caste person. Consider the following description of black/white relations in the Deep South:

> Negroes and whites must not shake hands when they meet; the white man must start the conversation (although the Negro can hint that he wants to talk); the Negro must address the white person as Mr., Mrs., or Miss, but he must never be addressed by these titles himself (Negroes are addressed by their first name, or called uncle, aunty, darky, nigger, or in some cases — for politeness sake — may be called by their last name or by such titles as doctor, professor, or preacher). The topic of conversa-

tion must be limited to specific job matters or to personal niceties (e.g., inquiries after one's health); it must never stray over to bigger matters of politics or economics or to personal matters such as white husband-wife relationships. Negroes should never look into the eyes of white people when they talk to them but generally keep their eyes on the ground or shifting, and their physical posture in front of white people when they talk to them should be humble and self-demeaning.[7]

Classic examples of paternalistic roles can be seen in American movies of the 1920s and 1930s. In a typical example of these, a white child calls her black plantation servants by their first names and treats them as house pets. The blacks are always ready to sing and dance at her birthday parties or on other occasions.[8] Stereotypes are not only reinforced, but are created by system requirements.

In some paternalistic systems the role relationships are bolstered by racism, the belief that innate biological qualities of a racial group determine aptitudes or behavior patterns such as evilness, intelligence, or the capacity to produce a "high culture." Highly crystallized racism often develops late in the career of a paternalistic system to justify or rationalize the often brutal exploitation of a racial stratum by claiming that members of that stratum are something less than human beings. Early forms of paternalism may involve only ethnocentrism: devaluation of a peoples' culture without implying biological inferiority.[9]

From Paternalistic to Competitive Race Relations

As multiracial societies have changed from rural agricultural plantation economics to highly complex urban industrial systems, paternalistic race relations have given way to competitive relations. In a competitive society one race is rarely completely superordinate and another completely subordinate (though the wealth and power of a society are still concentrated in the hands of the original ruling group). Rather, the situation is more fluid, open, and, as a result, competitive. Criteria such as skill and performance become as important as race. As a result, racial roles are less clear and open competition develops as the subordinate racial group attempts to secure a larger share of wealth and power in the system. The stereotype of the subordinate race changes from a picture of happy, contented children to one of violent, aggressive, pushy persons. Van den Berghe notes:

> In . . . a dynamic industrial society with its great geographical mobility and its stress on impersonal market mechanisms and universalistic and achieved criteria of occupational selection, race relations are quite different from what they are under agrarian conditions. The master-servant model with its elaborate caste etiquette and its mechanisms of subservience and social distance breaks down to be replaced by acute competition between the subordinate caste and the working class within the dominant group.[10]

The exact causal sequence from paternalism to competitive relations varies from society to society according to unique historical events. However, certain patterns do stand out. Ideologies stressing liberty, equality, and fraternity were taking hold in Western European countries as well as in the United States during the early 1800s. The changes in political structure that occurred in many countries at this time tended to undermine paternalistic relations. Oligarchic, aristocratic, and colonial political structures shifted toward representative democracies with a much wider participation in the polity. Even so, blacks in the United States have until recently been excluded from this democratic participation.[11] Industrialization and urbanization no doubt contributed to the dissolution of paternalistic race relations, though this factor often may be given more casual significance than the facts warrant.

It is true that industrial economics tend to emphasize rationality, efficiency, and the use of achieved rather than ascribed criteria for assigning general status to persons. Industrial manufacturing systems require a free and mobile labor force rather than a mass of unskilled workers tied to a plantation. The greater impersonality and diversity of norms in the urban setting mean that subordinate racial groups can escape some of the traditional patterns of etiquette and deference. In such a system it becomes inefficient and detrimental to production to make race the primary criterion for determining job position.

Herbert Blumer has argued that industrialization per se does not necessarily upset the existing racial order. It takes internal and external power pressures to bring about a total racial realignment. Drawing from data dealing with industrialization in the South, he concludes that, when industrialization is introduced into a racially ordered society, social organization conforms to the alignment and code of the existing racial order. Industrial slavery may substitute for agrarian slavery.[12]

Though Blumer is correct in pointing out that the process of industrialization does not automatically destroy a racial stratification system, it is also true that during periods of extreme need for production and skilled manpower, a subordinate race does make definite gains. Thus, during World Wars I and II, when factories were operating twenty-four hours a day and there was an extreme need for manpower, the occupational structure "opened" sufficiently for many members of minorities to obtain semi-skilled, skilled, or white-color jobs. In times of critical need for economic rationality, widespread changes do occur. However, when the paternalistic lid is lifted it does not follow that subordinate racial populations are fully liberated or that a system of employment based solely on merit is fully realized. A major point in the van den Berghe typology is that a competitive system is not a completely open system. Rather, new means of coercion are instituted as a second line of defense to keep the dominant racial stratum in power. Instead of the intimate face-to-face control of the master-slave plantation, blacks, Chicanos, and Indians live in separate communities — ghettos, barrios, and reservations. Spatial separation and a duplicate set of inferior institutions replace the personal control of the plantation.

Internal Colonialism

Internal colonialism is the label often used today for separate and unequal minority communities.[13] Confinement of blacks to ghettos, Chicanos to barrios, and Indians to reservations represents the new forms of coercion found in competitive race relations. The separate institutions found in the internal colony or ghetto are typically inferior to those found in the dominant system. Police harrassment, schools of inferior quality, consumer exploitation, and overcrowded hospitals with perfunctory services are the trademarks of the barrio and the ghetto. The term internal colonialism focuses on one important fact: that ghettos and barrios are controlled and manipulated by dominant white outsiders. Viewed through the model of internal colonialism, policemen, social workers, teachers, and merchants are seen as custodians of the "colony." They enter the colony during the day to administer and return to suburbia in the evening. Unlike those of the white immigrant enclaves of the nineteenth century (e.g., Little Italy, etc.), the businesses of the ghetto or the reservation are not ordinarily controlled by blacks, Chicanos, or Indians.

RACIAL STRATIFICATION UNDER COMPETITIVE SYSTEMS

From the beginning of this synthesis, it has been stressed that racial stratification is based on power inequality. From the initial conquest of a racial population to plantation paternalism to the manipulation of internal colonies, a white power stratum has controlled the life chances and destinies of black, brown, and red people. However, a major theme of this book is that race relations in advanced competitive systems such as present-day United States involve an increasingly complex interaction of race and class. Black and Chicano populations are increasingly stratified with fairly sizeable upper-working and middle-class segments. This is occuring particularly where blacks and Chicanos have turned from persuasion, faith, and legal reforms to direct exertions of counter power, from the demonstrations of the Civil Rights Movement, to the ghetto riot-rebellions, to the institutionalization of black power. A major characteristic of competitive systems is that the caste system declines and class systems gain in importance.

Class Within Caste

Nearly half a century ago, Lloyd Warner presented his classic conceptualization of class within caste.[14] It is one of first statements that considers the idea of race and class in interaction, earlier works having assumed a unidimensional racial caste hierarchy. Warner and his colleagues studied a small city in the Deep South. Two black and two white social scientists lived in "Old City" for two years to study the class structure. Blacks and whites were separated by a definite caste line forbidding racial intermarriage, defining blacks as mentally inferior to whites, and reducing opportunities for black upward mobility. Even so, a socioeconomic structure existed within each caste; some blacks had achieved socioeconomic positions superior to some whites.

Figure 2-1 represents the caste-class model:

FIGURE 2-1. CLASS WITHIN CASTE

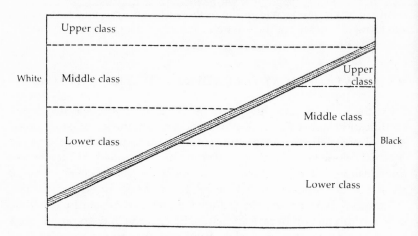

Adapted from *Deep South: A Social-Anthropological Study of Caste and Class*, by Allison Davis, Burleigh, B. Gardner and Mary R. Gardner, From an Introduction by W. Lloyd Warner, p. 10, by permission of the University of Chicago Press, Copywright© 1941 by the University of Chicago. See also the adaptation of this figure in Jopseph A. Kahl *The American Class Structure* (New York: Holt, Rinehart and Winston, 1957), p. 245.

Note the caste line is not horizontal as it would be in paternalistic relations but rather is slanted so that the highest class of blacks is higher in socioeconomic traits than the lowest class of white persons. Warner speculated that if trends continued the caste line would swing further on its axis until it reached a vertical line; there then would be a complete class hierarchy within each caste, with proportional numbers of each race in each socioeconomic stratum. The present status of this trend is a major concern of this book. However Warner did not clearly spell out all the possible results of internal differentiation within the black caste, leaving significant questions unanswered;

1) Does socioeconomic similarity produce a common value system so that middle-class blacks and Chicanos share more values, outlooks, and behavior patterns with middle-class whites than with lower-class people of their respective minority groups?

2) To what extent does class similarity take precedence over two

essential meanings of the caste line: differential power and social exclusion? For example, to what extent does class similarity between members of different castes break down social interaction barriers? To what extent is power socioeconomically achieved rather than caste ascribed?

3) Do the middle-class segments of the subordinate racial group turn to militant protest to bring about full equality or do they turn toward identification with the white Anglo middle-class and rejection of the lower strata of their own race?

4) What are the empirical possibilities of race and class in interaction? Under what conditions would race be expected to override class, class to override race, or the two to unite in producing special ethclass effects?

Application of Paternalistic Competitive Model to Different Societies

Van den Berghe's account of paternalistic-competitive race relations is presented as a comparative model applicable to emerging race relations in many countries. He notes that black-white relations in the United States and Brazil have followed this trend toward competitive relations rather closely. In Mexico and South Africa the model does not fit as well.

In Mexico there has been a shift from caste-based paternalism to a class system; the conflicts and differences have shifted from racial stratification to economic stratification. Miscegenation among Spaniards, Indians, and Africans in Mexico and the extreme degree to which Spanish culture was forced on the indigenous population has resulted in a high degree of homogeneity in both skin color and culture.

In contemporary South Africa one finds extreme contradictions in the racial stratification system. Because South Africa has evolved from an agricultural to a complex industrial economy, one would predict a more open society with competitive race relations. Instead is found apartheid, a rigid caste system involving ruthless repression of socioeconomic mobility by any means, with complicated and formal — even legal — rules of etiquette and deference for black people. Van den Berghe notes that:

> Apartheid in my opinion ought to be interpreted as an endeavor to reestablish the old paternalistic master-servant relations that prevailed in the pastoral Boer Republics of the nineteenth century.[15]

It is only with great tension that an advanced industrial system (straining toward mobility, openness, and an efficient use of manpower) can practice a high degree of paternalism and keep blacks totally "in their places." To do so the ruling class must resort to open coercion. It is no accident that pass laws, police surveillance, job reservation, and other formal means of repressive control are found in South Africa.

APPLICATION OF PATERNALISTIC-COMPETITIVE MODEL TO BLACKS, CHICANOS, AND NATIVE AMERICANS

The paternalisic-competitive model has never been applied in a comparative way to summarize the treatment of minorities in the United States. A major purpose of this chapter is to superimpose the model on the experiences of three American minorities. Blacks, Chicanos, and American Indians are conquered minorities that have all gone through various forms of paternalism and are currently experiencing an awakening to the potentials of counter power in an industrial environment. There are some striking differences in the history of these three minorities. Our goal is not to rigidly force the experiences of blacks, Chicanos, and Indians into a common set of charateristics but rather to note the patterns that fit and diverge from the paternalistic-competitive trend. The study of these three minorities within a paternalistic-competitive framework allows one to see the development of independent power bases within each minority as well as the emergence of patterns of social stratification within each.

Blacks in the United States

The early subordination of black Americans follows rather closely the paternalistic-competitive conceptual scheme. Blacks were imported to the United States specifically for the exploitation of their labor on tobacco and cotton plantations. A pure case of paternalistic relations can be found in Southern plantation social organization. "Negroes were regarded as immature, irresponsible, unintelligent, physically strong, happy-go-lucky, musically gifted, grown up children."[16] American slavery was often brutal and harsh. A common explanation in the literature is that neither church nor state did anything to interfere with the arbitrary power of a plantation master.

Although the Civil War destroyed many of the paternalistic underpinnings, an extrimely rigid substitute system of coercion and control developed after Reconstruction. With the threat of equalitarian relations between the races occasioned by the Confederacy's defeat in the Civil War, a substitute form of coercion evolved that had primarily paternalistic, but also some competitive, characteristics.

> In the economic sphere, slavery gave way to share-cropping and debt peonage. After an initial exodus to the towns, many freedmen had to return to the land to find a basis of subsistence. The plantation owners broke up their lands into small plots to be cultivated by individual tenants. The slave barracks near the big house gave way to a pattern of dispersed wooden shacks. Money lendings or rather the loan of food, seeds, tools, and other necessities to be charged at arbitrary prices against the value of the tenant's share of the crop, became an economic substitute for slavery. Through perpetual indebtedness, the tenant farmer was nearly as securely tied to the land and to his landlord as he was to his master under slavery.[17]

Perhaps the Jim Crow laws and caste etiquette were the most dramatic examples of the new coercion. These laws and customs enforced a systematic separation of the races in all potential situations of public intimacy such as restaurants, schools, drinking fountains, toilets, and public transportation. One of the most intensely felt caste rules was that Negro men must never have sexual relations with white women. Violations resulted in black men being lynched and compliant white women being exiled. On the other hand, many white men did have sexual relations with Negro women with impunity; under state laws the children of these unions were usually classified as Negro, but those who could "pass" for white often did. Equally repressive were the many informal rules of etiquette to demonstrate Negro inferiority to the white man. Negroes and whites did not shake hands when they met and did not eat in the same room (breaking bread together denotes equality).

Arnold Rose notes that the black-white caste system was not fully formed until several decades after the end of slavery. It was legitimized by the famed Plessy vs. Ferguson decision of the U.S. Supreme Court some thirty years after the Civil War. It remained substantially unchallenged until the '40s.[18] Desegregation of the armed services in World War II, large scale migration from the South to more urban industrial environments, Civil Rights legislation, the mechanization of agriculture, and black protest all contributed to the disintegration of the caste system. Race relations in the 1960s and 1970s represent a classic example of competitive relations: there is opportunity within limits, some emphasis on skill and merit, and a rising black middle class, mixed with extreme spatial segregation, poverty, and inferior ghetto institutions. The open expressions of anger, pride, and militancy and the fact that blacks can increasingly exert collective and individual power to move the white system aptly fits the competitive frame. The relatively high degree of socioeconomic differentiation that has developed recently among blacks is often ignored in studies of race relations. A major purpose of this book is to go beyond a black/white model and to develop a race/class interaction model.

American Indians

Unlike black American who were involuntarily forced into the United States as slaves, American Indians were conquered as indigenous people and forced from their fertile lands onto barren reservations. In many cases, initial relations between Indians and Europeans (English, Spanish, and French explorers) were friendly and involved the exchange of culture and resources. Nancy Lurie notes:

> The establishment of permanent European settlements along the eastern seaboard and St. Laurence River in the early seventeenth century required the assistance of Indians in providing food, information, and skills to survive the first years in a new environment. As the fur trade took on importance . . . the Indian tribes enjoyed a good deal of bargaining power and learned to use it astutely in their own interests in regard to both commercial and military activities.[19]

Conflict and violence between white settlers and Indians was a result of the white European (and later American) effort to acquire choice land — fertile land for settlement, land teeming with timber and buffalo, and later in California, land containing the scarce yellow metal, gold. Thus, the conquest of American Indians represents an especially clear case of Noel's variable — competition for scarce resources. The expropriation of land involved a common pattern. Treaties were signed between the U.S. Government and Indian leaders. As the white settlers increased in number, they encroached further upon Indian Territory, continually breaking the conditions of their own treaties. For example, in 1829, Andrew Jackson, convinced that Indians and whites could not peacefully live together, proposed a separate Indian district west of the Mississippi as a *permanent* frontier. In 1834 Congress passed such a frontier act which stipulated that white persons would not be permitted to settle in the Indian country or to trade in that territory without a license. Moreover, the military forces of the United States would be employed to enforce provisions of the act.[20] The conditions of this act were not honored and the boundary of the "permanent frontier" was continually moved westward as white settlers negotiated new treaties and claimed new land. An extreme form of ethnocentrism (known as Manifest Destiny) was developed to justify the seizure of Indian land. Dee Brown, in *Bury My Heart at Wounded Knee*, notes:

> To justify these breaches of the 'permenent Indian frontier,' the policy makers in Washington invented Manifest Destiny, a term which lifted land hunger to a lofty plane. The Europeans and their descendants were ordained by destiny to rule all of America. They were the dominant race and therefore responsible for the Indians — along with their lands, their forests, and their mineral wealth.[21]

Soldiers marched into the southwest area to fight Mexico; gold was discovered in California. With the realization that government treaties were meaningless, Indian nations often combined into coalitions to fight white settlers and soldiers. With the increase of Indian raids and bloody fighting, the military force of the United States was employed. Indians were either slaughtered (as in the case of the Massacre of Sandcreek) or forced onto barren reserves.

The Reservation as a Form of Paternalism

In tracing the evolution of the relationship between Indians and the U.S. Government, Lurie notes that in an 1831 decision a Justice of the Supreme Court used the unfortunate term "ward " to describe the Indian, emphasizing the U.S. Government's obligation to protect Indians from hostile settlers and the U.S. Army. The term emphasized the federal government's acknowledgement of its responsibility to protect Indian tribes against "usurpation of their lands." Because the Indian Bureau sometimes became the uneasy and unhappy mediator between Indians and the U.S. Army, it was decided in 1862 to designate the members of Indian tribes as "wards" of the Indian Bureau rather than to let them be considered as sovereign or independent enemies. "Unfortunately and without ever really having legal sanction the term 'ward' took on administrative connotations by which the Bureau exercised incredible control over the lives and property of individuals much as a guardian would act for minors or helplessly retarded children." [22]

American Indians experienced a unique kind of paternalism as wards of the government, administered by their guardian, the Bureau of Indian Affairs. Much has been written about the paternalism of the Bureau. One of the more caustic accounts is found in Edgar S. Cahn's *Our Brother's Keeper:*

> From birth to death his home, his land, his reservation, his schools, his jobs, the stores where he shops, the tribal council that governs him, the opportunities available to him, the way in which he spends his money, disposes of his property, and even the way in which he provides for his heirs after death — are all determined by the Bureau of Indian Affairs acting as the agent of the United States Government. [23]

It may seem incorrect to cast the reservation Indian into a paternalistic framework since Indians are owners of land. However, Cahn notes that sales exchanges and transactions are all controlled by the Bureau.

> The Bureau prescribes the number of cattle which may graze on a parcel of land. It approves leases, controls prices, terms, and conditions. Often the leasing process is initiated not by the owner of the land but by the person desiring to lease it. Leases have been approved without the owner's consent, and *only* the Bureau — not the tribe or individual owner — is empowered to cancel a lease. [24]

On the Indian's personal affairs he comments:

> Mere supposition by a Bureau official that an Indian might prove indiscreet in handling money, might be exploited, or might at some future point be unable to provide for himself — any of these is considered reason enough to relieve the Indian of control over his possessions. Once the Indian is deemed incompetent he cannot even draw money from his own bank account without obtaining approval from a BIA guardian. [25]

Especially indefensible has been the separation of Indian children from their families to attend BIA boarding schools often located many miles from the reservation. In such schools there is often a forced denial of Indian culture, tradition, and values.

There are important similarities and differences between *reservation paternalism* and the *plantation paternalism* that van den Berghe describes. The overriding similarity is that in both cases the subordinate race is so completely dependent that it is impossible for identified members to build a collective power base or to acquire significant amounts of wealth, power, or prestige. The obstacles to upward mobility are virtually insurmountable. Thus in both cases the development of a highly differentiated socioeconomic hierarchy within the subordinate race is not likely.

The differences between reservation and plantation paternalism are also noteworthy: the Indian reservation is a self-contained unit. The Indians' relationship to BIA officials is not the symbiotic, intimate, face-to-face relationship that one finds between master and slave on a plantation. As a result, Indians have not been forced to adapt to the rhythms and routines of a white labor system — a point that explains partially why they have been able to keep alive and intact some degree of cultural continuity. Another significant difference is that while the paternalism of southern plantations revolved around the exploitation of labor, this has not been a primary feature of reservation paternalism. In fact, it can be argued that Indians have been so disengaged from the production system that national changes from agriculture to industrial manufacturing have not affected them as they have other minority groups. In many ways, the American Indian cannot be easily placed in an orthodox minority group conceptual framework. His peculiar legal status with the BIA and his traditional insistence on preserving Indian identity and tribal affiliation and culture make him unique.

So anxious are American Indians to protect their land and traditions that they have militantly opposed any action to do away with the BIA. Though the Bureau has taken advantage of the Indians again and again, the alternative — termination of this trusteeship and protective arrangement — is far less desirable. In those instances where termination has occurred, Indians have lost all their land, their special services and institutions and have become individual welfare cases. For example, with termination, Indian land comes under state and local property taxes. Indians are unable to pay the taxes and their land is absorbed or sold at public auctions.[26]

In spite of the nearly total control of Indian life on reservations, there has developed a rising degree of Indian militance in the last decade. Consistent with the competitive model, the activists tend to be young urban university students, rather than reservation dwellers. However, these Indian students have returned to their reservations to direct the action of others in protest. Commenting on the first "fish-ins" in the state of Washington, Robert C. Day noted:

> Protest efforts were initially blocked by the disunity, apathy, and traditional values of many tribal leaders (going to jail was perceived as undignified). Some questioned whether direct action was 'the Indian way.' Many worried about negative repercussions, but in the end there was no choice, the tribal leaders knew that if they lost their fishing rights they could not survive as a cultural unit.[27]

"Tribal Nationalism" is the name given to the reservation-based movement which has recently begun. In a meeting of young Indians the goals of the movement were defined: "Th(e) declaration stressing self government, sovereignty and nationalism made it clear that Indian people wanted complete autonomy to protect their land base from expropriation and to make their own plans and decisions in building an economic system to rid themselves of poverty while reasserting traditional cultural values."[28]

American Indians appear to be moving from a peculiar form of Federal Paternalism to the development of an independent power base on the reservation. Internal stratification of the community has not occurred to any great degree even though there are growing numbers of middle-class Indians in urban areas. Compared to blacks and Chicanos, class differentiation among Indians on reservations will be less likely to develop in the near future due to extreme poverty and strong communal ideologies that reject "political" climbing and internal differences.

Mexican Americans in the United States

Mexican Americans constitute the nation's second largest minority population. As in the case of American Indians, Mexicans were not forced into America as slave labor but rather conquered as an indigenous people. A unique fact about the conquest of the Mexicans is that paternalistic stratification systems were already intact and highly developed at the time white Anglos arrived. These were frontier extensions of Spanish colonialism in Mexico. They were caste systems based on "purity of blood," ranging from pure Spanish to Mestizo to Indian. The typical rancho consisted of a family of Spanish *gente de razon* and a legion of mestizo and Indian laborers.

The Americans often took advantage of the Mexican stratification system, identifying with the Spanish elite and thus acquiring a convenient supply of Indian and mestizo labor. As a result, Mexicans (Indians and mestizos) faced two systems of discrimination: internal Spanish colonial and external Anglo. It is interesting that the presence of aggressive American Indian tribes (that often attacked and raided Anglo and Spanish settlements) contributed to the view of the Mexican as inferior.

> The presence of Indians and their reputation for treachery and savagery probably had notable effects on the Anglo view of Mexicans. A conviction that Mexican immigrants in general were Indians in physique, temperament, character, and mentality is reflected in public documents spanning several decades in the nineteenth and twentieth centuries.[29]

The extreme conflict that developed between Mexico and the United States centered around competition for land. Through many border clashes and open warfare between the United States and Mexico, as well as by purchase of certain lands, the United States acquired what have become the states of Texas and New Mexico and parts of Colorado, Arizona, Utah, Nevada, and California.

Conquest of the Mexican Americans did not fall into a single pattern but followed several patterns in different parts of the Southwest. For example, Joan Moore identifies three kinds of colonialism in the Southwest: "classic colonialism" as exemplified by New Mexico, "conflict colonialism" (Texas), and "economic colonialism" (California).[30]

In New Mexico, Spanish colonial (paternalistic) stratification was developed to a high degree. The American conquest of this system was a bloodless takeover and a merging of traditions rather than a destruction of culture. Elite Spanish leadership was shared with Anglo domination to the extent that "sessions of the legislature were — by law — conducted in both languages."[31] At the lower class level in the villages, Moore notes a patron (go between) system existed that allowed for some representation of the lower class. Thus in the case of New Mexico "an intact society rather than a structureless mass of individuals was taken into the territory of the United States with almost no violence."[32]

But in Texas, violent, open conflict was the rule. Many years after the annexation of Texas by the United States, armed clashes occurred between the guerilleros of Northern Mexico and the U.S. Army. Moore notes that the more violent clashes in Texas meant a termination of political participation by the Mexican elite. Any possibility of lower-class political protest was ruthlessly suppressed by the Texas Rangers, a group of law enforcement officers organized in 1835 to protect the frontier. The Anglo political and economic dominance in Texas was at least in part attributable to the fact that there were five Americans for every one Mexican prior to the American conquest. Mexicans in New Mexico, on the other hand, retained the numerical majority for more than 100 years after being conquered. As a result of the pattern of conflict colonialism, it is not surprising that some of the most extreme versions of caste stratification developed in Texas.

Summarizing research done in Corpus Christi in the 1920s, Grebler, Moore, and Guzman note that

> Mexicans were 'overwhelmingly' laborers in the cotton fields and definitely lower class. Mexican clerks were hired only to attract the Mexican trade and the few Mexican American businessmen almost all served the ethnic populations. Mexican Americans went to segregated schools. Restrictive covenant clauses usually confined them to segregated neighborhoods. Discrimination in public accommodations was almost as stringent as it was against Negroes. Mexican Americans were allowed to sit at the drugstore fountain (though not at the tables) while Negroes would not be seated at all. Intermarriage was disparaged and the Anglo member of an intermarrying couple became socially a Mexican.[33]

California represents the extreme of economic exploitation. For it was in this area more than any other area of the Southwest that Mexican labor was manipulated to serve the interests of agricultural development. Attracted by the relatively high wages, hundreds of thousands of Mexicans entered the United States in the 1920s. During the depression a large fraction of these workers were forcibly deported ("repatriated") by California welfare agencies when their labor was not needed and many were on the welfare rolls. This pattern contrasts sharply with that in Texas. In Texas there were very few welfare provisons and, as a result, no need for forced deportation. With the tremendous economic expansion caused by World War II there was a heightened need for Mexican labor. Normal immigration was supplemented by a contract labor arrangement known as the Bracero Program, under which large numbers of Mexicans could find employment as farm laborers for a season. But, as during the depression, too many came to work in the United States, some without legal status. Again in 1954 massive sweeps of deportations eliminated Mexicans by the thousands in Operation Wetback — citizenship checks by the Border Patrol of the U.S. Immigration Service. "New Mexico was largely spared both waves of deportation; Texas was involved primarily in Operation Wetback rather than in the welfare repatriations. California was deeply involved in both." [34] Thus it is especially in California that we find conscious economic manipulation of the large pool of Mexican labor.

How well does the sketch of Anglo-Mexican conquest fit the paternalistic-to-competitive model and the resulting forms of stratification? A system of dependent laborers working in dead-end agricultural jobs with poor wages and no union representation is certainly one version of paternalism. However, it differed considerably from the experience of Black Americans. Since the indigenous systems were often modified rather than destroyed, Mexican Americans have a much more well-preserved culture than blacks. They retained their language, their Catholic religion, and their patterns of family organization.The proximity of the United States to Mexico and the continous back-and-forth immigration add to the persistence of their ethnic culture.

By definition, a paternalistic system necessitates a caste model of stratification. It is true that caste-like relations developed in certain areas (such as Corpus Christi, Texas) in the 1920s; but the Mexican Americans had more escape valves, more inconsistencies of status, and more opportunities for upward mobility than did the blacks. As has been reported for the blacks, there was always a degree of sexual contact between castes. Upwardly mobile Mexican Americans who did not have extremely Indian-like appearances could claim all or predominantly Spanish blood in communities where the caste sanctions toward Mexicans were extreme. Further, Mexicans who had middle-class occupations faced inconsistent caste status. San Antonio was seen as a relatively open place for the middle class — a very different milieu from Corpus Christi. [35]

In the last twenty years, the Mexican-American population has changed drastically in a competitive direction. Fernando Penalosa notes that World War II was a major factor in the change. At that time there was a great flow of people out of the barrios.

> Young Mexican Americans took industrial jobs in increasing numbers, went off to war, traveled around the world, and were treated as individuals, some for the first time. . . . Veterans especially returned to find themselves dissatisfied with the old ways and many went to college

under the provisions of the G.I. Bill. Occupational skills were upgraded because of wartime industrial experience and because of the additional educational opportunities made available to young members of the group.[36]

There is an out-of-date stereotype of Mexicans as being highly concentrated in migratory farm labor. It is true that prior to World War II the Mexican-American population in the Southwest was largely rural, but it was two-thirds urban by 1950 and four-fifths urban by 1960. In southern California, a large 83.7 percent of the Mexican population lives in urban areas.

Penalosa notes that the stratification system has changed dramatically in the last two or three decades. While formerly Mexican-Anglo relations leaned toward a caste system, Penalosa likens present-day Chicanos (in southern California) to "a European immigrant group of a generation ago such as, for example, the Italian-Americans in New York, Boston, or San Francisco."[37] The rigidity of caste barriers against intermarriage and equality of employment has diminished considerably. Consistent with a more competitive model, the Mexican-American population has developed a moderate degree of internal stratification. The modal occupation is semi-skilled or skilled blue-collar work.

CONCLUDING NOTE

The shift from paternalistic and competitive race relations for America's conquered minorities does not mean that all racial paternalism has disappeared from our institutions. Major pockets of paternalism continue to thrive in our advanced industrial society.

The welfare system in the united States has been strongly criticized as encouraging dependency and undermining self respect. In many states Aid For Dependent Children benefits are available only when there is no male living in the house. The "man-in-the-house rule" has encouraged the break-up of many homes and perpetuated dependence on welfare. The relationship between welfare workers and the poor is often filled with tension and paternalism as a result of complicated eligibility requirements and, in some instances, "flagrant invasions of privacy."[38]

Migratory farm labor represents one of the most extreme survivals of paternalism in this country. (See Chapter 6) A great many Mexican-

American farm laborers are locked into a system that provides bare subsistence and totally controls their lives. Steiner captures well the paternalistic relations between grower and worker:

> When a grower says 'my Mexicans' and 'my boys' he means it affectionately. He is sentimental about the 'old days,' when it was 'like a big happy family here' — men singing down by the camp at night. Women praying to their plaster saints. . . . Like a good father, the grower feels he has to be stern at times. . . . A father sometimes has to say no to his children for their own good and future well being.[39]

Although American Indians have entered a new period of militancy and self determination, illustrated by recent legal suits to recover land and fishing rights, and by the seizure of the township Wounded Knee, there are still many Indian tribes living in abject poverty with most of their affairs controlled by the Bureau.

The shift from paternalism to competition is an important *macro*-societal trend, but within this society residues of paternalism remain.

Notes to Chapter 2

[1] This definition comes from Max Weber's classic discussion of power. See Reinhard Bendix, *Max Weber: An Intellectual Portrait* (New York: Doubleday & Co., 1960), p. 294.

[2] Donald Noel, "A Theory of the Origins of Ethnic Stratification," *Social Problems* 16 (fall, 1968): 157-172.

[3] Ibid., p. 163.

[4] Pierre L. van den Berghe, *Race and Racism* (New York: John Wiley & Sons, 1967).

[5] Ibid., pp. 65-66.

[6] Gilberto Freyre, *The Masters and the Slaves* (New York: Alfred A. Knopf, 1964), p. 380.

[7] See Arnold M. Rose, "Race and Ethnic Relations," in *Contemporary Social Problems*, ed. Robert K. Merton and Robert A. Nisbet (New York: Harcourt, Brace, 1961), p. 358.

[8] One of the best films that I have seen on the portrayal of blacks in stereotypical roles in American movies is "Black History: Lost, Stolen or Strayed," narrated by Bill Cosby.

[9] An interesting example of paternalistic roles without extreme racism is found in van den Berghe's discussion of Spanish-Indian relations in early Mexico. Indians were regarded as "in need of enlightenment through exposure to the true faith, but they were basically human." That is, their culture was lacking but they were regarded as reasonably rational and intelligent members of the human race. In contrast, the attitudes of Spaniards toward Negroes constitutes a purer form of racism. They were regarded as intrinsically of unclean blood and low intelligence. Van den Berghe, op. cit., pp. 50-52.

[10] Van den Berghe, op. cit., pp. 29-30.

[11] Rose notes that white Southerners at this time wanted to be modern and democratic and at the same time retain their vested interests in the institution of slavery. Racism became a convenient vehicle to resolve this conflict of interests. Since blacks were judged biologically inferior, they were not capable of intelligent participation in the polity or the economy. However, they could enjoy some of the benefits of democracy and Western culture by "serving the white race." Rose, op. cit., pp. 355-357.

[12] Herbert Blumer, *Industrialisation and Race Relations, A Symposium* (London and New York: Oxford University Press, 1965), p. 245.

[13] See Robert Blauner, "Internal Colonialism and Ghetto Revolt," *Social Problems* 16 (spring, 1969): 393-408 and Robert L. Allen, *Black Awakening in Capitalist America* (New York: Doubleday & Co., 1969).

[14] See W. Lloyd Warner's Introduction in Allison Davis, Burleigh R. Gardner and Mary R. Gardner, *Deep South* (Chicago: University of Chicago Press, 1941).

[15] Van den Berghe, op. cit., p. 109.

[16] Ibid., p. 82.

[17] Ibid., pp. 87-88.

[18] Rose, op. cit., p. 359.

[19] Nancy Oestreich Lurie, "The American Indian: Historical Background," in *Majority and Minority*, ed. Norman R. Yetman and C. Hoy Steele (Boston: Allyn & Bacon, 1971), p. 209.

[20] Dee Brown, *Bury My Heart at Wounded Knee* (New York: Holt, Rinehart & Winston, Bantam Books, 1972), p. 6.

[21] Ibid., p. 8.

[22] Lurie, op. cit., p. 221.

[23] Edgar S. Cahn, *Our Brother's Keeper* (New York: World Publishing Co., 1969), p. 5.

[24] Ibid., p. 9.

[25] Ibid.

[26] Ibid., pp. 14-26.

[27] Robert C. Day, "The Emergence of Activism as a Social Movement," in *Native Americans Today: Sociological Perspectives*, ed. Howard M. Bahr, Bruce Chadwick, and Robert C. Day (New York: Harper & Row, Publisher, 1972), p. 508.

[28] Ibid., pp. 511-512.

[29] Leo Grebler, Joan Moore, and Ralph Guzman, *The Mexican American People* (New York: Free Press, 1970), pp. 44-45.

[30] Joan W. Moore, "Colonialism: The Case of the Mexican Americans," *Social Problems* 17 (spring, 1970): 463-472.

[31] Ibid., p. 466.

[32] Ibid.

[33] Grebler, Moore, and Guzman, op. cit., p. 323.

[34] Moore, op. cit., p. 469

[35] Grebler, Moore, and Guzman, op. cit., pp. 323-324.

[36] Fernando Penalosa, "The Changing Mexican American in Southern California," in *Majority and Minority*, ed. Norman R. Yetman and C. Hoy Steele (Boston: Allyn & Bacon, 1971), p. 327.

[37] Ibid., p. 332.

[38] For a good summary of the welfare issue see Otto Kerner, *Report of the National Advisory Commission on Civil Disorders* (New York: Bantam Books, 1968), pp. 457-466.

[39] Stan Steiner, *La Raza: The Mexican Americans* (New York: Harper & Row, Publisher, 169), p. 260.

Chapter 3

THE INTERACTION BETWEEN RACE AND CLASS IN CONTEMPORARY AMERICA

In viewing race relations in the United States as moving from paternalistic to competitive, one examines the foci of history on a time-scale of increased status differentiation *within* minorities and finds an increasing need for reconceptualizing social organization on a race-class perspective. The paternalistic-competitive model clarifies and illuminates the trend from rigid racial castes to a more fluid situation in which a) several economic-power strata form within each race, and b) there is increased competition and conflict between ethnic groups (as well as classes) for scarce resources. Marvin Olsen has summarized this trend well.

> This paternalistic pattern may give way to a more 'competitive' type of race relations . . . as a society becomes more industrialized and urbanized, as slavery is declared illegal, and as members of the subordinate class become more physically mobile and slowly gain education, occupational skills, and wealth. In place of wholly superordinate and wholly subordinate racial populations, two parallel racial categories develop each having its own organizational structure, division of labor, and socioeconomic status graduations. The formerly dominant population may continue to enjoy numerous advantages in power, privilege, and prestige for a long period of time, but it no longer totally controls the previously subordinate racial population. The old patterns of paternalism and voluntary subservience give way to competition and conflict between the two racial categories as the subordinate one struggles to increase its share of power, privilege, and prestige in society. Race relations are no longer static and 'peaceful'; dynamic conflict and change now prevail.[1]

However, the specific ways in which ethnicity and class interact in such a competitive society appear to be an open frontier for exploration. Though there are several excellent essays and empirical studies on the subject,[2] on the whole, "race and class in interaction" is a remarkably understudied conceptual area. Moreover, the ethnic

31

power and ethnic identity movements of the last decade make the topic especially intriguing when the ethnic groups under study are Chicanos, blacks and American Indians.

Does the upwardly mobile Chicano or black reject or minimize his ethnicity and become a middle-class consumer, as some accounts would suggest, or have the ethnic pride movements generated a whole new set of constraints encouraging middle-class black, Chicano, or urban Indian persons to retain their ethnic identifications — even their commitments to their respective movements — at the same time that they enjoy a middle-class life style? Further, it is quite possible that class differentiation has distinctly different meanings and consequences for each minority group. For example, upwardly mobile Mexican Americans (who have reached a skilled or white-collar stratum) may both resemble and differ from upwardly mobile blacks in such areas as perceived discrimination, assimilation options, and propensity toward militant action. Our point is that many of the traditional concepts and theories in the study of class and ethnic relations are not adequate to explain the simultaneous emergence of an increased skilled and white-collar stratum coupled with heightened ethnic consciousness among American ethnic minorities.

TWO HIERARCHIES

Our basic perspective is that racial-ethnic qualities and socioeconomic characteristics result in two distinct but interacting hierarchies. Although there are significant differences between these two orders, they share a common basis — both determine access to power, economic privilege, and social honor. The basic assumption of ethnic stratification is that *physical* and/or *cultural* distinction from the dominant ethnic stratum results in power inequality and limited access to important rewards. Quite apart from one's wealth or education, membership in an ethnic group *per se* determines to some extent one's life chances. This is especially the case when the ethnic minority has gone through a long-standing paternalistic relationship in which beliefs of inherent inferiority have developed and in which unequal power has become highly institutionalized. In contrast, the socioeconomic hierarchy deals with the economic earnings, education, and occupational status of persons.

A given socioeconomic stratum (often used interchangeably with social class in our discussion) refers to a category of people with roughly comparable levels of occupational attainment, education, and income. One sometimes finds the term "achieved rank" used when referring to SES or socioeconomic status (as opposed to ascribed rank in the case of race). But SES is not always entirely "achieved," since initiative, effort, and ability are not the only determinants.

Equally important are inherited wealth and privilege. An upper middle-class child typically inherits not only material wealth and possessions but a high achievement motivation from his home environment. He also attends the best schools, and has parental connections with the most influence. Diagramatically, the two-hierarchy perspective would look like this:

Socioeconomic Hierarchy
(comparable levels of occupational attainment, education, and income)

Race-Ethnic Hierarchy
(strata distinguished by cultural and physical characteristics)

Differential Access to

Power (ability to influence one's own and others' lives)
Economic Life Chances (probability of maximizing economic accumulation)
Social Honor (prestige in the eyes of others)

FIGURE 3-1: A Two-Hierarchy Perspective

Until recently, the correlation between race (black, Chicano, native Americans) and low socioeconomic position was so consistent that the two categories were rarely separated. That is, it was assumed that practically all blacks, Chicanos, and Indians were lower class. Though the poverty rate is still high for all three groups, increasingly large numbers of urban blacks and Chicanos have managed to attain better socioeconomic positions in the last two decades. The 1970 Census indicates that somewhere between 30 percent and 45 percent of the employed black and Spanish-surname populations (depending upon region of the country and the age and sex of the respondent) are either in skilled blue-collar positions (craftsmen or foremen) or white-collar occupations.[3] As one would expect, minority persons in white-collar positions tend to come from stable working-class or middle-class homes rather than from poverty backgrounds. The child who faces the dual barrier of poverty and race has extremely limited chances for substantial socioeconomic advancement while minority children from stable working-class or middle-class homes do inherit some advantages.

My major point is that in black, Chicano, and Indian populations the correlation between "race" and lower-class status is no longer .95 (as it would be under a paternalistic system) but has dropped to something like a moderate .50. This means that race and class increasingly interact in interesting and complex ways. A middle-class black person may have very different outlooks and battles to fight than those of a lower-class black.The dual-hierarchy model allows for the possibility of a middle or upper-class black person having greater power and wealth (though not necessarily greater social honor) than a lower-class white person. However, before examining these interaction possibilities, the ethnic race hierarchy needs to be more clearly defined.

There are many excellent discussions of social class ranking in the United States, but ethnic and racial ranking are less commonly viewed as hierarchical. In particular, blacks, Chicanos, and American Indians have not been commonly distinguished from other ethnic groups in hierarchical conceptions. Accordingly, a more extensive discussion of the ethnic-race hierarchy is presented below, followed by some important comparisons between race and class stratification.

RACIAL-ETHNIC STRATIFICATION

The term "Ethnic group" is used by today's authors to include peoples distinguished primarily by visible physical criteria (blacks), cultural populations, distinguished by language, heritage, or special traditions (American Jews) as well as groups differentiated both by cultural and physical differences (Mexican Americans and Indians). The three groups discussed most in this book — blacks, Chicanos and American Indians — have either a high degree of visiblity or a combination of physical and cultural differences. To separate clearly the "conquered minorities" from white ethnic groups we will frequently use the term "race" when referring to blacks, Chicanos, and Indians. Orientals, Italians, Irish, Scandinavians, Jews, Samoans, and uncounted other identifiable people are simply not whom this book is about.

Following the approaches of Lenski and Olsen, we view *power inequality* as the key variable for distinguishing strata in an ethnic-race hierarchy. That is, power inequality comes first, is the prime mover of the system, and determines the distribution of economic privilege and prestige (social honor). From this viewpoint, better economic chances or prestige for minority persons are only likely to occur when basic institutional arrangements are changed by the exertion of power. As Olsen puts it: "If racial inequality is in fact largely a consequence of power exertion by whites, it follows that *blacks seeking to change the situation so as to gain greater equality of privileges and prestige must in turn exercise power against the dominant whites.*"[4] Similarly, prejudice is viewed as the result or outcome of power inequality institutionalized (e.g., segregation). Olsen argues that one is far more likely to reduce racial prejudice by minority power action that affects these institutions (eliminates segregation, brings black and white into equalitarian contact with each other, etc.) than by education or persuasion. In terms of power inequality and differential access to rewards, a racial-ethnic stratification order in the United States would look like this:

> *White Anglo Saxon Protestants*
> *White Ethnics (e.g., Italians, Irish, Jews)*
> *Asian-Americans*
> *American Indians and Mexican Americans*
> *Blacks*

FIGURE 3-2: United States Stratification Order

Descending the scale in Figure 3-2, we find increasing degrees of political powerlessness, economic oppression, and social exclusion.[5] Note that the top stratum of WASPS possesses the dominant physical characteristics as well as the dominant culture (white, Protestant, English-speaking, achievement motivation, and competition orientation). White ethnics, because of cultural differences in religion and traditions as well as minor physical differentation, face slightly limited access. Asian-Americans represent an interesting intermediate stratum between the WASP and the most oppressed minorities. Though they are certainly physically visible — they are technically a racial minority — and currently face some degree of social exclusion,[6] their cultural stress on personal achievement, duty to the community, emphasis on long-range goals, etc., is highly compatible with that of the dominant culture. Further, Japanese and Chinese-Americans did not enter this country as a conquered people. Compared with blacks, Chicanos, and Indians, Asian-Americans have not remained in a highly dependent paternalistic relationship for long periods of time. Though legal controls against them have often been harsh ("Gentleman's Agreement," "Yellow Peril," and the Acts of Oriental Exclusion), and though relocation during World War II was one of the most extreme temporary forms of total control that the white majority has exerted on a racial minority, Asian-Americans have not experienced the long-range powerlessness of the three "conquered minorities."

From the perspectives of unequal power and differential access to scarce rewards one finds American blacks, Indians, and Chicanos at the lowest end of the ethnic hierarchy. As noted in Chapter 2, not only were all three groups conquered but the unequal power relationship became institutionalized. All three groups experienced some version of a long-lasting paternalistic relationship with the white power structure (slavery, total control by the Bureau of Indian Affairs, the use of Mexicans as a commodity for farm labor). Such unequal power was not just an historical fact but continues to a large extent today with the low degree of power and autonomy in many ghetto, barrio, and reservation communities (i.e., externally manipulated colonies). However, there are differences between American blacks, Mexicans, and Indians on this dimension of differential access to scarce rewards. Chicanos and Indians face unusual victimization due to cultural factors, blacks due to visibility and the stigma attached to that visibility.

Some segments of the Mexican-American and Indian populations have a distinctive culture that is at wide variance with the dominant culture. For example, Spanish language, greater emphasis on family cohesion, less stress on individualistic achievement and materialistic acquisition separates to some degree Anglo and Mexican-American outlooks. (However, the differences between Anglos and third generation urban Chicanos on these dimensions are probably very small.) Moreover, these cultural differences are not neutral or without consequence.

Moore notes that there has typically been a gross and insensitive reaction to Mexican language and culture in most Anglo institutions.[7] In the schools Mexican-American culture is often viewed as inferior in the sense that it causes bilingualism (assumed to be detrimental to education) and a lack of motivation. Federal financial assistance to schools in barrio communities is often based on the assumption that we must " . . . help Mexican-American children compensate for certain inadequacies they display compared to a 'standard' middle class child."[8] Such efforts are aimed at changing the child rather than changing the system. Cultural differences in the case of Chicanos and American Indians have become further means of limiting opportunities and enacting oppression.

Black Americans, in contrast to Chicanos and Indians, have fewer cultural differences in language and values, but are more "locked in" by physical visibility and by the stigma that is attached to that color. Though the extreme racist ideologies that developed during slavery and the era of Jim Crow (blacks were defined as biologically inferior and were assessed as three-fifths of a man for determining the number of seats a state got in Congress) have subsided, many white Americans continue to cling to milder versions of inherent black inferiority. Racial stratification that is tied to belief in black inferiority is likely to be especially rigid, making upward mobility much more difficult. In contrast, skin color and physical features in the Chicano group are more variable and hence there is more inconsistency in status assignments based on visibility. There are tremendous differences in skin color among Mexican Americans. Dark-skinned Chicanos often face more prejudice than light-skinned persons. Those with distinct Indian physical features are objects of more discrimination than those with a more classical Spanish appearance. In terms of self-definition, the concept of a "brown" race is a rather new development in the Mexican-American community. In the sense of the permeability of a color line, upwardly mobile Mexican Americans and American Indians have more options for mobility than black Americans.

In sum, American blacks, Chicanos, and Indians are lowest on the ethnic hierarchy (have the least access to scarce rewards) because of combinations of these factors:

1) Pronounced cultural differences (especially Chicanos and Indians);
2) High visibility (especially blacks);
3) Conquered status and long-lasting paternalistic relationship with the white majority;
4) Relatively powerless communities controlled and manipulated by white society;
5) Highly crystallized ideologies of inerradicable inferiority (especially blacks).

DOMINANT WHITE STRATUM OR POWER ELITE?

As we talk about power inequality being the essential fact of a racial stratification order, it is important to clarify several points dealing with the dispersal of power in the white population and in the minorities. Who has the power in this country? A widely held theory is that a small group of men at the top of major institutions make things move. C. Wright Mills argues that at the highest levels of the political, economic, and military hierarchies a small elite group have an inordinate amount of control over the destinies of individual citizens of *all races.* "For they are in command of the major hierarchies and major organizations of modern society. They rule the big corporations. They run the machinery of the state and claim its prerogatives. They direct the military establishment."[9]

From this power elite model, it would seem inappropriate to use the terminology of "dominant white group" since some whites (the elite) have far more control over the racial stratification system than rank and file whites. One could even argue that the white and minority masses are equally dominated by a powerful few. However, from the perspective of this book, a group of whites much larger than a power elite have controlled the destinies of black, Chicano, and Indian peoples. Systems of racial inequality initiated by a small group of powerful whites (as in colonialism and Manifest Destiny) allowed for a wide dispersal of authority resulting in middle-class, working-class, and, to some degree, poor whites acting out the racial order. Consider C. Vann Woodward's statement about the wide dispersal of power occasioned by Jim Crow laws:

> The Jim Crow laws put the authority of the state or city in the voice of the street-car conductor, the railway brakeman, the bus driver, the theater usher, and also into the voice of the hoodlums of the public parks and playgrounds. They gave free rein and the majesty of the law to mass aggressions that might otherwise have been curbed, blunted, or deflected.[10]

Currently, many whites of modest status and economic attainment have prevented black encroachment in their trade unions and neighborhoods. Indeed, it is commonly noted that the white working class has most rigidly acted out the discrimination norms of the old caste order since they face the greatest status threat and economic competition from an upwardly mobile black population. Sociologists having an internal colonization perspective also emphasize the fact that white agents (e.g., the white police) of powerful ruling groups enforce the system of inequality.[11] Thus, large numbers of whites far in excess of the power elite have been and continue to be involved in racial discrimination. But to refer to the white population as dominant in power and the conquered minority populations as subordinate in power is only partially accurate. One exception worth noting is that some segments of the white majority have identified with the ethnic liberation movements and actively participated in them (one of the major support groups in Cesar Chavez's farm worker movement is white and middle class). The white majority group cannot be viewed as one homogeneous oppressor. Another very important fact is that increasingly some members of the minority populations have more personal influence and control over their environment than some whites. Not all whites are dominant over all blacks.

TWO KINDS OF POWER

If power is defined as control over major institutions and, in particular, control over the economy, then few minority persons have such top power compared with whites. Even at upper middle levels of institutional power (for example, mayors or senators) whites have far more representation and influence than blacks, Chicanos, and Indians. However, if power is thought of in more personal terms as the probability of exerting control over one's own life, then middle-class blacks often have more control than working and lower-class whites. That is, middle-class blacks, in contrast to lower-class whites, typically have more money, influence in the context of their jobs, knowledge of redress channels when they face inequities, and general life chances. The terminology of dominant and subordinate racial strata completely misses this possibility.

COMPARISONS AND DIFFERENCES BETWEEN THE SOCIAL CLASS ORDER AND THE RACE-ETHNIC ORDER

1)The Marxian Prediction

If both class and race hierarchies involve an unequal distribution of power, what, then, is the difference between them? Three important distinctions can be made: 1) The clarity of the stratum boundary lines; 2) the opportunities for mobility from one stratum to another; and 3) the resulting potential for stratum solidarity and collective action to move the social structure in ways favorable to the lower stratum.

Social strata in the United States have been characterized by vague boundary lines, at least a moderate amount of social mobility from one stratum to another, and rather low degrees of shared fate, stratum solidarity, and collective action. For a hundred years scholars have debated why a proletarian revolution has not occurred, i.e., why the working class has not been a more radical force for social change as Karl Marx predicted. The fluidity of the system and resulting mobility of individuals coupled with unlimited faith in the "American Dream" are possible explanations.

As Marvin Olsen notes, "to the extent that numerous opportunities for individual mobility do occur in a society, there is little impetus for the members of a subordinate class to organize for collective power exertion and class conflict. . . ."[12] However, racial-ethnic stratification often comes much closer to a Marxian model. For the visible minorities, the stratum boundary lines are extremely clear and mobility to a higher ethnic stratum is virtually impossible in one lifetime. Moreover, power inequality is perceived as great by the minorities in the case of white-black, Anglo-Chicano, and white-Indian relations. The potential for collective action is further heightened by spatial segregation, that is, ghetto, barrio, and reservation communities in which frustrations and perceived wrongs can be easily shared and disseminated. Finally, blacks, Chicanos, and American Indians have faced severe economic oppression. In short, racial stratification in the United States has a much greater potential for producing stratum consciousness and stratum conflict than does socioeconomic stratification. There are, however, major differences between blacks and Chicanos on this dimension. There is tremendous diversity among the Mexican Americans — by class, generation, and geographical area — as well as very diverse reactions from the white majority. This diversity tends to mute the potential for a sense of shared fate as a separate oppressed minority. Discrimination against Mexican Americans has been more inconsistent than it has against blacks. To the extent that blacks are more visible, more stigmatized, and more "locked in" to their racial stratum, the long-range potential for collective action will be greater for blacks than for Chicanos or American Indians.

2) Differences in the Concept of Social Honor

In Weber's classic discussion of the status hierarchy, a variety of criteria for social honor were mentioned: reputation of family, status attached to a particular occupation, manners, refinement and etiquette, and educational attainment.[13] High status groups with commonality on these characteristics tend to band together and exclude others without the proper qualifications. Race or ethnic status is another characteristic that may result in low social honor and social exclusion. However, a low racial status has been accompanied by more intense social exclusion in American society than a lack of refinement or than a lower-class family origin. This is because race has been accompanied by beliefs in inherent differences and inferiority (e.g., Chicanos are naturally lazy and less ambitious), while among Anglos social honor can be acquired (the nouveau riche can become accepted by the "right" friends and donations to the "right" charities). To develop this point further, in both the class and ethnicity versions of social honor there is the element of exclusions. Prestigious upper-class persons tend to restrict entrance of lower-class persons into their elite clubs and associations; whites tend to exclude blacks (and, to a lesser extent, Chicanos[14]) from their peer groups. But social exclusion based on color is often more intense than that based on class; it frequently is accompanied by strong emotions, and violation of its unwritten rules involves more severe sanctions. No upper-class white person living in an exclusive residential area would consider burning a cross on the lawn of a newly entering white machinist. The same cannot be said with certainty in the case of a black machinist or even a black doctor.

Another consideration makes the assignment of social honor to minority persons far more complex than to majority persons. Social honor due to achieved merit may be constantly interacting with social honor due to race. A black doctor may receive a high degree of deference and esteem as a result of competence in his occupation, but when he leaves his office and his insulated occupational role, he may be accorded the same low level of prestige in his social contacts as that accorded less successful blacks. His social honor may be constantly shifting as he moves from social situations that acknowledge his achieved rank to social situations where his racial status is most important.

THE LACK OF RESEARCH ON RACE-CLASS INTERACTION

A major thesis of this work is that sociologists have not adequately explored the ways in which ethnicity and class combine in the contemporary (post-Watts) ethnic power era. The failure to consider race and class conjointly stems from two kinds of overemphasis: the stress on race to the exclusion of class and the stress on class to the exclusion of race.

Primacy of the Race-Ethnicity Dimension

Quite often the minority group is viewed as one homogeneous, impoverished, lower-class group. If the middle class of a minority is mentioned, it is usually depicted as a small peripheral segment, despite current census evidence that 30 to 45 percent of black and Spanish-surname persons hold skilled or white-collar occupations. It is as if being black in America is such an overriding factor that the class position of the person is unimportant or peripheral. For example, it is currently in vogue to use the analogy of internal colonialism when speaking of American blacks, Chicanos and Indians. The model is important in that it clearly distinguishes between white ethnic communities of choice (e.g., Italian, Polish, and Irish enclaves) and ghettos, barrios, and reservations that are externally controlled and manipulated by white persons (white merchants, police, eligibility workers, etc.). Internal colonialism does not stress social class differences. All members of the colonized group tend to be seen as facing the same degree of exploitation, racism, and reduced life chances. This approach misses — or at least de-emphasizes — some crucial points. The middle-class and upper working-class strata have far greater resources (money, connections, knowledge of redress channels, physical health) to challenge the system individually when facing personal discrimination, and collectively (for broad institutional reforms) than the lower-class stratum. Further, middle-class blacks have discrimination battles to fight that are very different from those of lower-class blacks. For example, Stanley Lieberson suggests that middle-class blacks face especially the problem of converting their incomes into the same economic privileges that middle-class whites automatically enjoy (quality housing, good schools) whereas lower-class blacks may be far more concerned with the "gut" issues of steady employment and survival.[15]

Primacy of Class

Some theorists hold the extreme view of social class as being such a powerful steam roller variable that it overrides all race-ethnic effects.

Some have even asserted that racial discrimination is no longer a major problem; they suggest instead that poverty, lower-class apathy, and hopelessness create the actual barriers. Edwin C. Banfield comments that:

> If overnight Negroes turned white most of them would go on living under much the same handicaps for a long time to come. The great majority of New Whites would continue working at the same jobs, living in the same neighborhoods, and sending their children to the same schools. There would be no mass exodus from the blighted and slum neighborhoods where most Negroes now live. By and large New Whites would go on living in the same neighborhoods for the simple reason that they could not afford to move to better ones. [16]

One interesting version of this line of reasoning is that there is a natural sequence from racial to class stratification. Initally, race-ethnicity is extremely important in determining differential power and privilege; however, once members of a race have been denied access to good jobs, education, and positions of power, the subordinate position of the race may continue because of class and poverty, rather than because of racial barriers.

> Once this has happened, once these discriminating lines of opportunities have been drawn, a process of impersonal but effective discrimination has been put into motion that endures often without much formal enforcement at all. For one generation of disadvantaged parents breeds a second generation of disadvantaged children, bereft of education, choices, and the capacity to raise *their* children in ways that might make it possible for *them* to move up the socioeconomic ladder. . . . [17]

Although such an approach makes an important point (that poverty and powerlessness are automatically recycled without the repeated stimulus of the initial cause) the special joint effects or complex blends of race and class discrimination are ignored. At lower-class levels, ethnic and class discrimination often are combined to produce unique barriers that cannot be explained by either class or race discrimination alone. What is needed then is the development of models that explicitly take into account the joint effects of race and class. The following chapter attempts to do this.

Notes for Chapter 3

1. Marvin E. Olsen, "Power Perspectives on Stratification and Race Relations," in *Power in Societies*, ed. Marvin E. Olsen (New York: Macmillan Co., 1970), p. 301.

2. See, for example, Milton M. Gordon, *Assimilation in American Life* (New York: (Oxford University Press, 1964), chs. 2-3; Andrew Billingsley, *Black Families in White America* (Englewood Cliffs, N.J.: Prentice-Hall, 1968); Pitirim A. Sorokin, *Society, Culture, and Personality*, New York; Harper & Brothers, 1947), ch. 15; Stanley Lieberson, "Stratification and Ethnic Groups," in *Social Stratification: Research and Theory for the 1970s*, ed. Edward O. Laumann (Indianapolis: Bobbs-Merrill Co., 1970), pp. 172-181.

3. See chapter 5 of this book for a more specific discussion of the demographic characteristics of the black and Spanish Surname populations.

4. Olsen, op. cit., p. 302.

5. John R. Howard defines social exclusion, economic oppression, and political powerlessness as the three crucial variables in an ethnic stratification system. See John R. Howard, *Awakening Minorities* (New York: Trans-action Books, Aldine Publishing Co., 1970), pp. 1-9.

6. See Harry L. Kitano, *Japanese Americans: The Evolution of a Subculture* (Englewood Cliffs, N.J.: Prentice-Hall, 1969), pp. 50-51.

7. Joan W. Moore, *Mexican Americans* (Englewood Cliffs, N.J.: Prentice-Hall, 1970), p. 81.

8. Ibid., p. 81.

9. C. Wright Mills, "The Higher Circles," in *The Impact of Social Class*, ed. Paul Blumberg (New York: Thomas Y. Crowell Co., 1972), p. 278.

10. C. Vann Woodward, *The Strange Career of Jim Crow* (New York: Oxford University Press, 1957), p. 93.

11. Robert Blauner, *Racial Oppression in America* (New York: Harper & Row, 1972), pp. 97-99.

12. Olsen, op. cit., p. 300.

13. Max Weber, *From Max Weber: Essays in Sociology*, ed. and tr. Hans H. Gerth and C. Wright Mills (New York: Oxford University Press, 1946), pp. 180-195.

14. Consistently, social distance research shows that Anglos are more willing to admit Chicanos into situations of social intimacy (same club, neighborhood, and marriage) than they are blacks. For example, in a recent survey in Texas, 50% of the Anglos were willing to admit a Mexican American to close kinship by marriage contrasted with only 10% of the Anglos willing to admit a Negro. See Chandler Davidson and Charles M. Gaitz, "Ethnic Attitudes as a Basis for Minority Cooperation in a Southwestern Metropolis," *Social Science Quarterly* 53 (March, 1973): 738-748.

15. Lieberson, op. cit., p. 180.

16. Edward C. Banfield, *The Unheavenly City* (Boston: Little, Brown & Co., 1968), p. 73.

17. Melvin M. Tumin, *Comparative Perspectives on Race Relations* (Boston: Little, Brown & Co., 1969), p. 16.

Chapter 4

THREE MODELS

Three race-class perspectives are developed in this chapter. We refer to them as: "Open Marketplace of Status Configurations," "Minority Subcommunity," and "Ethclass."

I. AN OPEN MARKETPLACE OF STATUS CONFIGURATIONS

According to this approach, individuals come into a marketplace of social interaction, each simultaneously asserting many different statuses. Most individuals will attempt to maximize rewards and "payoffs" and minimize barriers and stigma. (It is of course not only possible to consider ethnic and class stratification within such a model, but age and sex stratification as well. We are simply limiting this discussion to the two possibilities of race and class.)

The open marketplace model is designed to explain the interaction of minority persons in racially integrated settings. This model is therefore especially appropriate for the upper working-class and middle-class segments of the minority population, where a large part of each person's lifetime may be spent outside of the ghetto or barrio. Increasingly, the skilled and white-collar strata of the minority group are employed in the general societal occupational structure (e.g., civil service jobs) rather than in separate all-black or all-Chicano unions, schools, or other institutions.

In such an open marketplace of status claims, a number of important things can happen. A relatively high social class position can undermine or considerably offset (in terms of power, privilege, and prestige) a low ethnicity position. Many status audiences, both white and black, accord more deference and respect to a black high school principal or scientist than to a white construction worker. Furthermore, regardless of what people think of him, a high-achieving minority person may have more objectively measured power and economic life chances than some Anglos. Stated in more general terms, class and race may overlap to the extent that the life chances, power, economic options, and prestige of a high-achieving black, Chicano, or Indian person are greater than those of a low- or moderate-achieving white person.

One extreme version of the "open market" model suggests that race is but one kind of status that can be offset by socioeconomic achievement. That is, an industrial society functioning rationally will reward performance rather than skin color. Such an approach leads to the conclusion that high-status segments of racial minorities will become an undifferentiated part of the American middle class, or at least that skin color and ethnic status will pose no serious barriers. This option — assimilation — is more immediately open to middle-class Chicanos and urban Indians than to middle-class blacks, largely because of the lower "visibility" of the first two groups.

A second version of the open market model appears to be far closer to reality for the majority of blacks, Chicanos, and Indians. Although socioeconomic advancement increases the power and the economic life chances of minority persons, there are yet likely to remain some racially-associated differentials between majority and minority persons holding the same degree of socioeconomic achievement. It is often observed that the high-achieving black person has difficulty in consistently "cashing in" on all power and status fronts. He may have the same education as the white person but be paid less. Even with the same education and income as comparably trained white persons, he may have less power as a result of exclusion from social cliques in which policy decisions are made. Also his status is multivalent. The status of a black doctor will shift and vary as he moves from group to group. Among his medical peers he may be fully respected as a very competent doctor and may easily enter into social relationships with other doctors; while among prejudiced white patients, the same physician may receive minimal deference in the doctor-patient relationship and complete social exclusion in any other relationship. Indeed, one aspect of the marketplace model is that low status crystallization (a lack of fit or consistency among different statuses) in the combination of low ethnic position and high socioeconomic position creates very uncomfortable situations for the individual. The middle-class black or Chicano is seen as laboring under conflicting expectations in contemporary society. It is not surprising that several studies have shown that a low position on the ethnic hierarchy in combination with high socioeconomic achievement is associated with "liberal" political persuasions or other attempts to change the social structure in ways that would bring a more consistent and equitable flow of rewards.[1]

Our point, again, is that although a black, Chicano, or Indian person who achieves a higher social class position is likely to have greater life chances than a lower-class Anglo, ethnic differentials and barriers are still likely to remain at comparable levels of socioeconomic achievement. Further, the ethnic gap no doubt varies according to the minority group in question. Because of the uniquely high visibility, stigma, and prejudice that blacks have faced, the high-achieving black person is likely to face a greater residue of ethnic barriers and inconsistent treatment than the high-achieving Chicano or American Indian.

The Open Market Place and the White Majority

Not only does socioeconomic advancement bring greater control and privilege to minority persons but such advancement is beginning to have effects on the total society. It is important, therefore, to stress the term "open." Although a great many studies have noted the increased differentiation within minority groups, the emphasis has been on differentiation in the encapsulated ghetto; the achievement of blacks and Chicanos is not seen as having wide ranging effects on the society as a whole. Classic race-class formulations such as Warner's "class within a caste" and Drake and Cayton's "Bronzeville" are primarily intraethnic (e.g., black doctors only treat black patients).[2] The word "open," then, is a purposeful attempt to break out of this tradition and note how the development of larger skilled and white-collar minority strata will have important effects on the broader society.

How does the socioeconomic advancement of blacks and Chicanos change the larger society? Recent small group research provides a vehicle for discussing such changes. Several studies involving black and white students in task-oriented game activities show that in "untreated" groups, equal status interaction is not likely to occur.[3] Even with social class held constant, white persons are consistently more likely to dominate game situations and to exert far more lasting influence on group decisions. The interpretation is usually that strong racist beliefs are still embedded in our sentiments, so that blacks are generally felt to be less competent than white persons. Thus, in an open situation of status interaction, prior racist expectations structure the situation — white persons become more assertive, black persons more docile. A recent (and very "tight") study indicates that equal status interaction among black and white high school boys is possible, but only when the expectations of both whites and blacks are "treated" before the game.[4] In this experiment, black subjects were teachers and white subjects their students; the task was the building of a transistor radio. In addition, "clear evidence of black competence was presented to both black and white subjects by the use of video tapes which recorded and played back the competent behavior of the black subjects. . . ."[5] In a subsequent game situation (having nothing to do with radios) there was found a transferral of the treatment in that whites did not dominate the new situation; the flow of influence was equalitarian. A comparison or control group in which only black expectations were treated did not result in equalitarian interaction — white persons again dominated.

The small group research cited has wide-ranging societal implications. Specifically, it suggests how the development of skilled and white-collar strata in the minorities under discussion will effect broad change in race relations. Our thesis is that the socioeconomic advancement of blacks and Chicanos into the dominant occupational structure means that there will be an increase in "conventional" role relationships in which black persons are dominant and white persons subordinate. By "conventional role relationships" we mean complementary roles in which rights, duties, prerogatives, and obligations are clearly spelled out, and where there is a clear dominance-submission pattern.[6] Examples would be:

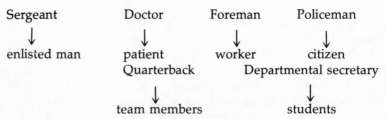

Sergeant	Doctor	Foreman	Policeman
↓	↓	↓	↓
enlisted man	patient	worker	citizen

Quarterback	Departmental secretary
↓	↓
team members	students

When a minority group is largely impoverished, or when all mobility takes place only within the minority community, there will be no conventional role relationships in which blacks or Chicanos are in dominant positions. However, upward mobility into the more general occupational structure greatly increases the probability of blacks and Chicanos being in at least some conventional role relationships in which they are dominant. When such role relationships occur, the results are likely to be striking for both minority and white participants. White persons are given a kind of stereotype-breaking "treatment" much like the white subjects in the Cohen-Roper small group study.[7]Black participants are likely to feel an increased sense of confidence and assertiveness. The reader may argue that such "treatments" would be extremely rare in a racist society. However, it is increasingly possible that many whites experience blacks in position of authority in military institutions, as teachers of their children, as professors in their classes, as policemen giving them tickets. For those white persons not directly experiencing minority persons in the course of their work or in some kinds of formal organizations, many experience blacks in positions of authority indirectly, through the mass media.

The increased number of black newscasters is an interesting example of "treatment" through the media. A good newscaster is articulate, has good diction and presence, and, most important, is *informing* the audience. Although there are no black quarterbacks in professional football at the time of this writing, the lack of them is frequently asserted as a sign of racism. When such a role relationship does occur, millions of viewers, both black and white, will be observing another black person in a position of dominance.

An interesting example of indirect experience with black ascendance was seen in the 1972 Democratic Convention. Yvonne Braithwaite, a black woman and chairperson for the convention, moderated it with great skill and confidence. It would be fascinating to know what was going on in the minds of millions of white viewers. No doubt many could never before have imagined a black women in such a role. In this case, although the viewers were not the direct subordinates in the role relationship, they were viewing subordinate role relationships between chairperson and delegates. We are postulating that the increase of role relationships in which blacks and Chicanos are in superordinate positions should have strong leverage effects on traditional race relations. Assessment of the exact effects of these "treatments," however, awaits further research. It is quite possible that the immediate effect will be to equalize the flow of power and influence in many interracial situations; this may or may not result in reduced social distance or a greater willingness for or interest in social intimacy on the part of either majority or minority persons.

To summarize our thesis, black and Chicano socioeconomic achievement in the dominant occupational structure is seen as having strong leverage effects on contemporary society. However, socioeconomic achievement *per se* is too gross a concept to measure all of the changes. The fact that there are more black foremen or electricians or teachers or parole officers does not, in itself, explain all of the recent changes in race relations. The conventionalization of occupationally linked role relationships, in which blacks or Chicanos are in dominant roles (vis-á-vis whites), forms a crucial intervening link between minority occupational mobility and changed race relations — changes in attitudes toward black competence, greater tendencies toward equalitarian power, interaction in open non-structural situations, greater confidence for the minority persons playing the dominant role. Diagramatically, the picture looks like this:

Results of Minority Status Due to Socioeconomic Change
FIGURE 4-1

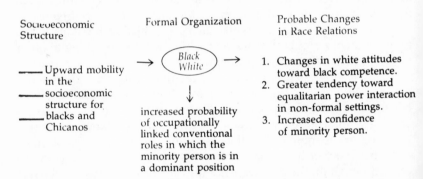

Socioeconomic Structure	Formal Organization	Probable Changes in Race Relations
____ Upward mobility in the ____ socioeconomic structure for ____ blacks and Chicanos	→ Black / White → ↓ increased probability of occupationally linked conventional roles in which the minority person is in a dominant position	1. Changes in white attitudes toward black competence. 2. Greater tendency toward equalitarian power interaction in non-formal settings. 3. Increased confidence of minority person.

Three additional points are crucial to this formulation. 1) What gives the black person a dominant position in a conventional role relationship is most typically his position in some formal organization (e.g., civil service, school, hospital, or military organization). White persons do not willingly grant greater power to black persons as a matter of course. Rather, minority persons have fought and collectively pushed for increased racial representation in dominant positions. Such positions by definition grant the incumbents a certain amount of legitimate authority. As blacks and Chicanos achieve these positions they automatically have authority over subordinates. 2) For many years blacks have played prominent roles in television and cinema. In a few cases, the black actor is the star of the show (e.g., "The Bill Cosby Show," "The Flip Wilson Show," or "Julia"). However, we are not just emphasizing the increased number of blacks in T.V. and movie roles as "indirect treatments." Rather, we are stressing the increased frequency of role sets in which blacks and whites are both involved and blacks are in dominant positions. 3) The small group research noted above suggests that equal status between black and white participants in games is not sufficient to upset traditional racial roles. White persons may exhibit no changes in attitudes when they experience blacks in the same occupational position that they have. Being exposed to minority persons in positions of greater power, however, is likely to upset traditional race roles and stereotypes.

II. THE MINORITY SUBCOMMUNITY PERSPECTIVE

The "open marketplace" model of race relations stresses the interaction of ethnicity and socioeconomic class in integrated situations and the common importance in both majority and minority communities of occupation, education, and income. However, it is likely that spatial segregation and isolation may have produced distinct black and Chicano subcultures which include different — even radically different — evaluations of status from those found in the dominant culture. The obvious implication of this possibility is that there may be a high degree of error in applying "uncorrected" white stratification theory or indices to the black or Chicano communities.

Milder versions of the "minority subcommunity" perspective accept occupation, education, and income as important, but postulate that either a) there are significant differences in the relative importance of these factors between the black and the white societies,[8] or b) there are more limited ranges in each of these hierarchies in minority communities resulting in evaluations different from those of the white society for the same position — e.g., a high school principal may be middle class in white society and upper class in black society.[9] The more extreme separatist versions of this perspective stress the need for a totally different set of criteria in understanding stratification in the black community. For example, family "respectability," unique ghetto life styles, and community participation in organizations have been suggested as alternatives.[10]

This last version of the race relations model has a strong black nationalist ring; it implies that the ghetto has generated its own status dynamics and that culturally unique criteria should be applied to the black community. All the issues that emerge from this approach cannot be discussed in this chapter; however, several points can be brought up which have special significance for the concept of race and class in interaction.

1. The minority subcommunity probably has its strongest effect on class and status evaluations made by lower-class blacks and Chicanos. When color and poverty unite one is likely to find a very high degree of spatial segregation, a low degree of participation in racially integrated institutions, and a somewhat separate set of status criteria. An updated version of Warner's "class within caste" model (see chapter 2) for blacks and Chicanos may be helpful in conceptualizing this difference.

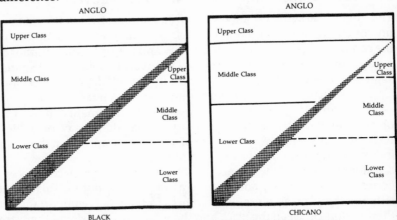

Revised "Class Within Caste" Model of Stratification

FIGURE 4-2

In Figure 4-2 the diagonal colorline represents the social distance between castes. It is not of uniform width but is only thick at its lower-class end. At the middle-and upper-class end, the colorline funnels down to indicate a moderate barrier for middle- and upper-class blacks and an almost permeable barrier for middle-class Chicanos. The greater the socioeconomic achievement, the more permeable is the caste line. The "open marketplace" model is more applicable at the middle and upper end of the color-caste line. But the lower-class stratum is likely to be so physically and socially segregated that intra-ethnic contacts are more crucial for one's status or identity. The indexes of occupation, education, and income, which are useful for determining status in the white world, may be incomplete measures of status, respect, or acceptance for lower-class blacks and Chicanos.

In a lower-class section of the Washington, D.C., black ghetto,Ulf Hannerz found that a number of status-graded life styles existed that were unknown to outsiders.[11] He found "mainstreamers," "swingers," "street families," and "streetcorner men" who were assigned discrete ghetto-specific statuses. Hannerz found that blacks who are denied status and male ego satisfaction through steady employment and support of a family (the norms for the "mainstreamers") may alternately attain respect and status through a unique ghetto-specific masculinity (dressing well, talking well, fighting well, etc.). These alternative sources of identity and status-satisfaction have developed in the ghetto (especially in the lower-class sections) as a result of closed access to the dominant society. This is not to say that the minority subcommunity is *only* important at the lower-class end of the spectrum.

In analyzing Los Angeles data, Grebler, Moore, and Guzman found that not all higher-income Chicanos move away from the barrio. Some may choose to stay in the barrio for status-related reasons. One kind of person who may remain in the colony is the upwardly mobile Chicano who has a relatively high income but low or moderate occupational prestige — that is, a person with imperfectly crystallized statuses. "For example, a highly paid truck driver of Mexican descent may be able to get more out of life by staying in a predominantly Mexican area where both his income and his occupation receive deference because they are above the norm."[12] Status inconsistency may be reduced by remaining in the barrio. Though black and Chicano minority communities have developed and persisted because of residential segregation, they may offer certain kinds of desirable status definitions to both the moderate and the low achiever.

Of course there are reasons other than status gains that encourage identifiable minority persons to remain in the ghetto: there are warmer friendships, more sincere contacts in neighborhood shopping, and more helpful neighbors than the minority person is likely to find outside the ghetto.

2. Given the strong possibility that alternative stratification systems exist in the minority subcommunity, some scholars have suggested that attempts at class comparisons across majority and minority communities — using the traditional measures of class, occupation, education, and income — are meaningless and futile. We do not agree. Such comparisons seem simply to be incomplete or in need of further *specification* by the minority subcommunity. A number of studies have shown that occupation, education, and income are important measures of prestige in both black and white communities.[13] Money will enable an individual to attain many goals. Since it is the societal medium for the exchange of goods and services, money is important for both majority and minority persons regardless of subcommunity evaluations of honor. The minority person who is high on occupation, education, and income scales *objectively* has more power to control his life than the lower-class minority person, and this holds regardless of microcultural evaluations.

3. Even if occupation, education, and income are accepted as important status determinants in both minority and majority communities, it is still quite possible that the three are weighted differently in different racial groups. A great many studies have shown that education has a uniquely important place in the black community.[14] (Black parents' stress on educational achievement perhaps originates from attitudes inherited from slavery; unlike a job, education is something the white man can't take away). But in most widely used general indices of social class (e.g., Warner's ISC or Hollingshead's ISP), occupation receives the highest weight.[15]

Research shows that blacks often do not receive the same occupational returns for their educational investment as white persons.[16] As a result of such job discrimination, it is quite likely that occupation is a less valid measure of socioeconomic status for black persons than for white persons. There appear to be serious problems in the comparability of occupations between races. One should be wary of studies that apply uncorrected indices across different racial groups.

4. The significance of the minority community is far greater than simply the physical space called a ghetto or barrio. There is, in addition, a *psychological* concept of a black or Chicano community. For some, this may be simply an identification with others of the race who

have suffered common oppression. For those blacks and Chicanos who have a more developed ideology, a separate community may symbolize the development of a unified group with a heightened sense of pride and cultural nationalism. The idea of community then, may mean that blacks, Chicanos, and Indians exert *collective* rather than individual power toward attaining their civil rights.

Harold Cruse, writing in support of a strong, unified black community, separates individual and collective mobility:

> If 'we' — the great unskilled, uneducated, un-middle-class, unintegrated, and uninvited masses — staged an all-black-American super boycott merely to get a scattering of hand picked Negroes jobs in big corporations, it just would not be worth the bother. Such are *class* aims, integrationist class aims; they are not *group* economic aims.[17]

Similarly, Alfredo Cuellar, in discussing the growing ideology of Chicanismo, writes:

> *Chicano* ideologues insist that social advance based on material achievement is, in the final analysis, less important than social advance based on *la raza*; they reject what they call the myth of American individualism. . . . If Mexicans are to confront the problems of their group realistically they must begin to act along collective lines.[18]

The idea of a unified community is extremely important for understanding race-class interaction. To what extent does a strong identification with one's racial stratum outweigh class differences? Enough that lower and middle-class segments of that stratum hold common outlooks and are willing to engage in common action? That is, how potent are the black and Chicano ideologies in uniting their respective races toward common outlooks and actions? Empirical explorations of race and class should, at a minimum, consider the possibility that a common racial ideology is more significant than a common class ideology.

III. ETHCLASS

The ethclass model is a third major construct on the way ethnicity and class interact. This approach is especially concerned with stratification outcomes and correlates, that is, the values, the primary group interaction, and the behavior that emerge from the joint occupancy of two hierarchies. According to the ethclass concept, it is fallacious to assume that either class variables or ethnicity variables will alone consistently predict values, interaction, or behavior. To assume that middle-class black persons will have outlooks identical to middle-class white persons is to accept the melting-pot ideology — i.e., that the functional goal of society is assimilation. However, to assume that race or ethnicity always sweeps aside class differences (especially in a united black community or a "black power" ghetto) is equally unsupported by data.

One of the more balanced presentations of this discussion is found in Milton Gordon's *Assimilation in American Life.*[19] Gordon views both class and ethnicity as powerful forces that profoundly affect identity, social participation, and cultural behavior. As a determinant of cultural behavior, life style, and taste, social class is likely to be more important than ethnicity. People of the same social class have similar interests, tastes, and occupational experiences even if they are from different ethnic groups. However, when it comes to collective identity — a sense of peoplehood in which a common sense of destiny and heritage is shared with a large number of people of the same racial or national descent — ethnicity will be more salient than class position.

Ethnic identification is viewed as a powerful source of collective identity that does not disappear with class mobility. Many blacks, Chicanos, and Indians who make substantial gains will still retain a sense of shared fate with their respective ethnic or racial fellows. However, just as class does not completely override race, the ethnic factor is not so powerful that it overrides *all* class differences. Instead, class outlooks and ethnic identification often unite or blend into what Gordon calls the ethclass or the "social space created by the intersection of the ethnic group with the social class."[20] . . . This is illustrated by Figure 4-3 below, in which the four ethnic populations of this discussion are cross-tabulated with social class.

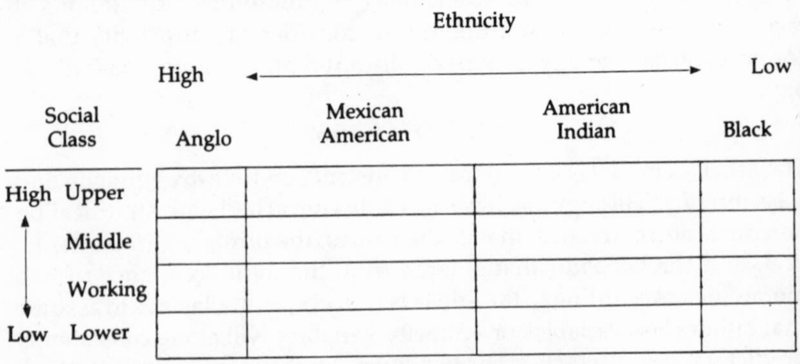

Ethnicity

Social Class	High ◄——————————————————————► Low			
	Anglo	Mexican American	American Indian	Black
High Upper				
▲ Middle				
Working				
Low Lower				

Ethnicity and Social Class

FIGURE 4-3

Each cell of the Table represents a unique social space, a kind of sub-society. Gordon suggests that "ethclass" has the greatest salience for primary group participation.

> With a person of the same social class but of a different ethnic group, one shares behavioral similiarities but not a sense of peoplehood. With those of the same ethnic group but of a different social class, one shares the sense of peoplehood but not behavioral similarities. The only group which meets both of these criteria are people of the same ethnic group *and* same social class.[21]

Following Gordon's logic, middle-class blacks would be far more likely to enter into relaxed, trusting relationships with other middle-class blacks than with lower-class blacks or middle-class persons of other ethnic groups. Gordon hypothesizes that *cultural behavior* is best predicted by class, *sense of peoplehood* is most often a reflection of ethnicity, and *participation in primary groups* is confined to ethclass.[22]

Surprisingly, the concept "ethclass" has received very little attention in race or stratification literature in recent years. It appears to be an especially provocative concept for analyzing current race-class interactions among blacks and Chicanos. Class stratification within the black and Mexican-American populations appears to be developing rapidly while black pride and "la raza" are producing heightened ethnic identifications. A concept that posits that unique "social spaces" are determined by a blend of race and class has special relevance to the contemporary scene. Gordon's version of ethclass is chiefly confined to primary group participation. However, Gordon's concept may be expanded to suggest that an "ethclass effect" is *any* instance in which the behaviors or attitudes of individuals result from the joint effect of ethnicity and social class; this could be cultural outlooks or political behavior as well as the primary group interaction that Gordon suggests. Our expanded version of the concept means that the values and tastes of individuals are not necessarily due to their social class positions alone.

Since blacks, Chicanos, and American Indians are asserting their cultural uniquenesses (as illustrated by "soul," chicanismo, and tribal nationalism) but at the same time have distinct class structures, it seems likely that there may be unique blends of ethnicity and class that will be reflected in attitudes and values. Many urban middle-class and working-class Mexican Americans may have an orientation toward mobility and materialistic success that is a blend of the ethnic tradition of family cohesion and solidarity and the middle-class orientation toward individualistic mobility. An often posed question is why lower-class blacks and Chicanos have not united into "Third World" coalitions since their class interests are so similar. "Ethclass" would suggest that common class oppression (economic discrimination and unemployment) is not a sufficient condition to produce such unions; there must be commonality on both class and ethnic dimensions. There are many perceptions of the social system (such as feelings of ability to affect city government, distrust of government officials, and beliefs in the openness of the system) that may be profoundly affected by peculiar ethnic-class attitudes rather than solely by either ethnic or class attitudes. Working-class blacks sharing a common occupation (e.g., postal workers) may have an especially high potential for political protest since perceived class exploitation and racial identification reinforce each other in the direction of a unique sense of a shared fate and common grievances.

Ethclass can be a powerful tool for analyzing the society as a whole. The *white working class* (blue-collar workers) is one of the most widely discussed ethclass groups of recent years. White workers are seen as having unique complaints and grievances over the special reparations and dispensations granted to blacks. The white worker who can barely afford to send his son or daughter to college often feels that blacks are given an unfair advantage in both preferential admission and financial aid. He is expressing an ethclass outlook. That is, his intense grievances and anger are due to a combination of his race and his socioeconomic status.

An important feature of the ethclass model (in its expanded version) is that it takes into account two often discussed race relations outcomes — assimilation versus a separate united ghetto or barrio. We have frequently heard that the ultimate fate of minority groups in American society is upward mobility and assimilation into the dominant middle class. More recently, with the Black power ideology of the late 1960s there has been a call for complete control over ghetto institutions and a united (non-integrated) black community that can effectively wield power against the white majority. The concept ethclass suggests an outcome between these extremes. Class need not eradicate racial identification so that middle-class blacks become carbon copies of middle-class whites. Rather, the ethclass perspective focuses attention on the retention of both race and class identities, a combination which produces unique joint effects for each distinct cell.

SUMMARY

A great many points have been covered in the discussion of three models of American race relations and a brief summary may be helpful to keep important points in focus. The following (Figure 4-4) summarizes major perspectives that emerge from each of the three models.

Figure 4.4: Summary of Three Models

1. Open Marketplace of Status Interaction

Possible Outcomes
a) *Assimilation*
   Class achievement completely overrides racial status in terms of power, wealth, and honor (least likely alternative).
b) *Remaining Ethnic Differential*
   Social class achievement greatly improves power and life chances of minority persons to the extent that middle-class blacks, Chicanos, and American Indians have greater power in the general society than lower-class whites. However, some racial barriers, strain, and inconsistencies remain vis-à-vis middle-class whites.
c) *Changing Role Relationships*
   Majority group's tendency to dominate racial interaction and to perceive minority people as incompent is weakened by exposure to conventional role relationships in which minority person is in superordinate position.

2. Minority Subcommunities

a) Subcommunity provides alternative sources of honor and prestige (especially for lower-class minority persons).
b) Persons completely identify with their respective ethnic communities. Ethnic position is more important than class.

3. Ethclass

Race and class intersect to form subsocieties with unique attitudes, perceptions of the social system, and primary groups.

THE THREE MODELS AND PREDICTION

An important goal of this book is the prediction of attitudes, behavior, and social participation from the joint interaction of race and class. Chapters 6 through 9 will compare the attitudes of whites, blacks, and Chicanos of different socioeconomic levels. The three models — open marketplace, minority subcommunity, and ethclass — help in making these predictions.

It should be noted that the three models are not mutually exclusive but rather focus on different aspects of race-class interaction. It is quite possible for individuals or groups to be shifting across these three "worlds." A Chicano or black employed in a skilled or white-collar occupation may spend part of his time in an integrated or mostly Anglo work situation, his job and position in the hierarchy being crucial to his power, self-esteem, and his effect on whites. [23] Yet he may also be a part of a barrio stratification order and have a thoroughly compartmentalized self-concept in that "world." He may also have attitudes and self-concepts that could only be explained by ethclass. For example, he may feel that he is personally doing all right but that his race as a whole is not getting fair treatment.

Open Market and Prediction

The open market model constantly brings us to the question of the degree to which social class achievement *changes, modifies,* or *overrides* ethnic status. Two questions are to be explored in later chapters:

(1) To what extent does socioeconomic similarity reduce racial barriers to friendship? That is, does a common class position (similarity in education, tastes, and occupational experiences) reduce the social distance of the color line such that many middle-class blacks, Anglos, and Chicanos could enter into friendship contact?

(2) To what extent does class similarity produce the same values and outlooks in majority and minority persons? For example, are there particular value sets that middle-class parents emphasize in the socialization of their children, regardless of whether the parent is white, black, or Chicano?

Ethclass and Prediction

Although the concept of ethclass has great explanatory potential (and a kind of mystical ring) it has not been made operational or tested empirically. Several empirical directions for the concept are used in later chapters:

1) In Chapter 6, it is suggested that the values, aspirations and outlooks of middle-class blacks often represent a complex blend of materialism, racial militance and racial identification; 2) data in Chapter 8, indicate that lower-class black and Chicano children face a pile-up of ethnic and class barriers in obtaining a quality education.

To qualify as an ethclass analysis, there must be, at a minimum, a two-way comparison: a vertical comparison with persons of the same ethnic group and different classes, and a horizontal comparison with persons of the same class but different ethnic groups. However, if we take all the ethclass cells (Figure 4-1) as our operational matrix, there are a great many horizontal and vertical comparisons to be made. That is, to be completely exhaustive in determining an ethclass effect we would need to show that middle-class blacks are different from middle-class whites, lower-class Chicanos, upper-class Indians, etc. For obvious reasons (such as the cost to include this many subgroups in a survey and the difficulty in locating certain subgroups in representative numbers) the complete study of ethclass effects would be nearly impossible. To trim the equation down to one essential comparison, a minority group ethclass (such as middle-class black or lower-class Chicano) should differ both from the same class in the Anglo majority and a different class in the minority group. For example in Figure 4-5 middle-class blacks (the ethclass under study) must be shown to be different from middle-class whites as well as from lower-class blacks.

FIGURE 4-5: Ethclass comparisons

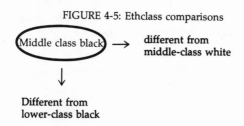

The horizontal comparison measures the class effect (middle-class black vis-a-vis middle-class white) while the vertical comparison measures the race effect. If middle-class blacks contrast with both comparsion groups we can assume an ethclass effect.

A third and fascinating possibility of ethclass prediction would deal with race and class consciousness. Barely explored is the possibility of race and class consciousness uniting into special ethclass combinations. For example, a revised Marxian conflict perspective might lead us to the hypothesis that blacks or Chicanos who identify strongly with both their race and a working-class socioeconomic position will be especially radical in their outlook and behavior. (The idea is explored in Chapter 7). In this example, a particular combination of subjective race and class are combining to determine political attitudes and behavior. Note, in this case, a single racial group is involved but both race and class are varying in terms of degrees of attachment and shared fate with the two strata.

FIGURE 4-6: Race and Class Identification
Among Blacks

Race Identification Among Blacks

		Low	High
Class Identification Among Blacks	Low		
	High		X

Minority Subcommunity as a Specification Variable

The minority subcommunity may provide important specifications in our race-class predictions as illustrated in Figure 4-7.

FIGURE 4-7: Race-Class Predictions

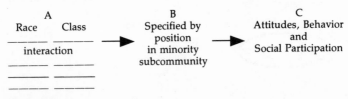

a) open market
b) ethclass

Suppose we were interested in the relationship between race, class, and self-esteem. Taking an ethclass approach, we might predict that lower-class blacks will be "uniquely low" in self-esteem. The prediction would involve the A and C components of Figure 4-4. However, the minority subcommunity would provide an important specification. Lower-class blacks who are highly integrated into a minority subcommunity and have a very solid reputation in the street culture may not have low self-esteem at all. That is, the ghetto community serves as a strong buffer against reduced self worth due to being poor and black. Our revised prediction, taking into account A, B, and C, would be that lower-class blacks will have low self-esteem only when they have no alternative sources of self-respect from ghetto life. The ghetto community is a crucial specification variable in this prediction because the outcome of self-esteem is largely derived from *social honor* in various stratification orders. However, if we were predicting action such as willingness to file suit in the face of discrimination, class position in the dominant society (A) would be more directly related to the outcome (C) irrespective of the minority community (B). High occupation, education, and income increase the probability of filing suit regardless of ghetto honor.

NOTES TO CHAPTER 4

[1] See Gerhard E. Lenski, "Status Crystallization: A Non-Vertical Dimension of Social Status," *American Sociological Review* 19 (August, 1954): 405-413.

[2] St. Clair Drake and Horace R. Cayton, *Black Metropolis: A Study of Negro Life in a Northern City* (New York: Harcourt, Brace, 1945). See also W. Lloyd Warner's Introduction in Allison Davis, Burleigh R. Gardner, and Mary R. Gardner, *Deep South* (Chicago: University of Chicago Press, 1941).

[3] See I. Katz, Judith Goldston, and L. Benjamin, "Behavior and Productivity in Biracial Work Groups," *Human Relations* 11 (May, 1958): 123-141, and I. Katz and L. Benjamin, "Effects of White Authoritarianism in Bi-racial Work Groups," *Journal of Abnormal Social Psychology* 61 (November, 1960): 448-456.

[4] Elizabeth G. Cohen and Susan S. Roper, "Modification of Interracial Interaction Disability: An Application of Status Characteristic Theory," *American Sociological Review* 61 (November, 1972): 643-657.

[5] Ibid., p. 646.

[6] This conception of "conventional role" is taken from Shibutani's discussion. See Tamotsu Shibutani, *Society and Personality* (Englewood Cliffs, N.J.: Prentice-Hall, 1961), pp. 46-54.

[7] Cohen and Roper, op. cit.

[8] See, for example, Norvel D. Glenn, "Negro Prestige Criteria: A Case Study in the Bases of Prestige," *American Journal of Sociology* 68 (May, 1963): 645-657.

[9] See, for example, Andrew Billingsley, *Black Families in White America* (Englewood Cliffs, N.J.: Prentice-Hall, 1968), p. 122.

[10] An excellent summary of this separatist approach is found in Donald I. Warren and Patrick C. Easto's "White Stratification Theory and Black Reality: A Neglected Problem of American Sociology" (paper presented at the sixty-seventh Annual meeting of the American Sociological Association, August 28-31, 1972), pp. 8-15. See also, Billingsley, op. cit., p. 124; Ulf Hannerz, *Soulside* (New York: Columbia University Press, 1969), especially chs. 2 and 4; and Jay R. Williams, "Social Stratification and the Negro American: An Exploration of Some Problems in Social Class Measurement" (Ph.D. diss., Duke University).

[11] Hannerz, op. cit., chs. 2 and 4.

[12] Leo Grebler, Joan W. Moore, and Ralph C. Guzman, *The Mexican American People* (New York: Free Press, 1970), p. 329

[13] For example, Siegel, after an exhaustive study of occupational prestige with Negro and white samples, concluded: "The assertion that there is a community-wide prestige hierarchy of occupations within the Negro community, based upon Negro experiences in occupations, just does not square with the facts. Instead, Negros appear to be evaluating occupations in the same world as everyone else evaluates them and to be employing essentially the same information and the same combination of criteria as everyone else." See Paul M. Siegel, "Occupational Prestige in the Negro Subculture," in Edward O. Laumann, ed., *Social Stratification: Research and Theory of the 1970's* (New York: Bobbs-Merrill Co., 1970): 169.

[14] Drake and Cayton, op. cit.; Glenn, op. cit.; Seymour Parker and Robert J. Kleiner, *Mental Illness in the Urban Negro Community* (New York: Free Press, 1966).

[15] W. Lloyd Warner, Marchia Meeker, and Kenneth Eells, *Social Class in America: Manual of Procedure for the Measurement of Social Status* (New York: Harper & Brothers, 1960); August B. Hollingshead and Frederick C. Redlich, *Social Class and Mental Illness* (New York: John Wiley & Sons, 1958).

[16] One of the most sophisticated studies on this point is Peter M. Blau and Otis Dudley Duncan's *The American Occupational Structure* (New York: John Wiley & Sons, 1967), ch. 6.

[17] Harold Cruse, *The Crisis of the Negro Intellectual* (New York: William Morrow, 1967), p. 312.

[18] Joan W. Moore with Alfredo Cuellar, *Mexican Americans* (Englewood Cliffs, N.J.: Prentice-Hall, 1970), p. 153.

[19] Milton M. Gordon, *Assimilation in American Life* (New York: Oxford University Press, 1964), especially chs. 2 and 3.

[20] Ibid., p. 51.

[21] Ibid., p. 53.

[22] Ibid., pp. 52-53.

[23] See Alfred McClung Lee, *Multivalent Man* (New York: Braziller, 1964).

Chapter 5

DEMOGRAPHIC TRENDS: THE RISE OF BLACK AND CHICANO UPPER WORKING AND MIDDLE CLASSES

BLACK AMERICANS

A variety of data from the 1970 Census and reports from samples for 1971 and 1972 presents evidence for sizeable and growing working and middle-class segments of the black population, especially outside the South. For example, although the 1971 median family income for blacks (and small proportions of other non-whites) was only $6,714 (compared to the white median of $10,672), 30 percent of all black (non-white) families were making over $10,000; 40 percent of black families in the North and West were making this amount.[1] Thus, excluding the South, approximately four out of every ten black families were earning an income considered middle class in the early 1970s. Moreover, there has been a definite increase in this middle-class stratum in the last five years. In constant 1971 dollars, the proportion making over $10,000 increased from 12 to 20 percent in the South and 31 to 40 percent in the North and West (1966-1971).[2] In addition, 18 percent of blacks in the nation (South included) were in the $7-10,000 category, a category that might be roughly labelled "working-class" income. Combining this category with that of the families making over $10,000, it can be stated that about 48 percent of all black families in the nation earn over $7,000 and are, therefore, either in the "stable working-class" or middle-class segments of the population.[3] Another way of approaching this topic is by way of income differentials between median income of black families and median income of white families. The overall ratio of Negro (excluding other non-whites) to white family income is a discouraging 60 percent in 1970. In other words, the average black income is only 60 percent of the average white income. This is a closing of the gap when compared to the 1959 ratio of 52 percent or the 1964 ratio of 54 percent.[4] However, there are tremendous variations in the gap by region of the country and the age of the respondents. What is extremely interesting from the point of view of a rising middle class is the finding that "there was no apparent difference in 1970 between the incomes of white and Negro husband-wife families outside the South where the head was under thirty-five years old. For these young families, the ratio of Negro to white income was about 96 percent in 1970, up from 78 percent in 1959."[5] However, one qualification must be added to these optimistic findings: the income parity observed among young white and black families in the North and West holds true only for families in which both husband and wife worked. For these families, one actually finds that blacks are making more than whites with a ratio of 104 percent. Young black families in the North and West with both husband and wife working have a median income of $11,045 compared with $10,578 for comparable white families.[6] Note, however, that young black families in which just the husband worked were making about 75 percent of comparable white families. In other words, the black working wife was a crucial fact in the income parity finding. Young black wives in the North and West earned approximately 30 percent more than their white counterparts, one explanation being that young black wives were more likely to hold a job the year round (52 percent of the Negro wives vs. 36 percent of the white wives).[7] The point of these somewhat complex findings is that for the first time in American history, one segment of the black population is earning the same income as a comparable segment of the white population. However, young black two career families outside the South accounted for only about 10 percent of all Negro families in the United States. Although this is a rather small category of families it is also a very strategic one in terms of the future of the black working and middle classes: it is likely that the proportion of such young Northern and Western families will increase. It remains to be seen whether the present generation of young black families that has achieved parity with young white families can hold onto that equality as they grow older.

Occupational Status

Table 5-1 presents data from a current population report on the occupational status of employed blacks and whites in 1972.

TABLE 5-1
Occupational Distribution of White and Negro, 1972

	Negro*		White	
Professional	9.5%		15%	
Managers and Administrators	4		11	
Sales Workers	2	30%	7	51%
Clerical	14		18	
Craftsmen and Foremen				
Operatives	9		14	
Laborers	22		16	
Farmers and Farmworkers	10	71%	5	51%
Service (excluding private	3		4	
household)	20		11	
Private household workers	7		1	

*Includes very small proportions of other non-white groups.

Source: U.S. Bureau of the Census, *The Social and Economic Status of the Black Population in the United States, 1972*, Current Populations Reports Series P-23, no. 46 (Washington, D.C.: Government Printing Office, 1973), p. 49.

What is immediately apparent is that sharp differences continue to exist between the black and white distributions of occupational position. About 41 percent of employed Negroes (and other non-whites) were engaged in the most physically exhausting, poorly paid, and least prestigeful jobs (service, private household, farm and laboring jobs), about double the 20 percent for whites. On the other hand, from the perspective of a rising middle class, it can be seen that 30 percent of all employed blacks are in white-collar occupations and another 9 percent in the most challenging and rewarding blue-collar jobs (craftsmen and foremen). This means about 39 percent of employed blacks are in skilled and white-collar occupations. In predominantly urban industrial areas outside the South, these proportions are higher. For example, in California (data reviewed later in this chapter) 38 percent of blacks in 1971 were in white-collar occupations; 48 percent were in skilled or white-collar.[8] Such occupations provide at least a moderate degree of work challenge, financial reward, and social status. Further, a comparison with the 1960 Census shows a definite increase in the white-collar segment (from 16 percent in white-collar occupations to the 1972 30 percent).[9] Nor are all the white-collar increases in the lowest paid clerical jobs; the percentage of black persons in clerical jobs shifted from 7 percent in 1960 to 14 percent in 1972, but the professional proportion also increased from 5 percent to 9.5 percent.[10] However, some have cautioned that when observing white-collar statistics among minority persons, one must make a distinction between males and females since these statistics often include the many black female clerical workers who have low salaries and little chance for advancement. For the nation, the 30 percent proportion of blacks in white-collar jobs drops to 22 percent when only black males are considered (vs. 40 percent of blacks females).[11] Similarly, in the 1970 California census the 38 percent figure drops to 27 percent when only black males are considered.[12] In other words, our findings on the size of the black middle-class are not quite as striking when only black males are considered. However, it still appears that about 1 in 4 black males are in white-collar jobs, the greatest proportion of this category in non-clerical work. Further, when the craftsmen-foremen category is added to the white-collar category, we find that 37 percent of employed black males in the nation (1972) and 48 percent of black males in California (1970) are in either white-collar or skilled jobs.

Education

In general, blacks made gains in the last decade in the percentages completing high school and attending and completing college. Table 5-2 shows the percent of persons twenty to twenty-nine years old who completed four years or more of high school from 1960 to 1972*. Though the differences between black and white are substantial, a steady increase in blacks completing high school can be noted: in 1960 only 38 percent of young black males and 43 percent of young black females had completed high school compared with 64 percent of black males and 61 percent of black females achieving this education level in 1972. The proportion of young black adults completing college has also increased. Thus, the proportion of blacks twenty-five to thirty-four years old who had completed four or more years of college increased from 4 to 8 percent in 1972 (compared to a white increase from 12 to 19 percent).[13] Finally, it can be noted that college attendance has increased among those in the eighteen to twenty-four year-old bracket. In 1972, 18 percent of the young blacks (21 percent of males, 16 percent of females) were enrolled in college as compared to about 13 percent in 1967. In contrast, the proportion of young whites has remained about the same — 27 percent in 1967 compared to 26 percent (31 percent males, 22 percent females) in 1972.[14]

TABLE 5-2

Percentage of Persons 20 to 29 years old who have completed at least four years of High School

Year	Male		Female	
	Black*	White	Black	White
1960	38%	64%	43%	66%
1967	52	77	56	77
1970	59	81	63	80
1972	64	84	66	83

Source: U.S. Bureau of the Census, *The Social and Economic Status of the Black Population in the United States, 1972,* Current Population Reports Series P-23, no. 46 (Washington, D.C.: Government Printing Office, 1973), p. 64.
*Includes small proportions of other non-whites.

The statistics here summarized from the 1970 Census suggest that a fairly sizeable middle-class and upper working-class group has developed in the black population and is likely to show continued growth in the future. However, a number of recent studies suggest that not all blacks are making progress; a large segment of the black population is moving up while another segment of the black population is becoming more firmly entrenched in poverty and dependency. Aggregate data may mask these counter trends. For example, Daniel Moynihan, in a provocative article, speaks of the "up and down" pattern, noting that the "down" (or poverty) population is inextricably associated with specific patterns of family structure. "During the 1960's the number of children living in poverty declined sharply — except for those in female-headed families . . . "[15] Though the trend was true for white families as well as blacks, it was most pronounced among blacks and other new arrivals to the cities (such as Puerto Ricans). Another example of the up-down pattern has to do with education. Blacks with any college experience (even one year) made sharp gains in income in recent years as contrasted with the small or nonexistent gains made by those with a high school education or less. "This variance is striking in young families. In 1968 the Negro family headed by a twenty-five to thirty-four year-old person with one to three years of college had a median income 111.1 percent higher than one headed by a person with only one to three years of high school. For white families, this gap was only 29.6 percent."[16]

The main thrust of this chapter and the next is the growth of middle-class and stable working-class segments of the black and

Chicano populations — people often ignored in the studies of race relations. In developing this thesis of a rising middle class, however, I want to be sure that statistics presented above do not create a one-sided optimism. It is true that many blacks and Chicanos have experienced gains in the last decade. It is also true that many have made no gains or are perhaps even more firmly entrenched in poverty and dependency. Our discussion is simply emphasizing the former; the reader should not forget the latter. The normal processes of urbanization, even with special black power programs operating, are not likely to affect those persons most deeply involved in poverty. Large-scale structural overhauls, such as guaranteed income, are one possible policy for affecting the poverty strata.

SOCIOECONOMIC CHARACTERISTICS OF SPANISH SURNAME PERSONS IN CALIFORNIA, TEXAS, LOS ANGELES METROPOLITAN AREA AND EAST LOS ANGELES

As in the case of blacks, there appears to be a fairly sizeable and growing stratum of Mexican-Americans earning over $10,000 in skilled and white-collar positions. However, there are special problems in describing Mexican Americans as a result of the census classificiation, "Spanish language/Spanish surname." In most census reports, Mexican Americans are not separated from other persons with Spanish surnames. In 1970, the "Spanish surname/language" population was composed of (1) persons who reported Spanish as their mother tongue, the language spoken in the home during childhood and (2) all members of a household related to a head or wife reporting Spanish as their mother tongue, plus (3) all other persons with Spanish surnames (the Bureau refers to a list of about 8,000 Spanish surnames). This definition is rather broad; for example, it might include Anglo wives of Mexican Americans as well as all Latin people other than Mexican Americans (e.g., Spanish surname persons from Cuba, Central and South America, Puerto Rico, etc.) and their wives regardless of ethnic origin. It is extremely difficult to estimate exactly the discrepancy between the Spanish surname/language and Mexican-American categories. But to give a rough idea, data from the five Southwestern states (1970) indicate that 84 percent of persons of Spanish origin (slightly different than language/surname) were of Mexican descent.[17] However, the discrepancy between "Spanish" and "Mexican" varies by area of the Southwest. In California, particularly the Los Angeles-Long Beach metropolitan area, there are special problems since many third generation and higher-status Mexican Americans marry outside their ethnic group.[18] It is a fact that the Spanish surname/language definition is masking a number of Anglo wage earners in Los Angeles. There are also a fair number of Cubans and other non-Mexican Latinos in the Los Angeles and San Francisco metropolitan areas. On the other hand, there is known to be far closer correspondence between "Spanish surname" and "Mexican-American" in Texas and the east side or San Gabriel Valley sectors of Los Angeles. The point is simply that, in the following discussion, though most Spanish surname/language persons are Mexican-American, there is an unknown degree of variance between the two terms and our findings on a rising skilled and middle-class are likely to be inflated in California and the Los Angeles metropolitan area as a whole. If we find, for example, one-third of the persons with Spanish surnames in white-collar occupations, not all these persons are upwardly mobile Mexican Americans from the barrio. Some (presumably a small percent) may be Latinos not of Mexican descent who move to middle-class neighborhoods directly and in no way identify with the Mexican-American group.

We have chosen to concentrate on Spanish-surname persons in two states, California and Texas, and on three specific areas within these states, Los Angeles-Long Beach SMSA (Standard Metropolitan Statistical Area), San Antonio SMSA, and East Los Angeles. The two states were chosen because they contain by far the largest number of Spanish-surname persons (almost half of all Spanish-surname persons lived in California in 1970[19]) and because they contain the extremes of discrimination and caste-like barriers. For example, Grebler, Moore, and Guzman frequently allude to South Texas as an area in which Mexicans have historically faced the most consistently rigid racial barriers. In contrast, California (particularly Southern California) is seen as a relatively open area with a larger working and middle class, a lower degree of traditional folk culture, a more highly rationalized economic system, and a more permeable color line for upwardly mobile Chicanos.[20] This optimistic statement, however, must be balanced with the realities of the East Los Angeles barrio where one finds a high degree of poverty, tense police-community relations, and the failure of the school system to educate large numbers of Chicano children.

Before moving to socioeconomic data, a stereotype of Mexican-American people needs to be corrected. With the exception of the very latest accounts, Mexican Americans have often been depicted as rural migratory farm laborers. This stereotype of the Mexican American has probably been accentuated by the widely publicized boycott of grapes and head lettuce inspired by Cesar Chavez. Though migratory farm laborers are an extremely important population in terms of social justice and ethnic solidarity, they are an atypical minority. Mexican Americans are most highly concentrated in urban areas and occupations. The 1970 Census shows that nine-tenths of California's Spanish-surname population lived in urban areas. If one were to characterize Mexican Americans in terms of a modal occupation, they would be blue-collar workers in semi-skilled or skilled jobs in an urban setting.[21] This does not necessarily mean that all discrimination battles have been won, for as Pēnalosa notes " . . . to assert that Mexican-Americans have largely left behind the problems associated with migratory agricultural labor is not to say that they have no problems. It is rather that now their problems have become those of an under-privileged urban minority group."[22]

Comparing Occupation by States

In table 5-3 we find the distribution of Spanish surname persons in the states of California and Texas compared with whites and Negroes. Consistent with our theme of rising skilled and white-collar strata, we are particularly interested in the proportions of Spanish-surname persons in white-collar and craft positions. The data show that about one-third of the employed Spanish-surname persons in California are in white-collar positions with an additional 14 percent in skilled blue-collar (craftsmen-foremen) positions. In other words, roughly half of the employed Spanish-surname people (most of whom are Mexican-Americans) in California are in skilled or white-collar occupations. Of male wage earners, 28 percent are in white-collar jobs (21 percent professional, managerial, and sales and 7 percent clerical) and 20 percent are craftsmen or foremen. Again the totals show about one-half of the population in skilled or white-collar jobs. This is certainly a very different picture from the lower-class migratory farm labor image.

However, before asserting the emergence of a large new Chicano middle-class stratum in California, we need to return to the problems of the Spanish-surname category. At the time of this writing there are no data published on the occupational distribution of *Mexican-American* persons in California. But there is a current population report (1972) in which occupational data are presented separately for those of Mexican origin in the U.S.[23] The report shows that about 18 percent of employed Mexican-American males are in white-collar jobs with another 21 percent in the craftsmen-foremen category. (The corresponding proportions for females are approximately 40 percent — mostly clerical — and 1 percent.) It is apparent that there are lower proportions of white-collar males in the national Mexican-origin data than the California Spanish-surname data (18 percent versus 28 percent). However, one can still summarize that about four out of ten persons of Mexican heritage in the U.S. are in either *white-collar* or *skilled* positions.

Even if we accept the California statistics (Table 5-3) as moderately accurate, one should balance the one-third of the population in white-collar jobs with the much larger percentage of Anglo persons (56 percent) in such positions. Further, it should be noted that the proportion of Anglos in the most challenging, prestigious, and well-paid white-collar jobs (professional and managerial) is double that of the Spanish-surname proportion (28 percent versus 14 percent). The occupational distribution of blacks in California is somewhat similar to Spanish-surname persons (38 percent white collar) except that there are higher proportions of blacks in managerial and sales jobs and far higher proportions of blacks in service occupations.

Turning to the Texas data (Table 5-4), it is surprising to find that the occupational distribution of Spanish-surname persons is quite similar to that of California. For example, 32 percent of Spanish-surname persons are in white-collar positions compared with the 34 percent in California. This finding is not simply an artifact of female clerical workers. (Twenty-five percent of the males are in white-collar occupations — about the same proportion as in California.) However, striking differences emerge between the blacks of California and those of Texas. Among Texas black persons, the proportion in white-collar occupations is only about half of what it is in California — 20 percent vs. 38 percent. In Texas there are consistently more blacks in the least skilled positions — operatives, laborers, and service. From an occupational standpoint, in Texas it is blacks rather than Mexican Americans who face the most extreme racial barriers and have the least developed socioeconomic range.

Income by States

Income data for California and Texas are in Tables 5-5 and 5-6. For convenience in discussing these data, incomes of over $10,000 will be designated "middle class," incomes in the $0-4,999 category are labeled "at or near poverty," and the two categories in between ($5,000-7,000 and $8,000-9,999) will be called "lower working class" and "upper working class" respectively. In California, forty-one percent of the Spanish-surname families (and unrelated individuals) are in the middle-class income range as compared with 56 percent of the Anglo families. In California blacks have a noticeably lower proportion in the middle class with one-third making over $10,000. At the other end of the scale, blacks are more likely to be in the poverty category than Spanish-surname persons. The median incomes of families are also interesting; whites, of course, lead with $10,969 median income, followed by Spanish surname ($8,791) and black ($7,484).* In sum, the California income data show that although there are sizeable proportions of blacks and Mexican Americans at a poverty level or with very modest incomes (lower working class) there are also fairly sizeable percentages in the middle-class category — four out of ten families for Spanish surname, three out of ten for blacks. Again, however, we face the nagging problems of Spanish surname/language classification. Could it be that the fairly large middle-class "Spanish" proportion represents a gross overinflation of Mexican-American income in California? Probably not — though there is, no doubt, some degree of inflation. For example, a recent national report notes that 31 percent of U.S. families of *Mexican origin* were making an income over $10,000.[24]

---

*Relative sizes and composition of families must be taken into consideration in interpreting these data. Mexican-American families are more likely to be structurally intact over a longer period of time, and hence have more potential wage earners than either black or Anglo families.

Texas, however, is a very different world of income distribution. Before looking at detailed statistics, it is noteworthy that the median incomes of all three categories (including Anglos) are considerably lower in Texas than California. However, the extremely low incomes of Spanish-surname and black families cannot be totally attributed to a generally lower state income. For example, comparing income differentials in the two states, we find that in California Spanish-surname families are making about 80 percent of the income of Anglos, while in Texas, Spanish-surname families are making only 66 percent of the Anglo families' average income. Similarly for blacks, the respective percentages are 68 percent (California) and 60 percent (Texas). Historically, Chicanos in South Texas have faced unusually severe caste-like relations with Anglos. Blacks also have faced the same strong racial barriers in Texas as they have in the South generally. The largely rural area of South Texas also contributes to these low incomes. Note the large proportion of Spanish-surname and black families in the poverty category (41 percent and 47 percent). At the other end of the scale, only 21 percent of Spanish-surname families (vs. 41 percent in California) and 16 percent of black families (vs. 33 percent in California) are in the middle-class income group. No doubt these differences need to be somewhat corrected for the cost of living in the two states. However, even with such corrections, it is safe to say that the proportion of blacks and Mexican Americans with middle-class incomes is far greater in California than in Texas. The fact that Spanish-surname income distribution in Texas shows a large poverty category and a small middle class category is somewhat curious when we recall that the occupational distribution in Texas did not suggest such depression: forty-seven percent of Spanish-surname persons in Texas are in white-collar or skilled jobs. However, Mexican Americans in Texas are in skilled or white-collar positions with the lowest degree of economic reward. Moore has noted that Mexican Americans often hold the poorer jobs inside a broad occupational classification: "Professional and technical job holders, for example, are far more likely to be medical technologists than surgeons; draftsmen than architects; social workers than lawyers. In the managerial classification there are far more managers of small, marginal restaurants than corporate executives." [25]

TABLE 5-3

State of California

Occupational Distribution of Spanish Surname, Negro, and White,
1970 Census Employed Persons 16 years and older

	Spanish language/surname %		Negro %		White %	
Professional-technical	8.7		11.1		17.7	
Managers-administrators	4.8		3.2		9.8	
Sales	5.0	34.1	3.4	38.2	8.4	55.6
Clerical	15.6		20.5		19.7	
Craftsmen-foremen	14.0		9.6		13.4	
Operatives	24.7		18.6		13.3	
Laborers (non-farm)	7.0		7.3		3.8	
Farm Managers	.5		.1		.6	
Farm Laborers	5.6		.8		1.5	
Service Workers	12.5		20.2		10.7	
Private Household	1.3		5.0		.9	

Source: U.S. Bureau of the Census, *General Social and Economic Characteristics*, Census of the Population 1970, Final Report PC(1)-C6 California (Washington, D.C. Government Printing Office, 1971). Percentages computed from Table 54, p. 397.

TABLE 5-4

State of Texas

Occupational Distribution of Spanish Surname, Negro, and White,
1970 Census Employed Persons 16 Years and Older

	Spanish language/surname %		Negro %		White %	
Professional-technical	7.5		7.2		14.4	
Managers-administrators	5.0		2.1		8.9	
Sales	5.6	31.7	1.9	20	7.8	48.5
Clerical	13.6		8.8		17.4	
Craftsmen-foremen	15.0		8.8		14.3	
Operatives	21.5		21.3		15.1	
Laborers (non-farm)	8.7		11.3		4.8	
Farm Managers	.7		.4		2.0	
Farm Laborers	5.8		2.3		2.0	
Service Workers	13.8		23.5		11.1	
Private Household	2.5		12.1		2.1	

Source: U.S. Bureau of the Census, *General Social and Economic Characteristics*, Census of the Population, 1970, Final Report PC(1)-C45 Texas (Washington, D.C.: Government Printing Office, 1971). Percentages computed from Table 54, p. 445.

TABLE 5-5

State of California

Income Distribution of Spanish Surname, Negro, and White,
1970 Census for Families and Unrelated Individuals

	Spanish language/ surname		Negro		White	
At or near poverty						
$0-4,999	22.0%		31.2%		15.8%	
Lower working class						
$5-7,999	21.8		22.6		15.5	
Upper working class						
$8-9,999	15.1		13.0		12.4	
Middle and upper middle						
$10-14,999	26.0 ⎫		21.4 ⎫		28.4 ⎫	
$15-24,999	12.6 ⎬ 41%		10.2 ⎬ 33.1%		21.3 ⎬ 56.2%	
over $25,000	2.4 ⎭		1.5 ⎭		6.5 ⎭	
Median =	$8,791		$7,484		$10,969	

Source: U.S. Bureau of the Census, *General Social and Economic Characteristics*, Census of the Population, 1970, Final Report PC(1)-C6 California (Washington, D.C.: Government Printing Office, 1971). Percentages computed from Table 57, p. 403.

TABLE 5-6

State of Texas

Income Distribution of Spanish Surname,Negro, and White, 1970
Census for Families and Unrelated Individuals

	Spanish language/ surname		Negro		White	
At or near poverty						
$0-4,999	41.3%		46.8%		23.0%	
Lower working class						
$5-7,999	26.3		25.8		20.3	
Upper working class						
$8-9,999	11.7		11.4		13.8	
Middle and upper middle						
$10-14,999	14.3 ⎫		12.1 ⎫		24.8 ⎫	
$15-24,999	5.0 ⎬ 20.5%		3.4 ⎬ 16%		13.9 ⎬ 42.9%	
over $25,000	1.2 ⎭		.5 ⎭		4.2 ⎭	
Median =	$5,897		$5,334		$8,930	

Source: U.S. Bureau of the Census, *General Social and Economic Characteristics*, Census of the Population, 1970, Final Report PC(1)-C45 Texas (Washington, D.C.: Government Printing Office, 1971). Percentages computed from Table 57, p. 451.

State Education

Tables 5-7 and 5-8 present two kinds of educational data for California and Texas. The first is the proportion of males twenty-five years old and over who have completed a given educational level; the second deals only with younger and young middle-aged males (ages twenty to forty-nine) so as to capture the most recent trends in educational attainment. We are especially concerned with the proportion who have completed at least one year of college. Increasingly, persons need at least some college to obtain skilled and white-collar jobs. In California, among males twenty-five years old and over, 35 percent of whites, 20 percent of blacks and 19 percent of Spanish-surname persons have attended college. These proportions increase slightly when considering only males twenty to forty-nine years of age. Then, about one-fourth of Spanish-surname and black males have experienced (or are currently enrolled in) college. Thus, in a relatively "open" area (California) about one in four Spanish-surname males in the young and middle-aged group has attended college. At the other end of the educational scale, 38 percent of the Spanish-surname males have not even attended high school. Generally, the Spanish-surname population has lower mean educational attainment than either blacks or whites. California schools (especially in East Los Angeles) have been criticized for their failure to educate Mexican Americans. The high school dropout rate is said to be as high as 50 percent in some schools. Looking at younger males (twenty to forty-nine years old) we see that about half of the Mexican Americans (54 percent), two-thirds of the blacks (64 percent), and three-fourths of the Anglos have achieved high school graduation or more. Although educational attainment of Spanish-surname males in California is clearly less than blacks and whites, a large proportion have at least a high school education. Texas, in contrast, shows the educational attainment of Mexican Americans to be far more depressed. A whopping 60 percent of Mexican-American males (twenty-five years or over) have not attended high school and only 12 percent have attended college. Though things improve somewhat among younger males, the Spanisn-surname population in Texas stands out as unique in low educational attainment.

The Spanish-Surname Population in Urban Centers: Los Angeles-Long Beach and San Antonio Metropolitan Areas and East Los Angeles

The data presented for California and Texas in the previous section are valuable as summary socioeconomic information. However, it is important also to look at areas where Mexican Americans are most highly concentrated. As population centers with high concentrations of persons of Mexican descent in California and Texas, the Standard Metropolitan Areas of San Antonio, Los Angeles-Long Beach, and the East Los Angeles sectors are especially significant units for analysis.

TABLE 5-7

State of California, Educational Attainment of
Spanish Surname, Negro, and White 1970 Census

Males 25 years old and over	Spanish language/ surname %	Negro %	White %
0-8 years	38.3	27.8	19.5
High school 1-3	19.2	23.2	16.6
High school 4 years	23.4	28.6	28.8
College 1-3	11.9	14.3	17.3
College 4 or more	7.2	6.0	17.7
Median years completed	10.8	11.9	12.5
Males 20-49			
No high school	25.0	11.6	8.8
High school 1-3	25.0	24.0	15.1
High school 4 years	30.0	38.2	33.0
College 1 year or more	23.6	26.1	43.1

Source: U.S. Bureau of the Census, *General Social and Economic Characteristics*, Census of the Population, 1970, Final Report PC(1)-C6 California (Washington, D.C.: Government Printing Office, 1971). Percentages computed from Table 51, p. 391.

TABLE 5-8

State of Texas, Educational Attainment
of Spanish Surname, Negro and White
1970 Census

Males 25 years old and over	Spanish language/ surname %	Negro %	White %
0-8 years	59.7	47.7	29.7
High school 1-3	13.5	23.6	20.0
High school 4 years	14.9	18.6	23.0
College 1-3	6.3	6.1	12.6
College 4 or more	5.6	3.9	14.8
Males 20-49			
No high school	42.5	23.6	16.1
High school 1-3	18.3	29.1	17.4
High school 4 years	22.7	31.8	29.5
College, 1 year or more	16.5	15.5	37.0

Source: U.S. Bureau of the Census, *General Social and Economic Characteristics*, Census of the Population: 1970, Final Report PC(1)-C45 Texas (Washington, D.C.: Government Printing Office, 1971). Percentages computed from Table 51, p. 439.

It has been noted that Los Angeles has more people of Mexican descent than any other city in North America with the exceptions of Mexico City and Guadaljara.[26] Far more than simple population concentration makes Los Angeles interesting; one finds a great range of life styles, differential identification with the Chicano movement, attachment to Mexican culture, and residential patterns in Los Angeles.

The East Los Angeles sector of the metropolitan area is the barrio. As in many black ghettos, life in the barrio is often harsh. There are frequent complaints of consumer exploitation, of the existence of a separate and inferior school system that tracks Mexican students into low paying vocational job training, of police harassment, and of a lack of legal redress channels that the poor can use to fight the bureaucracy. A recent riot occurred in East Los Angeles (following the death of Reuben Salazar) that left two dead and many injured. It was also in East Los Angeles that large-scale demonstrations and walkouts took place over the inferior quality of the schools.

Since World War II, Mexican Americans "who have made it" often move completely out of the barrio into housing tracts in the larger Los Angeles Metropolitan area (our second comparison group). Although there are certain residential concentrations of middle-class Mexican Americans (for example, in Monterey Park and Montebello) many move to primarily Anglo areas. Middle and upper income Mexican-Americans face fewer barriers to residential movement than middle and upper income blacks. Survey researchers in the Los Angeles area often complain that they have trouble finding middle-class Mexican Americans because this group is too randomly dispersed. Not all successful Mexican Americans, however, move from the barrio. In a Los Angeles survey, Grebler, Moore, and Guzman found that a fairly high proportion of middle income persons choose to live in (or on the periphery of) the barrio, presumably to retain a more Mexican style of life and to remain near their extended families.[27]

San Antonio provides a third interesting comparison group. In contrast to Los Angeles, San Antonio has a smaller population, a much less diverse ethnic population ("there is no Negro Watts, Jewish Fairfax, Little Tokyo or other ethnic shopping and residential center."[28]), an economy depending more on tourist trade (occasioned by its historic past) than on large-scale manufacturing or industry, and more survival of the racial etiquette of dominance and subordination.[29] In short, San Antonio is not the large, cosmopolitan, diverse industrial center that one finds in Los Angeles.

In making socioeconomic comparisons between these three areas, one may ask how different is the socioeconomic distribution in the East Los Angeles area from the larger metropolitan area (which contains middle-class as well as lower-class Mexican-Americans). Another question is whether the average socioeconomic returns of Mexican Americans living in a separate depressed barrio community in a highly industrialized urban setting (East Los Angeles) will be higher than the returns of Mexican Americans in a less industrialized, more traditional Mexican-Anglo milieu (San Antonio).

Table 5-9 presents a selective summary of occupation, income, and education data for the three areas. Again, we view white-collar occupation, income over $10,000 and some college as middle-class criteria. The occupational summary shows East Los Angeles Mexican Americans with the lowest proportion in white-collar jobs and the highest proportion in service, labor, and operative jobs. Still, from the perspective of a rising upper working and middle class, it is noteworthy that 41 percent of East Los Angeles Spanish-surname persons are in craft or white-collar jobs. The San Antonio and Los Angeles (SMSA) data are similar with a little over one-third in white-collar jobs.

TABLE 5-9

Selected Occupation, Education, Income Data for
Spanish-Surname Population in San Antonio (SMSA)
Los Angeles-Long Beach (SMSA) and East Los Angeles.

Occupation	% white collar	% craft	% service/ labor operatives
San Antonio SMSA	36	18	46
Los Angeles-Long Beach SMSA	35	15	50
East Los Angeles	26	15	59

Income	% over $10,000	% 0-$4,999
San Antonio SMSA	22	35
Los Angeles-Long Beach SMSA	42	21
East Los Angeles	37	25

Education: Males 25 years and older	median years	% some college	% high school or more	% no high school
San Antonio SMSA	8.4	11	29	55
Los Angeles-Long Beach SMSA	11.0	20	43	36
East Los Angeles	8.4	7	24	55

Education: Females 25 years and older	median years	% some college	% high school grad or more	% no high school
San Antonio SMSA	7.5	6	23	62
Los Angeles-Long Beach SMSA	10.4	12	38	40
East Los Angeles	8.0	3	19	59

Source: U.S. Bureau of the Census, *General.Social and Economic Characteristics*, Census of the Population: 1970, Final Report PC(1)-C6 California and PC(1)-C45 Texas (Washington, D.C.: Government Printing Office, 1971). Percentages computed from pp. 686, 687, 718, 719, 734, and 735 for California. Percentages computed from pp. 619, 717, and 730 for Texas.

The income data from San Antonio are very different from those of Los Angeles. As in the Texas-California analysis above, San Antonio has a far lower proportion making over $10,000 than is found in East Los Angeles or the general Los Angeles-Long Beach SMSA. Surprisingly, 37 percent of the employed families (and unrelated individuals) in East Los Angeles are making over $10,000, compared with 42 percent in the Los Angeles-Long Beach area but compared with only 22 percent in the San Antonio area. In terms of dollar income reward, the East Los Angeles Mexican-American family is typically much better off than the San Antonio Mexican-American family. The highest proportion in the middle-class income category is among Mexican Americans in the Los Angeles Metropolitan area with fully 42 percent of families receiving an income over $10,000.

The eduation data show low average attainment for all groups except the Los Angeles Metropolitan males, the latter having 20 percent with some college experience and 43 percent with four years of high school or more. In contrast, East Los Angeles and San Antonio have amazingly high proportions of persons with no high school background at all (e.g., 55 percent of San Antonio males and 62 percent of San Antonio females). In East Los Angeles only 7 percent of all males twenty-five years and older have experienced some college and only a fourth of this group has four years of high school or more.

SUMMARY AND DISCUSSION

This brief and selective review of 1970 Census data suggests a number of important points that contradict the image of blacks and Chicanos as predominantly lower-class populations.

In more urban industrial areas without an historical past of extreme caste-like race relations (as the apartheid of blacks in the South and of Spanish-surname families in Texas) between one-third and 40 percent of black and Spanish-surname families are making over $10,000. About one-fourth of the employed black and Spanish-surname males are in white-collar occupations; this proportion increases to one-third when female workers are also considered. Moreover, not all the gains have been made at the lowest-paid clerical level; there appears to be a substantial growth in the numbers of those white-collar workers in both the professional *and* clerical levels. If we add the craftsmen-foremen category to the white-collar statistics, it appears that some-where between 40 percent and 47 percent of black and Spanish-surname males were employed at either the skilled or white-collar levels in 1970. Those with some college education do not reach the same proportions. Considering only the U.S. data on younger males (aged eighteen to twenty-four years), and the California data for younger and middle-aged males (aged twenty to forty-nine), it appears that 20 to 25 percent of blacks and Spanish-surname persons have attended or are presently attending college.

In the less urbanized and industrialized areas with an historic past of conquest and caste relations, and in the urban barrios such as East Los Angeles, there is a far more truncated socioeconomic range. In the state of Texas only 16 percent of blacks and 21 percent of Spanish-surname persons were making over $10,000 in 1970. An extremely large percentage of younger and middle-aged males (twenty to forty-nine years) have only a grade school education (43 percent) and this proportion increases to an unbelievable 60 percent among all Texas males over twenty-five years. Obviously, there is a strong regional variation in the size of the observed rising skilled and white-collar strata.

FURTHER MEANINGS

When presenting findings that show a developing upper-working and middle-class stratum among blacks and Chicanos, the specific meanings of these statistics must be clearly delineated. They do *not* mean that the system is now as open for minority persons as for the population as a whole. These data do not mean that the American Dream is being fully realized to the extent that every lower-class black or Chicano can (with a little Yankee initiative) make large gains in the class structure. Chicano and black persons typically face multiple barriers and must expend more effort to overcome these barriers than their white counterparts. Chicanos and blacks with middle-class incomes often must invest a much greater household input of time and effort to get the same economic outputs as white families. For example, we can interpret the data on page 66 as indicating that both husband and wife must work full-time, year-round in many black families to receive the same income as a white family in which only the husband works or a white family in which the husband works full-time and the wife works only part-time. In other words, though there is a growing middle-class stratum, it remains clear that many non-white persons have to work harder and longer than white persons to achieve positions equal in comfort and life style. However, even when this income is achieved, there are special problems in converting it into the same privileges that white persons automatically enjoy. For example, middle-class blacks living on the periphery of the ghetto do not get the same quality of schools or city services found in white suburbs. Blacks in certain middle-class occupations face special problems. Black doctors, veterinarians, and lawyers in private practice, for example, will typically have a smaller and economically poorer clientele from which to draw (mainly black). It is not surprising then, that some income data show that the gap between white and black income is greatest among the best educated.[30] Though the black professional may be far better off economically than lower- and working-class blacks, his long-range chances for economic advancement are often far more limited than those of his white counterpart.

THE RISING MIDDLE CLASS AND
THE COLLAPSE OF THE WAR ON POVERTY

An important point to consider is the effect of the recent elimination of poverty programs on the ability of those in white-collar and skilled employment to maintain their middle-class positions. The "War on Poverty" created a new "opening" in the occupational structure. Many talented poverty and working-class minority persons acquired jobs as directors and supervisors with incomes far higher than their educations would warrant on the general market. Many had their first taste of middle-class living and life styles. In a sense, the poverty programs of the 1960s could be compared with the upgrading of minority employment during World War II. Both represented new opportunities for skilled and white-collar work in the occupational structure. But both were followed by a decrease in structural opportunity* for minority persons. To what degree are the rising upper working and middle-class data reported in this chapter a function of poverty-agency jobs and to what extent will program-employed persons with relatively high incomes fall in socioeconomic level when the programs are terminated?[31] Those with college educations are likely to maintain their middle-class positions. But the talented community worker with low educational attainment is likely to fall in both income and occupational status. In the longer view many theories and data suggest that a significant increase in structural opportunity, followed by a sharp decline in such opportunity, leads to a high degree of frustration and discontent. That is, whenever our society is involved in a cyclical opportunity, an intolerable want-get gap is created; the result is heightened tension, alienation, and conflict in the society.[32]

* "Structural opportunity" can be defined as the ratio of available vacant positions to eligible job-seekers.

NOTES TO CHAPTER 5

[1] U.S. Bureau of the Census, *The Social and Economic Status of the Black Population in the United States, 1972,* Current Population Reports Series P-23, no. 46 (Washington, D.C.: Government Printing Office, 1973), pp. 17, 20.

[2] Ibid., p. 20.

[3] Ibid., p. 19.

[4] Ibid., p. 17.

[5] U.S. Bureau of the Census, *Differences Between Incomes of White and Negro Families by Work Experience of Wife and Region: 1970, 1969, and 1959,* Current Population Reports Series P-23, no. 39 (Washington, D.C.: Government Printing Office, 1971), p. 1.

[6] Ibid., pp. 1, 8.

[7] U.S. Bureau of the Census, *The Social and Economic Status of the Black Population in the United States, 1971,* Current Population Reports Series P-23, no. 42 (Washington, D.C.: Government Printing Office, 1972), p. 35.

[8] U.S. Bureau of the Census, *General Social and Economic Characteristics,* Census of the Population ,1970, Final Report PC(1)-C6 California (Washington, D.C.: Government Printing Office, 1972). Derived from Table 54.

[9] U.S. Bureau of the Census, no. 46, op. cit., p. 49.

[10] Ibid., p. 49.

[11] Ibid., p. 50.

[12] U.S. Bureau of the Census (California), op. cit. Derived from Table 65.

[13] U.S. Bureau of the Census, no. 46, op. cit., p. 65.

[14] Ibid., p. 62.

[15] Daniel P. Moynihan, "The Schism in Black America," *The Public Interest,* no. 27 (Spring, 1972): 3-24.

[16] Ibid., p. 12.

[17] U.S. Bureau of the Census, *Selected Characteristics of Persons and Families of Mexican, Puerto Rican, and other Spanish Origin: March 1972,* Current Population Reports Series P-20, no. 238 (Washington, D.C.: Government Printing Office, 1972). Calculated from data presented in Table 2, p. 3.

[18] Frank G. Mittelbach and Joan W. Moore, "Ethnic Endogamy: The Case of Mexican Americans," *American Journal of Sociology* 74 (July, 1968): 50-62.

[19] *Los Angeles Times,* July 6, 1972.

[20] Leo Grebler, Joan W. Moore, and Ralph C. Guzman, *The Mexican-American People* (New York: Free Press, 1970), ch. 13.

[21] See Fernando Penalosa, "The Changing Mexican-American in Southern California," in *Majority and Minority,* ed. Norman R. Yetman and C. Hoy Steele (Boston: Allyn & Bacon, 1971), p. 329.

[22] Ibid., p. 329.

[23] U.S. Bureau of the Census, *Persons of Spanish Origin in the United States: March 1972 and 1971,* Current Population Reports Series P-20, no. 250 (Washington, D.C.: Government Printing Office, 1973), p. 23.

[24] Ibid., p. 4

[25] Joan W. Moore, *Mexican Americans* (Englewood Cliffs, N.J.: Prentice-Hall, 1970), p. 62.

[26] Ibid., p. 110.

[27] See Grebler, Moore, and Guzman, op. cit., p. 327; and Moore, op. cit., p. 113.

[28] Grebler, Moore, and Guzman, op. cit., p. 300.

[29] Ibid., ch. 13.

[30] Peter M. Blau and Otis Dudley Duncan, *The American Occupational Structure* (New York: John Wiley & Sons, 1967), p. 211.

[31] I am grateful to Joan W. Moore for insight on this point.

[32] See James Davies, "Toward a Theory of Revolution," *American Sociological Review* 27 (February, 1962): 5-19.

PART II

EMPIRICAL EXPLORATIONS AND REVIEWS OF CURRENT RESEARCH ON THE JOINT EFFECTS OF RACE AND CLASS

Chapter 6

MILITANCE AND THE PERCEPTION OF DISCRIMINATION: COMPARISONS BETWEEN BLACKS AND CHICANOS OF DIFFERENT CLASSES

THE BLACK MIDDLE CLASS: MATERIALISTIC BOURGEOISIE CONSUMERS OR MILITANT ACTIVISTS?

As recently as the mid-1960s, middle-class black persons in America were profiled as individuals who: accepted unconditionally the values of white people — "their canons of respectability, their standards of beauty, and their consumption patterns" [1] — despised lower-class members of their own race and maintained social distance from them, and were afraid to endorse or participate in militant action that might jeopardize their precarious position in the general society. E. Franklin Frazier's *Black Bourgeoisie* is perhaps the classic account.[2] He maintains that middle-class Negroes (those in white-collar and craft occupations) are ambivalent, both toward the wider Negro community and the white middle class with which they tend to identify. They disassociate themselves from the masses of their own group because they view lower-class black behavior as the reason for prejudice and blocked mobility. Frazier makes an important distinction between the "old" and the "new" middle class. Members of the old middle class are predominantly descendants of house slaves or free Negroes — "men and women who had purchased their freedom by diligent effort or who had been set free by some liberal planter, because of some heroic deed, or more frequently because of long years of faithfulness."[3] Due to sexual exploitation of black women under the slavery system, many of these Negroes were lighter in skin color. A very special segment of the Negro group was created, in which lighter-skinned or more Caucasian appearing blacks were given special privileges and freedoms. The descendants of this group were unusually careful to marry someone of the same class level and skin color. The behavior of this old bourgeoisie, Frazier notes, was based on a "genteel tradition" patterned after the ideal of the Southern lady and gentleman. They placed great stress on stable and conventional family life, and on frugality and industry in economic matters. However, a major new segment of the middle class emerged in the 1940s and 1950s. Unlike the old bourgeoisie, the new recruits to white-collar occupations came from the black masses. These were the actors, entertainers, and professionals who managed to fight their way into better positions. It is this "new" middle class of which Frazier is most critical. This new class rejected both the folk culture of the Negro masses (e.g., the singing and preaching styles found in the Baptist Church) as well as the stable standards and genteel tradition of the old bourgeoisie. The new class was rootless, lacking a cultural or economic base. Bennett summarizes Frazier well when he notes:

> Frazier is critical of the manners, morals, and political values of the new class which, he says, is characterized by its psychological insecurity, its material dependence on the white propertied classes and its frantic quest for status. Worse yet, the new class composed essentially of 'the successful members of the rising black masses,' lacks a base in the economic system. Its wealth is too inconsequential, he says, for it to wield any political power. It is a lumpen, a fake bourgeoisie. . . .[4]

Moreover, Frazier asserts that the new middle class suffers from an inferiority complex that leads to a fear of competing with whites on an equal level, a conspicuous display of wealth, and an escapism in which Negro achievements and Negro wealth and business success are greatly exaggerated. Finally, Frazier (and many others) stresses the fact that middle and upper-class blacks may have vested interests in perpetuating the segregated ghetto since black professionals and businessmen often service the separate and unequal institutions of the ghetto as doctors, teachers, morticians, etc. The black professionals in private practice, for example, may be unable to establish a large clientele in both the black and white communities. A racist society combined with personal ambition thus leads him to search for success by maintaining an exclusively black practice. According to this view the middle-class black stratum has not been active in breaking down discrimination barriers since many of them have a stake in the continued survival of the ghetto.[5]

No doubt there are life-style residues of Frazier's "old" and "new" middle classes; however, as will be suggested in this chapter, neither group is an accurate characterization of middle-class blacks in the 1970s. The Civil Rights Movement, Black Power, and ghetto riots have generated new tendencies toward racial identification and militance. The class interest of acquisition, exemplified by a display of wealth and status, has been reshaped and modified by an intense movement of ethnic identification. Recent empirical evidence indicates that the black middle class of the 1970s is a complex blend of individualism, careers, militant attitudes (and sometimes action), and racial identification. In ethclass terms, there is a complex blend of class interests and race interests in the black middle class of today.

Changes in the Composition of the Labor Force

As the 1970 demographic data discussed in Chapter V show, there is a growing upper-blue-collar and white-collar segment in the black population. Much of the growth of this new middle class is due to upward mobility from manual occupations rather than to a growth of the light-skinned aristocracy of which Frazier spoke. In a recent study of the black middle class, two-thirds of the white-collar respondents were sons whose fathers were in blue-collar manual occupations.[6] Many of the newer arrivals to the middle class have not come from a tradition of separation or social distance from the black masses. Further, the skin-color composition of the middle class is changing. Edwards, in a study of Negro professionals, finds that the most common skin color is brown, rather than very light or very dark.[7] Similarly, Kronus reports that three-fourths of his middle-class sample were brown or dark brown.[8] Increasingly, the black middle class is not a highly visible (light-skinned) sub-group anxious to protect its color status.

Another major change in the last twenty years is that upwardly mobile blacks have moved in increasing numbers into occupational categories that were formerly exclusively "white" rather than remaining in specific "ghetto" occupations. There has been an increase in the number of black teachers and social workers and, more generally, Civil Service employees. At the same time there has been a decline in the number of black-owned businesses.[9] The large number of blacks employed by federal and county governments is an especially important factor in the upward mobility story. Kronus reports that although blacks in 1964 comprised about 10 percent of the labor force they accounted for 13.2 percent of all federal workers.[10] Agencies such as the Government Printing Office, the Veterans Administration, and the Department of Health, Education and Welfare now have as many as 20 percent to 40 percent black employees.[11]

Many in the new black middle class are salaried, white-collar workers who have no special stake in segregation or in the establishment of an exclusively black clientele.

The Middle Class and Militant Attitudes and Behavior

There is now overwhelming evidence that the Civil Rights movement had its birth and most consistent support in the black middle class rather than the lower class.[12] The earliest activists tended to be black students from fairly comfortable middle-class homes, though there was some participation from older segments of the black middle-class population.[13] Many accounts of the Civil Rights struggle speak of a generation gap between the direct protest tactics of the well-educated young and the more moderate intra-system methods of their parents.[14] However, once the Civil Rights (and later Black Power) movements were in motion, new constraints toward racial identity, action, and loyalty were generated that spread the base of support both age and class-wise. It is no longer correct to assume that only young black students have militant attitudes. Although the most militant ideologies of revolution and self-determination may still be found among black college students, today many blacks over thirty also have rather militant orientations. In fact, most of those people who were involved in the Civil Rights demonstrations of the late 1950s and early 1960s are now over thirty, and most likely have not been completely co-opted into system conservatism.

There are many good reasons why the black middle class should be most active in both individual and collective protest of the organized, programmed variety. When a person attains a middle-class position, he has greater resources with which to fight discrimination than has the lower-class person. The attainment of wealth, education, and high occupational position is clearly related to increased personal influence, knowledge of available channels of redress, enough money to hire a good lawyer or enough knowledge to file suit, and adequate personal connections for reaching the system. Empirical support for the notion of increased resources can be seen in Table 6-1, in which black respondents (interviewed by black interviewers shortly after the Watts riot) were asked, "what would you do if you went into a restaurant and were refused service because of your race?"[15] Placed in this hypothetical situation of race discrimination, blacks in white-collar jobs, those with incomes over $7,000, and those with some college education, were far more likely than those lower in SES to say that they would take definite action such as "organize a demonstration," "tell all my friends to boycott the restaurant," "report it to the NAACP or CORE," or "sue." Lower-class blacks were more likely to make statements such as "I would walk away," or "there's nothing you can do in situations like that."

In a recent study by Gary Marx,[16] social class was found to be strongly related to a militant orientation (for example, support of civil rights demonstrations). Similarly, Ransford found that middle-class blacks were significantly more likely to score high in a militant-behavior index (measured by participation in militant organizations, boycotts, and demonstrations) than lower-class blacks.[17] Consistent with the "higher resources" point, Marx explains that those higher in SES have " . . . the energy, resources, morale, and self-confidence needed to challenge an oppressive and powerful system. The mental and physical energy of severely deprived people is occupied in simply staying alive."[18]

But it is also true that the attainment of a middle-class position involves factors that mute the potential for extremely radical action. As a person attains a better occupational position, acquires property, buys a home, and provides a comfortable living standard for his family, he has more to lose by participating in a riot or other action that may lead to arrest or a jail record. The acquisition of a piece of the "good life" is likely to moderate the kind of protest that takes place and prevent a truly revolutionary movement from spreading across the middle-class stratum. Although significant percentages of middle-class blacks gave verbal support and approval to the riots in Watts,[19] actual participation in riots was far more likely to come from young (aged eighteen to twenty-five years) lower-class blacks with strong feelings of blocked mobility and distributive injustice. The Kerner Report describes these socioeconomic characteristics of the rioter:

TABLE 6-1

Action in the Face of Discrimination
By Education, Occupation, and Income

Item: "What would you do if you went into a restaurant and were refused service because of your race?"

	Non-Action Responses (e.g., walk away)	Action Responses (e.g., sue or organize boycott)
Education		
Less than High School	71%	29%
High School Graduate	58	49
Some College	28	72
Occupation		
Unemployed	61	39
Blue collar	53	47
White Collar	34	66
Income		
Under $5,000	59	41
$5-7,000	59	41
Over $7,000	29	71

Source: Ransford, Watts study. Three hundred twelve black males (ages 18-65) were interviewed after the Watts riot. Data in this table are unpublished. For further specifications on the sample and data collection procedures, see note 15 and H. Edward Ransford, "Skin Color, Life Chances, and Anti-White Attitudes," *Social Problems*, 18 (Fall, 1970), 167-168.

TABLE 6-2

Willingness To Go To Jail For A Civil Rights Cause
By Education, Occupation, and Income

	% Not Willing	% Willing
Education		
Less than High School	59	41
High School Graduate	58	42
Some College	69	31
Occupation		
Unemployed	58	42
Blue Collar	58	42
White Collar	72	28
Income		
Under $5,000	49	51
$5-7,000	61	39
Over $7,000	71	29

Source: Ransford, Watts study.

Although he had not, usually, graduated from high school, he was somewhat better educated than the average inner-city Negro, having at least attended high school for a time. Nevertheless, he was more likely to be working in a menial or low status job as an unskilled laborer. If he was employed, he was not working full time and his employment was frequently interrupted by periods of unemployment. He feels strongly that he deserves a better job and that he is barred from achieving it, not because of lack of training, ability, or ambition, but because of discrimination by employers. . . . He is more likely to be actively engaged in civil rights efforts, but is extremely distrustful of the political system and of political leaders.[20]

Other evidence for the muting effects of a stake in the system can be seen in Table 6-2 from the Watts Study. Although middle-class blacks in this study consistently expressed the need for militant civil rights protest, when asked whether they would be willing to go to jail for some civil rights cause, the middle-class respondents (those with incomes of over $7,000) were least willing. Similarly, in the Marx study, home owners (who had a greater stake) were less militant than the apartment dwellers (who had a lesser stake to lose).[21] In short, attainment of a middle-class position involves factors which encourage efforts to change a racist society but which discourage participation in violence or rebellions involving great risks or the loss of what has been gained through personal efforts and sacrifices.

Personal Career and Militant Attitudes

Some have suggested that the greater amount of individual and collective protest activity among middle-class blacks is only a function of selfish, personal career ambitions rather than a genuine concern for racial justice to the masses. Harold Cruse, in *The Crisis of The Negro Intellectual,* comments "No matter how you view it, the integration movement is run by the middle class, who, even when they are militant and sometimes radical, twist the meaning of integration to suit their own aspirations."[22] This is a difficult charge to test. It is probably true that some upwardly mobile members of any minority group may be more interested in the advancement of their own careers rather than in helping the masses. However, the two factors (personal career and racial concern and identification) may complement rather than oppose one another. The middle or upper working-class black with strong mobility aspirations may be most frustrated and impatient with color barriers that yet remain. He may be unusually sensitive to racial dis-crimination and thus maintain some identification and alliance with low-status Negroes. Further, the discrimination battles won by middle-class blacks may bring new openings that benefit blacks of all class positions. Some evidence for these ideas can be seen in the way middle-class blacks with different orientations toward mobility reacted to the Watts riot. Those in white-collar positions were asked a number of questions to measure their desire for upward occupational mobility. Table 6-3 shows that middle-class blacks who aspired to upward mobility were more likely to give a militant response (that is, to view the Watts riot as a justifiable expression of frustration and discrimina-tion) than middle-class blacks who expressed lower mobility aspira-tions. These data are extremely interesting in that they suggest that those blacks who were most intensely concerned with their own careers were also the ones more likely to sympathize and to identify with a lower-class ghetto rebellion. There is other evidence that some middle-class blacks combine career identification with racial identifica-tion. Billingsley notes:

TABLE 6-3

The Reaction of Middle Class Blacks to the Watts Riot By Two
Measures of Mobility Orientation

Item: I would probably turn down a promotion if it meant that I would have to be
away from my family a lot.

Riot Reaction	% Agree (Low Mobility) N=51	% Disagree (High Mobility) N=31
Militant response	22	36
Intermediate	23	16
Non-Militant Response	55	48
	100%	100%

Item: I really prefer to put my roots in solid in a community rather than move as the
chances for advancement come along.

Riot Reaction	% Agree (Low Mobility) N=51	% Disagree (High Mobility) N=34
Militant response	16	50
Intermediate	23	18
Non-Militant Response	61	32
	100%	100%

Source: Ransford, Watts study.

Negro physicians, social workers, teachers and other professionals are beginning to take special recognition of and special initiative on behalf of low income Negro families and children. At the University of Massachusetts . . . a group of Negro faculty members came together and designed a program for the recruitment and education of Negro students. A similar movement is under way at the University of California. In Berkeley, as in other cities, a group of Negro public school teachers came together and designed a special summer program for Negro children, combining a healthy amount of regular academic work with special learnings about the cultural heritage of the Negro people. . . . In financial ways, too, this racial consciousness or ethnic solidarity is manifesting itself. In 1967, for the first time, a group of the wealthiest Negroes in the nation came together in New York to consider how their money, their positions in the Negro community, and their influence in the larger society might be put into more effective efforts for improving the condition of underprivileged Negroes.[23]

Further, in the past five years, many middle-class blacks have linked themselves with the racial identity movement by engaging in or encouraging creative expressions in black art, black theatre, and black films. In a recent issue of *Newsweek* these interview comments were reported: "Black films give blacks much more opportunity to feel vicariously in control of their environment than whites get from James Bond movies." "And, indeed, control is first among virtues in these movies; grace under pressure (whether in bed or in the precinct house) mastery of self-defense (by karate or judo) and, above all, a hatred for heroin — the main tool of oppression and self-oppression."[24] In sum, there is an indication that many blacks in business, arts, or the professions are combining personal success with black identity; the two forces do not necessarily conflict.

The Kahl-Goering Study of Stable Workers, Black and White

A current study illustrates well the mix of race and class interests that are emphasized in this section.[25] In the summer of 1968, black and white males of middle-class (white-collar) and working-class (blue-collar) status were interviewed to determine their positions on such matters as job satisfaction, attainment of the "good life," and opinions on current political demonstrations. The blacks and whites were carefully selected according to common position in the class structure: respondents were neither poor nor rich but rather steadily employed with middle incomes. Additional controls were applied: both parents were living together, and there was at least one child present. The model is simple: with social classes in common, differences found between black workers and white workers could be tentatively attributed to race; whereas, if no differences showed up, one might infer that class was overriding race. By asking the same questions of blacks and of whites of comparable class positions one might locate the issues on which black and white middle classes differ and the issues on which they are alike. Comparison between black and white stable workers produced very few differences when the subject was job satisfaction, family life, attainment of the good life, and career ambitions. On a question about "what the good life means to you," both black and white workers reflected common attitudes toward security, family activities, material success, and consumerism. Further blacks and whites were about equal in their perceived attainment of the good life. Only two large differences were found on the questions dealing with job and career: blacks were much more aware of general unemployment than whites, and blacks were "more devoted to occupational success as a primary goal, even at the cost of time with family and friends. . . . "[26]

However, on questions in the Kahl-Goering study having to do with race, the opportunity structure, and political protest, the two groups were found to be worlds apart. For a number of questions designed to measure a sense of distributive justice (for the group as a whole) blacks clearly felt more deprived than whites — despite their feelings of personal satisfaction with their jobs, their careers and future prospects for their sons. Sixty-two percent of the stable working whites agreed strongly that "people like me have as good a life as anybody in this country" compared with only 10 percent of the blacks. "Apparently these men were content with their own personal progress but also identified with their race and reacted with a general sense of unfair deprivation."[27] Other striking comparisons can be seen in the reproduced table of attitudes (Table 6-4). Compared to white persons, black persons are far more likely to accept violent protest as legitimate (when a group has been denied a decent life for years), to reject the view that Negroes are pushing too fast, and to see demonstrations as sincerely trying to improve the government. These data are certainly in opposition to the view that middle-class blacks become conservative, "don't-rock-the-boat" supporters of the status quo. "Gone is the contentment of blacks about jobs and in its place appears a deep sense of wrongs that need to be righted, even by extreme methods, if necessary."[28]

The Kahl-Goering study suggests that stable black and white workers are very similar on matters of economic ambition and consumerism. However, the black middle (and stably employed working) class has not become completely bourgeois or gone through co-optation in a political sense. Rather, stable black workers reflect a blend of materialistic personal ambition, identification with the black masses, and orientation toward militant protest.

TABLE 6-4

Political Attitudes of Blacks and Whites With Middle Incomes
And Steady Jobs

PERCENTAGE OF AGREEMENT

	Blacks	Whites
1. Our country is in fine shape the way it is.	6	32
(Alternative: Our country is in bad shape and needs a lot of changes.)	(94)	(68)
2. Violence in political movements is un-American and should be firmly repressed.	35	88
(Alternative: When a large group of people has been denied a decent life for years and years, they have a right to violent protest.)	(65)	(12)
3. People who march in demonstrations are often agitators and communists.	7	51
(Alternative: People who march in demonstrations are sincere and trying to improve government policy.)	(93)	(49)
4. People who are very poor are mostly lazy people who should help themselves.	20	40
(Alternative: People who are very poor are mostly unlucky people who need help)	(80)	(60)
5. Negroes have been moving too fast, and should not push so hard.	4	58
(Alternative: Negroes are still not getting a fair deal in this country.)	(96)	(42)

Reprinted from Joseph A. Kahl and John M. Goering, "Stable Workers, Black and White," *Social Problems* 18, no. 3, p. 315, by permission of the authors, the publisher, and The Society for the Study of Social Problems.

Self-Determination and Black Control

Increasingly, the black movement has shifted from protests in favor of integration and civil rights to concern about black control over neighborhood institutions, self rule, and autonomy — demand for self-determination. There are limited data as to which socioeconomic groups are most supportive of this outlook. One of the few recent studies suggests that the strongest support for self-determination is found among younger (twenty to thirty-nine years old) black college graduates.[29] These persons were more likely to support black owner-ship of stores and control over black schools than any other age-education sub-group (20 to 30 percent supported these issues). Further, there is a clear generation gap on the issue of self-determination. A far smaller percentage of older (forty to sixty-nine years old) black college graduates supported these issues (3 to 13 percent). The mixture of younger generation and high degrees of educational attainment also profoundly affected how blacks viewed the riots. Sixty-seven percent of the younger (aged twenty to thirty-nine) college graduates felt that riots helped black progress as con-trasted with 28 percent of older college graduates. (Older college graduates were most likely to say the riots both helped and hurt.)[30]

Rejection of the Black Lower Classes — Seeking Acceptance in the White Middle Classes

One aspect of Frazier's thesis is that the middle-class black attempts to separate himself from the black masses and holds very disparaging attitudes toward this group. Given the numerous changes in this stratum, is this still the case? One of the few current studies that deals with this question is Kronus' *The Black Middle Class*.[31] He reports that the majority of respondents in his sample did not hold disparaging attitudes toward lower-class Negroes but neither did they express positive identification. More specifically, only 10 percent gave truly positive statements, 53 percent viewed lower-class black people as victims of forces beyond their control, while 15 percent were ambigu-ous and only 20 percent clearly negative.[32] Thus, there is nowhere near the amount of disparagement that the Frazier thesis would predict. On the other hand, these responses are a long way from demonstrating the existence of a united black community.

Another assertion is that middle-class black persons are seeking white acceptance. Kronus also asked questions about the frequency of contact with white persons in various situations. Contact on a frequent basis was most likely to take place in work situations. Some interracial contact took place in the home, at parties, or at voluntary organiza-tions; however, the latter occurred far less frequently (once a month or less). While 94 percent of the respondents had contact with white persons at least once a week on the job (most daily), only 15 percent of the black people interviewed had weekly contact with white persons in the home, parties, or voluntary organizations. What is interesting is that most of the blacks felt that the amount of contact they were having with whites was quite enough. Here is a sample of comments:

. . . Through no fault of my own I am in close contact with them in my work and this is enough. We have nothing in common and I know they are nice and polite only because they have to be.

. . . I'm not in love with white people and don't especially enjoy being around them. I just make a living that way.

. . . Every white person doesn't care to associate with Negroes, so I say everyone to his own taste. Those that I work with are regular and are as good friends as I could care to have.[33]

SOCIAL CLASS, PERCEIVED DISCRIMINATION AND PROTEST POTENTIAL AMONG MEXICAN AMERICANS

Compared with the numerous mass demonstrations, ghetto rebellions, and black power demands of blacks in the 1960s, most Mexican Americans have been less militant. It would be a great mistake, however, to depict Mexican Americans in the last decade as silent. There are many signs of a growing mood of militant protest and a willingness to bargain with the white majority with power tactics rather than simply to use persuasion. To mention but a few examples, we can note the highly effective grape and lettuce boycotts led by Cesar Chavez to bring union representation to farm workers, the militant claims to land rights led by Reies Tijerina in New Mexico, the numerous protests among Chicano college students for establishment of quotas for Chicano entrants, the young activists who walked out of several East Los Angeles high schools protesting what they called the inability of the educational system to deal with language and cultural differences, and the resulting 50 percent drop-out rate, and, most recently, the East Los Angeles riot of 1970 that left two dead and hundreds injured. However, much of the Chicano militance of the last decade had been overshadowed by black protest. The anger and grievances of Chicanos have not been burned into the public consciousness to the same extent as blacks. In several interviews following the East Los Angeles riot these comments were recorded: "The authorities didn't listen. They didn't believe that the frustrations in the Mexican American community would ever boil over. . . . " "Issue after issue has been laid to rest with nothing done about them because the feeling has been that the Mexican American would never be a violent person."[34]

The Chicano Movement

The "Chicano Movement" is the most current example of the attempt of Mexican Americans of the Southwest to redefine their common identity and their relations to the white majority. The "movement" began especially among middle-class students in the summer of 1966, but it spread quickly to others who were not middle-class. According to Cuellar the major force of the movement is the ideology — Chicanismo. To quote briefly from his discussion:

> Chicanos assume that along with American Indians and black Americans, Mexicans live in the United States as a conquered people. This idea allows *chicanismo* to explain the evolution of the Chicano as essentially conflictful. In each conflictual relationship with Anglos, the Mexicans lost out and were thus forced to live in the poverty and degradation attendant upon those with the status of a conquered people. . . . *chicanismo* emphasizes that the Mexican was transferred into a rootless economic commodity, forced either to depend on migrant farm work or to sell his labor in the urban centers, where his fate depended upon the vicissitudes of the economy. . . . It is argued that Anglo racism denies the Mexican his ethnicity by making him ashamed of his 'Mexican-ness.' Mexican ancestry, instead of being a source of pride, becomes a symbol of shame and inferiority. As a consequence, Mexicans spend their lives apologizing or denying their ancestry to the point that many dislike and resent being called 'Mexican,' preferring 'Spanish American,' 'Latin,' 'Latin American,' and similar euphemisms. For these reasons, the term 'Chicano' is now insisted upon by activists as a symbol of the new assertiveness. Advocates of *chicanismo* therefore hope to reconstruct the Mexican Americans' concept of themselves by appeals to pride of a common history, culture and 'race'. . . . Chicano ideologues insist that social advance based on material achievement is, in the final analysis, less important than social advance based on la raza, they reject what they call the myth of American individualism . . . if Mexicans are to confront the problems of their group realistically they must begin to act along collective lines. Hence the stirrings of new spirit of what *chicanismo* terms 'cultural nationalism' among the Mexican-Americans of the Southwest.[35]

With the rising mood of cultural nationalism, identity, and protest, one would expect that there would be many current studies of the political attitudes of the Mexican American population. Yet, there are only a few very recent studies that present any hard data on the consequences of identification with the Chicano movement, or the degree to which Mexican-Americans perceive discrimination and support militant protest methods. Even more rare are studies that take into account class and race (Mexican American vs. Anglo and black) in the prediction of militant outlooks. The discussion that follows is an attempt to summarize several of these recent studies and to present an original analysis of race and class reactions to the East Los Angeles riot with data from a current Los Angeles survey.

The Perception of Inequality

It would seem logical that one extremely important variable for heightened ethnic consciousness and political protest would be the perception on the part of minority group members of racial inequality. Mexican Americans must perceive a racial stratification system in which they are grossly discriminated against before militant attitudes and behavior are likely to ensue. A study by Davidson and Gaitz[36] (1973) presents some interesting data on this topic. A large sample selected and interviewed by the National Opinion Research Center was conducted in Houston, Texas, in the latter months of 1969 and the first few months of 1970. The sample N=1,441 was selected by quota methods, stratified by age, sex, ethnicity (Anglo, black, Mexican American), and occupation. To insure greater comparability across races, only a subsample (N=697) of currently employed, non-farm heads of households was analyzed in this article. To get at the minority group perception of position in a racial stratification order, blacks and Mexican Americans were asked the extent of inequality (full equality, some inequality, and great deal inequality) they felt when it comes to housing, schools, job training, wages, etc. Although about half of the Mexican Americans did perceive "some inequality" in the areas of housing, job training, job opportunities, and wages, they perceived on the whole their situation to be far better than blacks did theirs. For example, when one compares blacks and Chicanos on the category "great deal of inequality," these differences appear: while 45 percent of the blacks perceived a great deal of inequality in housing, only 17 percent of the Mexican Americans did. The corresponding percentages for schools are 30 percent (blacks) versus 10 percent (Mexican Americans). Similarly, in job opportunities, a full 39 percent of the blacks perceived a great deal of inequality versus only 15 percent of the

Mexican Americans. The Houston study shows for married, employed adults in that city at that point in time that Mexican Americans, on the average, view their situation to be one of moderate inequality rather than extreme oppression and they perceive far less racial inequality than do blacks.

Militant Attitudes

The same survey produced attitude data on various measures of political militancy. One issue that became of special importance in the late 1960s is the degree to which minority groups should be given special opportunities to redress past discrimination. The position that they showed would be antithetical to the rather entrenched American view that mobility and success should be won by individual effort. In response to the statement, "For a limited time, minority groups should be given special privileges because of past disadvantages and discrimination," 45 percent of the blacks approved, compared with 36 percent of the Mexican Americans, and only 14 percent of the Anglos. The Chicano stance appears to be in between blacks and Anglos but closer to blacks.

Two other questions in the Houston survey that tapped militant attitudes toward civil rights produced a similar pattern. In response to a question asking whether the (federal) government was pushing integration too slowly, 68 percent of the blacks agreed compared with 22 percent of the Chicanos and 5 percent of the Anglos. Similarly, 64 percent of the blacks felt there should be more civil rights demonstrations compared with 24 percent of the Chicanos and 2 percent of the Anglos. Again, the Mexican American response is in between blacks and Anglos but this time is closer to Anglo. The picture that emerges thus far is that, in comparison with blacks, smaller proportions of Mexican Americans perceive extreme ethnic inequality and fewer are ready to seek redress through militant protest. However, surveys of married adults only (which this study was) may be missing a large amount of militant potential. Many observers believe that the greatest feelings of cultural nationalism are to be found among high-school-age Mexican students who identify themselves as Chicanos rather than Mexican Americans. Guiterrez and Hirsch[37] conducted a study of the effects of Chicano identification. In May, 1971, data were gathered from 726 secondary school students (grades seven through twelve) in

Crystal City, Texas. Crystal City has become of special symbolic importance to the Chicano movement. Prior to 1969, the city reflected a common South Texas pattern. Though there was a substantial majority of Mexican Americans (four to one) in Crystal City, Anglos controlled the economic, political, and educational institutions. Relations between Anglos and Mexicans were paternalistic, the Mexican Americans being polite and obedient to the Anglos. Many were recent immigrants, poor, and lacking education, "connections," and "know-how" and were thus unable to challenge the *status quo*. The middle-class Mexican Americans often cooperated with Anglos rather than using their class resources for protest. Then, in 1969 and 1970, an almost complete transformation of power occurred. As a result of a school boycott and a high degree of Mexican- American organization in the City Council and School Board elections, Mexican Americans substantially changed the power structure and virtually took control of the school system. Amazing changes resulted: "Classes were conducted largely in Spanish. Chicano culture and heritage were taught freely. Emiliano Zapata's name was heard more often than George Washington's."[38] Crystal City has become a model of self-determination for the Mexican Americans in the whole Southwest area. It was in the middle of this mood of "control over our destiny" that the Guiterrez and Hirsch survey of high school students was conducted. If ever *Chicanismo* was to make a difference, one would expect to find it would occur in Crystal City at this time. The authors studied differences in political attitudes between those who were self-identified as "Chicano" versus those who preferred to be called Mexican American. There was an even split with 49 percent of the students calling themselves Chicano versus 47 percent choosing the term Mexican American. But what difference does ethnic identification make? Surprisingly, on questions dealing with the openness of the American system, there were absolutely no differences between "Chicanos" and "Mexican Americans." Seventy-seven percent of both groups felt that they had the same chance to succeed in life as anyone else. The American Dream is indeed a potent ideology! However, differences do emerge for certain political attitudes. Since some of the differences were moderate or large while others were very weak, I will review here only those differences in which the measure of association used — Gamma — showed a coefficient of at least .20. In comparison with Mexican Americans, Chicano identifiers were more likely to advocate public demonstrations and marches, were less likely to reject the use of violence to achieve ends, were more politically cynical, were more tolerant on issues of civil liberties, and more disbelieving that all persons get equal justice under the law. This is not to say that the young people who called themselves Mexican Americans were extremely conservative on all these issues. For example, fully 50 percent of those who identified themselves as Mexican American were politically cynical (vs. 65 percent of those who identified themselves as Chicano) and 40 percent agreed strongly or in part that demonstrations and marches were the best ways to move public officials (vs. 58 percent of the Chicanos). The findings suggest that Chicano students were somewhat more disposed toward the use of collective political action than Mexican-American students. The authors concluded:

> As Chicanos begin to experience political success in other parts of the country, their sense of identity will probably undergo a process comparable to that which we have seen in Crystal City. A strong sense of self leading one to identify one self strongly with one's cultural-racial group will increase the number of Chicano identifiers and will therefore increase political awareness. This awareness should then result in greater political activity. In other words, we have not heard the last from the Chicano movement — we may only have seen the beginning.[39]

Race, Class, and Perception of Police: Discrimination in East Los Angeles

The above data suggest that there is a growing mood of cultural nationalism in the Southwest that is felt especially by young people identifying themselves as "Chicanos." However, Chicanismo has not embraced the Mexican-American population to the same extent that Black Power and identity has the black population. Overall statistics on adults show that the black mood is more militant. To what extent does perception of discrimination and a militant mood vary by class as well as race? Do lower-class Chicanos living in the East Los Angeles barrio face an entirely different world of discrimination from middle-class Chicanos living on the periphery of or outside the barrio? Are middle-class Mexican Americans as likely to perceive discrimination and to engage in militant protest as middle-class blacks? While there are no definite answers to these questions at this time, some plausible trends are considered in the following discussion.

A great deal of evidence indicates that middle-class Mexican Americans face fewer barriers and have more integration-assimilation options than do middle-class blacks. Moore speaks of two common mobility patterns: upward mobility into more rewarding occupations but enjoyment of these economic and status rewards within a Mexican context (" . . . that is with Mexican associates, in a Mexican environment and quite familistic")[40] as compared with upward mobility into Anglo circles, often with an Anglo spouse. "In a city like Los Angeles a mobile Mexican American can make a choice." [41] In other words, some middle-class Mexican Americans choose an ethclass style, retaining a strong identification with their ethnic group, while others lean toward assimilation. The very fact that there are such options indicates that the Anglo majority has less intense feelings of social distance toward Mexican Americans than blacks. In Texas, Davidson and Gaitz find that while 50 percent of the Anglos would admit a Mexican American to close kinship by marriage, only 10 percent of the Anglos would admit Negroes. Similarly, while 86 percent of the Anglos would admit a Mexican American as a neighbor, a far smaller proportion would admit Negroes (56 percent).[42]

To add more conceptual leverage to this discussion, we can note John Howard's distinction between "partial" and "total" minority groups. By a partial minority, Howard means that "systematic impediments to group mobility are imposed by the dominant population, but individuals who manage to acquire the education, manner, and outlook of the dominant group are defined as members of the dominant group." [43] Though the term "partial minority" leaves a lot to be desired, it does make an important point: lower-class Chicanos probably face the same barriers as lower-class blacks, but middle-class Chicanos may fare considerably better. Thus the quality of life experienced by lower-class Chicanos in an urban barrio may be very similar to that experienced by lower-class blacks in the ghetto involving the same components of consumer exploitation, inferior schools, hostile police contacts, and a lack of institutions to redress discrimination. The middle-class Chicano, however, may face far less color prejudice than the middle-class black.

A Hypothesis

The distinction between persons of Mexican descent and persons of black descent in the permeability of the color barrier, no doubt, has a great deal to do with the "protest potential" of the rising middle-class segment of their respective minority groups. The following comparative racial hypothesis can be advanced: If a *rising* middle-class segment (as distinct from the old Spanish and black aristocracy) of an oppressed racial minority continues to face color stigma, social exclusion, and discrimination, the rising middle-class segment will often use its resources to engage in protest attempts to change that system. If the rising middle-class segment of an oppressed racial minority faces a much reduced level of color discrimination and greater opportunity for assimilation, much of the potential for protest will be splintered or drained off. That is, if class achievement more easily overrides racial status for Chicanos than for blacks, we can expect less militance from middle-class Chicanos.[44] It should be noted that this hypothesis applies mainly to the modal middle-class person. Evidence suggests that a new sector of the middle class is in the making. Some Chicano college and high school students (for example, those belonging to MECHA) are interested in mobility into a middle-class profession for the primary purpose of breaking down barrio inequities and contributing toward a more cohesive community. For example, some young Chicanos are entering law schools for the expressed purpose of returning to the barrio and offering new channels of legal redress for the Chicano poor. For these highly committed young persons, the ideology of Chicanismo would seem to override the assimilation possibilities noted in the above hypothesis.

Reactions to Police Force in a Period
Shortly After the East Los Angeles Riot

The following analysis compares Chicano, black, and white responses — with each race divided by three class (income) levels — to the police force used during the East Los Angeles riot. This analysis affords an opportunity to explore the hypothesis that the middle-class Chicano more easily escapes racial discrimination than the middle-class black.

In August 1970, a sizeable riot erupted in the East Los Angeles barrio. Two Mexican Americans were killed and hundreds arrested and injured. One of the dead men was a respected television commentator and a leading spokesman for Chicano rights, Reuben Salazar. Salazar was killed when police fired a tear gas projectile into a cafe where he was talking with barrio residents. The riot began with a rally of about 20,000 Mexican-American persons gathered to affirm the rights of Chicanos and to demonstrate against the Vietnam War, specifically against the disproportionate number of Chicano inductees in the war. According to newspaper accounts, confrontations first occurred between Sheriff Department Deputies and some demonstrators who looted a nearby liquor store. After several such confrontations the police apparently defined the situation as out of hand and marched on the large crowd in the park that was waiting to hear speakers. Tear gas was used in the crowd and a mass confrontation occurred, followed by several days of looting, arson, and vandalism. Militant Chicano groups were apparently motivated by what they believed to be excessive police force and especially by the accidental death of Salazar.

Shortly after the riot, a Los Angeles metropolitan area survey was conducted (LAMAS III).[45] In this survey several questions were asked of black, white, and Spanish-surname residents about the disturbance. The questions allow some comparison of a militant orientation by race and class. Since the behavior of the police was the major concern of the riot, questions dealt especially with this topic. One question tapped the perception of excessive police force in the context of the riot:

> "Would you say that the police used too much force, not enough force, or just the right amount of force during these demonstrations?"

Unfortunately, the number of Chicano and black respondents in this survey was small (Chicano, N = 102; black, N = 67; white, N = 398). However, it is possible to distinguish between three class levels for each race using family income as a measure of class. A lower-class category was defined as a family with an income of less than $5,000, a working-class category with family incomes ranging from $5,000-$9,000, and a middle-class stratum with incomes from $9,000-$20,000. In the following analysis our guiding logic is that middle-class Chicanos have an entirely different relationship with the police from that of lower-class Chicanos. In contrast, blacks will face a more uniform degree of police contacts with class differences making less difference. That is, middle-class Chicanos can more easily disengage themselves from color and class discrimination. Middle-class

Chicanos frequently move to the outskirts or completely out of barrio areas of greatest crime and police confrontations. Middle-class blacks, however, may continue to have many police contacts since they have more difficulty moving away from the ghetto and are generally more physically visible than middle-class Mexican Americans.

Excessive Police Force During the Riot

The confrontation between the police and the demonstrators involved a variety of interpretations. From the demonstrators' point of view, a predominantly peaceful rally had been interrupted by an oppressive, uncalled-for police sweep in which many innocent people were treated with brutality. However, the anger of militant youthful Chicanos appeared to be far more deep-seated than that produced by the one event. Many spoke of police harrassment and brutality that existed long before the riot. From a very different perspective, Chief of Police Davis spoke of communist subversives that had infiltrated the crowds, and he argued that the situation had demanded a firm control. The riot question in the LAMAS Survey is a rather crude index of the complexities of this event. However, for purposes of analysis we define the response, "the police used to much force," as an indication that violence resulted from the way justice and force are dealt out to Chicanos, rather than from any fault of the demonstrators. On the other hand, a person who answers "not enough force" is most likely giving an extremely "law-and-order" oriented response. Such a person is likely to have no sympathy with demonstrations (violent and non-violent) and an "order above all" approach to race relations. The intermediate response ("right amount of force") is difficult to interpret since some respondents could be sympathetic with non-violent protest yet at the same time have deplored the looting and vandalism that occurred in this disturbance. We view this response as intermediate between conservative and militant but leaning more toward the conservative end.

Table 6-5 presents the relationship between race and reaction to the disturbance. Sixty-six percent of the blacks complained of excessive police force (more militant answer) compared with 41 percent of the Chicanos and only 19 percent of the white respondents. Blacks are apparently more likely to perceive police malpractice against Mexican Americans than Mexicans themselves.

In terms of criticism of the police, the Chicano responses are exactly midway between black and white ones much like the data in the

Houston survey. Whites gave a far more conservative response; they tended to be most evenly split between "right amount of force" and "not enough force." Table 6-6 continues this analysis by controlling for family income, allowing us to compare the three races by different class levels. The overwhelming story appears to be that class does not change things much. Close to 40 percent of the Chicanos in all three income levels felt that too much force was used. Moreover, blacks of all income levels were more likely to perceive excessive force than either Chicanos or white respondents. The black response continues to be the

Table 6-5

The East Los Angeles Disturbance Involved:*

	% too much police force	% right amount of police force	% not enough police force	N
Black	66	26	8	(60)
Chicano	41	42	17	(81)
White	19	42	39	(275)

Source: LAMAS III (see note 45)
*Those answering "Don't Know" are excluded from the analysis.

TABLE 6-6

Perceptions of Police Force in the East Los Angeles Riot,
By Race and Class (Income)

The East Los Angeles Disturbance Involved:

	too much police force %	not enough police force %	right amount of police force %	N
Less than $5,000				
Black	65	6	29	(31)
Chicano	39	18	43	(28)
White	11	40	49	(53)
$5 - $9,000				
Black	69	0	31	(15)
Chicano	36	13	52	(31)
White	21	36	43	(80)
$9 - $20,000				
Black	55	27	18	(14)
Chicano	43	24	33	(21)
White	17	41	42	(142)

Source: LAMAS III (See Footnote œ 44)
Note: Those answering "Don't Know" and those making over $20,000 (mostly white) are excluded from the analysis.

most critical of police action regardless of class position. There is, however, a noticeable increase of higher-income blacks and Chicanos giving the response "not enough force" (27 percent of blacks, 24 percent of Chicanos). So the only class effect that exists is a slight tendency for an increased "law-and-order" response among upper income blacks and Chicanos.

The same LAMAS survey also asked respondents if they perceived that Mexican Americans were generally treated unjustly rather than only in the riot context. This question gets away from the multiple complexities of this particular riot and asks simply whether Mexican Americans are treated differently because of their race. In a poll conducted by the *Los Angeles Times*, many citizens of the East Los Angeles barrio expressed such a view.

> "Some times the police are too tough. In the 15 years I've been here I've seen a lot of things. Like the time I was standing here and I saw a Negro jay-walk. A motorcycle cop stopped for him to let him pass. Just then a Mexican jay-walked. The cop stopped him and gave him a ticket. I told him in Spanish — so the cop wouldn't understand to ask why he didn't give the black guy a ticket but he was too scared. He's in Vietnam now."

> "The cops harass everybody here. I watch them pick up Mexican people if they've had one beer and take them to jail. We can't do anything about it." [46]

From LAMAS data, we find that 51 percent of the black respondents, 37 percent of Chicanos and 13 percent of white respondents feel that the police treat Mexican Americans unfairly. Table 6-7 presents the joint effects of race and class on the perception of general police treatment of Mexican Americans. Unlike the riot questions, these data show a strong class effect among Chicanos in support of our hypothesis. Lower-income Chicanos are far more likely to feel unfairly treated (55 percent) than higher-income Chicanos (22 percent). This is not to say that higher-income Chicanos believe that Mexican-Americans always get fair treatment, since 39 percent say fair and 39 percent say mixed, fair and unfair. Nevertheless, there are strong differences among Chicanos, differences that are extremely important in terms of common community grievances and the propensity for mass action.

On the other hand, the race-class relationship for blacks is very different from that of Chicanos. Blacks of all income levels show that a rather high percentage feels that Mexican Americans receive unfair police treatment and higher-income blacks voice this view *more* than lower income blacks.[47]

In sharp contrast to blacks and Chicanos, white persons of all class levels voice support for the police with approximate 70 percent believing there is consistently fair treatment of Mexican Americans. Clearly, we have an issue in which race and class must be jointly considered. One possible interpretation is the following: we have suggested that a middle-class Mexican American living in Los Angeles may more easily escape discrimination and exclusion than a middle-class black person. As a result, middle-class Mexican Americans are less likely to feel the same degree of anger and outrage as middle-class blacks. Specifically, on the issue of police malpractice, the perceptions of our respondents may correspond, more or less, to their experiences. Lower-income Chicanos may live in areas where there is an unusually high degree of gang activity, violence, and hostile contact between the police and residents. Middle-class Chicanos may escape these relations with the police to some degree by moving from the barrio or being less visible by skin color and language though the data show that many do not shift all the way over to the "fair" responses, rather half choose "fair" and half choose "mixed good and bad" treatment. Blacks are more consistently hostile and higher-income blacks the more so. Middle-class

TABLE 6-7

General Police Treatment of Mexican Americans[1]

	Fairly %	Unfairly %	Sometimes Fair/ Sometimes Unfair	
			%	N
Less than $5,000				
Chicano	14	55	31	(29)
Black	31	47	22	(32)
White	68	7	25	(72)
$5-$9,000				
Chicano	44	31	26	(39)
Black	31	44	25	(16)
White	70	12	18	(87)
$9-$20,000				
Chicano	39	22	39	(23)
Black	8	67	25	(15)
White	77	11	12	(162)

Source: LAMAS III (see note 45)

*Those answering "Don't Know" and those making over $20,000 (mostly white) are excluded from the analysis.

blacks, because of their visibility, may continue to be stopped more by the police than other races or as a result of housing discrimination have greater difficulty in moving away from high crime rate areas. It may be especially insulting to the middle-class black person to be stopped and questioned by the police. Finally, more white persons may be more isolated from areas of crime and violence, and may in fact receive better treatment on the average than Chicanos or blacks.

Mexican American Farmworkers*

1 This discussion of Mexican-American farmworkers in the Southwest should be regarded as one interpretation of events.

Though "partial" minority may be a useful label for some of the options open to middle-class Chicanos, there is no more "total" or thoroughly oppressed minority group in the 1970s than the lower-class Mexican-American farmworkers. The plight of the present-day farmworkers is likened to pre-Civil War conditions of blacks on the plantations. As late as 1966, there was evidence that hundreds of farmworkers may be kept in virtual serfdom on remote ranches all over the southwestern United States, financially and physically unable to leave.[48]

Why is it that this very small fraction of one of the conquered minorities (about 6 percent of the Mexican-American population) asks for so few and such reasonable changes (like minimum wages and portable toilets on the job) that management reacts with such widespread, oppressive measures, thwarting the self-development of a rather unobtrusive power base?

The attempts to undermine the farmworkers' peaceful efforts to organize for benefits accorded other American industrial workers are not just isolated incidents or even a matter of deliberate consensus and planned action among agri-businessmen across the country. It is much more than that. It is not force and coercion that sustain, through time, one group's power over another, rather it is the institutionalization of that power — building into society a particular pattern of interaction. The farmworkers and growers are locked into a very old, traditional labor pattern. Agribusiness in the United States depends upon a massive, continuous, snag-free flow of cheap laborers.

Beginning with the Chinese immigrants in the 1870s, there have always been enough desperate, poverty-stricken people (either citizens already in this country, especially during the Depression, or people from abroad) willing to work in the fields without questioning the conditions. The Mexican American has been particularly available. For years, he was imported or deported, depending on the whims of economists, lawmakers, and businessmen. Other industries were not allowed to import foreign workers. (Farmers can still use "green-carders" to fill in if American farmworkers raise their voices in protest of working conditions. "Green-carders" are Mexican citizens with special work permit visas.) Other industries were forbidden to use child labor, were required to pay minimum wages, to make working conditions safe, to allow for the development of unions and worker representations. Farmworkers were excluded from these legal protections. They do not come under the jurisdiction of the National Labor Relations Board.*

Governmental exceptions and special privileges abound in agriculture. Farmers are given billions in Federal subsidies to protect them from fluctuations in the economy, to reimburse them for empty fields, but farm laborers receive nothing. Farmworkers, without any economic safeguards or rights guaranteed to other American workers are clearly at the bottom of the stratification system, class-wise. What about *eth*-class?

> You see, says Cesar Chavez, the farmworker is an outsider, even though he may be a resident worker . . . . His is an outsider economically, and he is an outsider racially. Most farm workers are of ethnic backgrounds other than white.[49]

Though growers are seldom heard referring publicly to farmworkers as "ignorant Mexicans," many paternalistic statements are still made, which imply a belief in inferiority. ". . . The idea that farmworkers are a different breed of people — humble, happy, built close to the ground

---

*There have been recent suggestions by politicians and growers that farmworkers should now be included under the NLRA, but few people realize that the time they should have been included was somewhere between 1935 and 1947. After the 1935 Wagner Act, unions became more and more organized and gained tremendous strength; the 1947 Taft-Hartley Amendment was aimed at curbing union power, and now would prevent the farmworkers from developing *any*. The Taft-Hartley Amendment limits the right to strike and to boycott — farmworkers would be caught with many conditions remaining unchanged once stripped of this kind of economic muscle. The farmworkers feel that they need a little catching-up with other industries. They liken the NLRA to Civil Rights legislation — unless a group has enough power to demand enforcement of laws, the laws mask the real, existing conditions of inequality; new laws only make the conditions look good on paper.

— still prevails," according to Chavez.[50] Growers often refer to "my boys" in a manner very similar to that of plantation owners talking about "their" Negroes.

> The Mexican is a child by nature, a grower explains. He has no sense of the future. He likes to enjoy himself. Sing. Dance. Drink. So he loves all those parades and flags and singing the union has. It's a fiesta to him, the damn union . . . . He doesn't know anything about farm economics.[51]

The Mexican-American farmworkers remain the last conquered minority group which still offers direct economic payoffs for exploitation. For example, it has become costly to exploit blacks. The costs, in terms of welfare rolls, national image, riots, and crime, increasingly has made large-scale, systematic exploitation of blacks unprofitable. There is no longer a nation-wide, systematic attempt to keep blacks economically "in their place." But any organization of power among farmworkers is seen as a threat to the highly lucrative business of agriculture, as well as a threat to the whole economic system. The implication of farmworkers with power does not mean just slightly higher wages and a few benefits: it suggests that the power elite might have to yield some of its exclusive hold on power over a heretofore docile, predictable work force upon which the economy is dependent.

In the 1960's farmworkers, for the first time, exerted a significant amount of counter-power. Under the leadership of Chavez, farm workers and their supporters appealed to consumers not to buy table grapes. *Boycott Grapes!* became an effective means to force growers to recognize the strength and legitimacy of the United Farm Worker's union and to sign contracts that would bring improved wages and benefits. A consumer boycott of a perishable crop has great power potential, yet such a boycott can only be successful when there is wide scale support in middle-class America.

How could such a voiceless minority as farmworkers ever organize a world-wide boycott against table grapes — the only world-wide boycott in history? Traditional Marxian class conflict theory would tell us that a totally powerless population often widely dispersed rather than in close proximity, disengaged from the conventional economic structure, with little hope or rising expectations for change would be overcome with hopelessness and despair, rather than ready to try actively to change the system through class action.[52]

There are probably three special aspects of the farmworker movement that account for its tremendous support and publicity, and help to explain why it is an exception from theoretical suppositions.

1) Cesar Chavez, the leader of the United Farmworkers Union, is to some, a saint, and to others, a dangerous power-monger. All who know of him are impressed by his outstanding ability to organize and his quiet charisma. Cesar Chavez is unequivocally dedicated to change through non-violence. He explains that though violence would certainly have won some union contracts, violence never wins respect.

2) The United Farmworkers have won respect — respect from some very respectful segments of our society — the National Council of Churches and many middle-class lay people. No other lower-class minority movement has managed to secure support from such groups. One reason for middle-class support is the *safety* of non-violence. Probably the timing of the movement too, has helped. During the 1960s (the beginning of the table grape boycott) our nation was fraught with riots and war. Aside from the moral and religious appeal of non-violence, a group pushing for change through peaceful means seemed, to many people, an isolated, perhaps vanishing, alternative to bloodshed, one that needed support and encouragement.

The grape boycott was another "safe" action, allowing for widespread support for farmworkers among middle-class segments of the society. Asking people not to buy grapes is a very small favor with which many people were able to comply. Few movements are able to incorporate more supporters than hardcore activists. The farmworkers movement has included millions of "mini-activists" as well. The California Migrant Ministry (under the direction of the Reverend W. C. Hartmire, with support from representatives of all faiths) asked for food and clothing and small donations of time and money from parishioners and friends. Again, these are items that middle-class people can give safely, but are very important for widely based support and subsequent public pressures for change.

3) The third aspect of the farmworkers' struggle that makes it unique is its *powerlessness*. That this low ethclass has been kept politically and economically powerless has been demonstrated. But, led by Cesar Chavez, they turned powerlessness — the very condition that should have spelled despair and apathy — into their most dynamic asset. The utter powerlessness and oppression of the Mexican-American farmworker is used as a device for extracting sympathy and

support from middle-class Americans. But much more important, the rock-bottom feelings of powerlessness of the farmworker account for his patient, unswerving, quiet, persistent push for change. The poverty-stricken Mexican American can say, "What have I got to lose? Things can't be worse." Growers and their foremen can't threaten him physically — he has known the pain of hunger too long. Jail probably is not worse than the poverty he has been locked into. He is not afraid of death — life is what has been hell.

Powerlessness becomes the very source of the farmworkers' power, his ability to endure unbelievable opposition to his requests for change and to persist in these demands against all odds. This third aspect of powerlessness as the most powerful non-violent weapon for change cannot be separated from the (1) leadership of Cesar Chavez. Neither can it be separated from (2) the unusual widespread support of so many non-Mexican American, non-farm-working, non-lower-class people. Cesar Chavez' words may best illustrate the uniqueness of the farmworker movement that seems to touch all of those who have been involved even slightly.

> When we are really honest with ourselves, we must admit that our lives are all that really belong to us. So it is how we use our lives that determines what kind of men we are. It is my deepest belief that only by giving our lives do we find life. I am convinced that the truest act of courage, the strongest act of manliness, is to sacrifice ourselves for others in a totally non-violent struggle for justice. To be a man is to suffer for others. God help us be men.[53]

In 1970, many large farm growers finally signed contracts with the United Farm Workers. The contracts brought health and retirement benefits for the first time as well as higher minimum wages. It appeared that self determination was at last becoming a reality for the powerless worker. However, in 1973, when contracts were to be renewed, California growers ignored or refused requests by farmworkers to hold elections for union representation. Completely bypassing UFW, growers secretly signed contracts with the Teamster's Union. Although the Teamster contracts are not without benefits (some of the benefits are comparable to the UFW contracts) the Teamsters are not oriented toward the unique problems of the farmworkers (the need for on-site medical facilities, pesticide protection for workers etc.) and their contracts reflect it. The issue is far more than the relative benefits of the two contracts; workers were once again not allowed to express their collective voice — the issue is self determination. Growers apparently found the Teamsters more appealing; they have in common a more business-like, less emotional, English speaking, middle classness. More important, Teamsters have a vested interest in a constant, uninterrupted flow of produce from the farm to the supermarket. Teamsters would want crops harvested under any conditions so that they could be guaranteed pay for transporting those crops.

The term *co-optation* is used when powerful organizations absorb the demands of dissedents in such a way that the social organization is not significantly altered. Contracts with Teamsters represent a kind of co-optation of worker demands. Such contracts do not alter the agribusiness equation. Two powerful groups (growers and Teamsters) are working together for their common economic interests and farmworkers, though given some increased material benefits, remain essentially outside and powerless. At the time of this writing, members of the United Farm Workers have called for a new boycott of head lettuce and grapes. The goal of this new boycott is simply to force growers to hold elections to allow workers to pick the union of their choice.

Farmworkers are striving to convert their lower-class status only to working-class position. This seemingly minor shuffling at the bottom of the hierarchy, however, threatens to shake the giants at the top — not enough to change noticeably the life styles of middle or upper-class persons but enough to demand a significant redistribution of power in a huge industry that is institutionalized about the *total* power of those at the top and the total voicelessness of those at the bottom. In their modest demands for traditional rights and privileges — self-determination, a voice in their future, secret ballot elections, choosing their own representatives, freedom from hunger and dangerous working conditions — farmworkers threaten another cluster of traditional American patterns — huge corporate power and bureaucratic insensitivities. Parallels of similar battles can be heard from the rumblings of consumers, from welfare recipients, and from American Indians. So far, indications of change, or redistribution of power (of even a tiny tokenism of power trickling down from the top) are more potential than actual. Success of the farmworker movement may mean not just the correction of injustices in that particular labor pattern, but application of a new economic pattern that could well affect other ethclass or lower-class or powerless people as well.

NOTES TO CHAPTER 6

[1] Tamotsu Shibutani and Kian M. Kwan, *Ethnic Stratification* (New York: Macmillan Co., 1965), pp. 494-501.

[2] E. Franklin Frazier, *Black Bourgeoisie: The Rise of a New Middle Class* (New York: Free Press, 1957).

[3] Sindey Kronus, *The Black Middle Class* (Columbus: Charles E. Merrill, 1970), p. 3.

[4] Lerone Bennett, Jr., "Black Bourgeoisie Revisted," *Ebony* 28 (August, 1973), p. 52

[5] See, for example, Shibutani and Kwan, op. cit., p. 498; Frazier, op. cit., p. 108; and Harry Edwards, *Black Students* (New York: Free Press, 1970), p. 11.

[6] Kronus, op. cit., p. 21.

[7] G. Franklin Edwards, *The Negro Professional Class* (Glencoe, Ill.: Free Press, 1959).

[8] Kronus, op. cit., p. 21.

[9] Leonard Broom and Norval Glenn, *Transformation of the Negro American* (New York: Harper & Row, 1965), pp. 135-143.

[10] Kronus, op. cit., p. 7.

[11] Ibid., p. 7.

[12] For example, see Harry Edwards, op. cit., pp. 5-16; Broom and Glenn, op. cit., pp. 172-192; Gary T. Marx, *Protest and Prejudice* (New York: Harper & Row, 1967), pp. 55-70; William Brink and Louis Harris, *The Negro Revolution in America* (New York: Simon & Schuster, 1964), p. 203; Ruth Searles and J. Allen Williams, Jr., "Negro College Students Participation in Sit-Ins," *Social Forces* 40 (March, 1962), pp. 215-220.

[13] Searles and Williams, op. cit., pp. 215-220; Edwards, *op. cit.*, pp. 5-16.

[14] For example see Harry Edwards, op. cit., pp. 5-16.

[15] The data in Tables 6-1 and 6-2 were gathered shortly after the Watts riot (August-November, 1965). A stratified random sample design was used to include both lower and middle-class blacks living in the Los Angeles area. The sample was composed of 312 black males between the ages of 18 and 65. The subjects responded to an interview schedule administered by black interviewers. Subjects were chosen by random methods and were interviewed in their own homes or apartments. The majority of the subjects were employed (N = 269) though there was a small sub-sample of unemployed persons (N = 43). For further specifications on the sampling procedure and data collection see H. Edward Ransford, "Skin Color, Life Chances, and Anti-White Attitudes," *Social Problems* 18 (Fall, 1970), pp. 164-179.

[16] Marx, op. cit., pp. 55-70.

[17] Data on the relationship between social class and the militant behavior index are unpublished. However, data on the relationship between class and the separate components of that index (e.g., boycott and demonstration behavior taken separately) are found in H. Edward Ransford. "Negro Participation in Civil Rights Activity and Violence" (Ph.D. diss., University of California at Los Angeles, 1966).

[18] Marx, op. cit., p. 68.

[19] See Raymond J. Murphy and James M. Watson, *The Structure of Discontent: The Relationship Between Social Structure, Grievance, and Support for the Los Angeles Riot* (Los Angles: University of California at Los Angeles, Institute of Government and Public Affairs, 1967 MR-92), pp. 82-87.

[20] Otto Kerner, *Report of the National Advisory Commission of Civil Disorders* (New York: Bantam Books, 1968), pp. 128-129.

21 Marx, op. cit., p. 65.

22 Harold Cruse, *The Crisis of the Negro Intellectual* (New York: William Morrow, 1967), p. 312.

23 Andrew Billingsley, *Black Families in White America* (Englewood Cliffs, N.J.: Prentice-Hall, 1968), pp. 11-12.

24 *Newsweek*, October 23, 1972, p. 78.

25 Joseph A. Kahl and John M. Goering, "Stable Workers, Black and White," *Social Problems*, 18 (Winter, 1971), pp. 306-318.

26 Ibid., p. 312.

27 Ibid., p. 313.

28 Ibid., p. 315.

29 Ann F. Brunswick, "What Generation Gap? A Comparison of Some Generational Differences Among Blacks and Whites," *Social Problems* 17 (Winter, 1970): 358-371.

30 Ibid., p. 368.

31 Kronus, op. cit.

32 Ibid., pp. 33-36.

33 Ibid., p. 30.

34 *Los Angeles Times*, August 31, 1970, p. 1.

35 Alfred Cuellar, "Perspectives on Politics," in *Mexican Americans* by Joan W. Moore, 1970. Reprinted by permission of Prentice-Hall, Inc., Englewood Cliffs, N.J.

36 Chandler Davidson and Charles M. Gaitz, "Ethnic Attitudes as a Basis for Minority Cooperation in a Southwestern Metropolis," *Social Science Quarterly* 53 (March, 1973): pp. 738-748.

37 Armando Gutiérrez and Herbert Hirsch, "The Militant Challenge to the American Ethos. 'Chicanos' and 'Mexican Americans,'" *Social Science Quarterly* 53 (March, 1973): 830-845.

38 Ibid., p. 833.

39 Ibid., p. 845.

40 Moore, op. cit., p. 113.

41 Ibid., p. 114.

42 Davidson and Gaitz, op. cit., p. 741.

43 John R. Howard, *Awakening Minorities* (New Brunswick, N.J.: Transaction Books, 1970), p.6.

44 I derived this hypothesis especially from two studies that link militant ethnic behavior and ethnic identification with acceptance in the majority group. See Kurt Lewin's essay "Leaders from the Periphery," in Kurt Lewin, *Resolving Social Conflicts* (New York: Harper & Row, 1948), pp. 195-197 and Alan C. Kerckhoff and Thomas C. McCormick, "Marginal Status and Marginal Personality," *Social Forces*, vol. 34, pp. 48-55.

45 Los Angeles Metropolitan Area Surveys (LAMAS) are conducted twice a year by the U.C.L.A. Survey Research Center. They represent probability samples of Los Angeles County. Adult respondents (persons twenty-one years or over) are selected by probability procedures and interviewed in their households. Interviewer and respondent are matched by race (blacks interview blacks, etc.) Latin respondents are given a choice of answering in Spanish or English. I am greatly indebted by the U.C.L.A. Survey Research Center for making these data available to me.

46 "Barrio Residents Describe Riot Reactions," *Los Angeles Times*, September 6, 1970, p. 1.

47 Other studies have produced similar findings when the object of discrimination is blacks. For example, Murphy and Watson found that blacks with more education tend to

perceive greater police malpractice than those with less education. See Murphy and Watson, op. cit., p. 64.

[48] Stan Steiner, *La Raza: The Mexican Americans* (New York: Harper & Row, 1970), pp. 247-248.

[49] Steiner, Ibid., p. 261 and conversation with Rev. W.C. Hartmire, Director, California Migrant Ministry: "In the Southwest, where most of the pioneering in organizing a farmworkers' union is taking place, about 70% of the farmworkers are Mexican American, others are Filipino, black and a few Anglos. Nationwide, the farmworker population is about 85% Mexican American (1970 census), but there are regional variations: almost 100% Mexican American in Texas, almost 70% black in Florida.

[50] Steiner, op. cit., p. 264.

[51] Ibid,, p. 260.

[52] For an excellent summary of the Marxian class conflict approach see Reinhard Bendix and Seymour Martin Lipset, "Karl Marx's Theory of Social Classes," in *Class Status and Power*, ed. Reinhard Bendix and Seymour Martin Lipset (New York: Free Press, 1966), pp. 6-11.

[53] Peter Matthiessen, "Profile: Cesar Chavez," *New Yorker*, June 21 and June 28, 1969 (original publication). This excerpt appeared subsequently in Peter Matthiessen, *Sal Si Puedes* (New York: Random House, 1970).

Chapter 7

VALUES, POWER, SOLIDARITY, AND INTERACTION: EMPIRICAL EXPLORATIONS IN RACE AND CLASS

When a stratification approach to the study of human behavior is taken, certain concepts or variables are commonly found. A hierarchical approach is one lens that illuminates or "focuses in" certain concepts. For example, when a stratification order is firmly established it is often asserted that persons of the same stratum will display (1) common values or belief systems, (2) similar feelings of power or control over their environment, (3) common feelings of solidarity and shared fate, and (4) a tendency to restrict their friendship context to those of the same stratum. These four concepts — values, power, stratum solidarity, and interaction — have roots in the classic theories of Marx, Weber, and Warner. They have been most commonly applied to a single class (or status) hierarchy. Some extremely interesting questions emerge when one considers these four concepts in the context of race and class hierarchies in dynamic interaction. As examples, these questions are explored in the following pages.

Values

Are middle-class blacks and Mexican Americans so acculturated that they share the value-orientation of middle-class whites? Or is there often some blend of class environment and racial experience such that the middle-class minority person will voice values that are very different from those of the middle-class white person?

Subjective Feelings of Power

If both race and class position determine one's power potential, then lower-class blacks and Chicanos should have the most intense feelings

123

of powerlessness. However, does higher income, educational attainment or the attainment of a white-collar occupation improve one's life-chances and power potential to the extent that middle-class black and Chicano persons will share the same feelings of control as middle-class white persons?

Stratum Solidarity

Are persons who identify strongly with their races as well as with a "working-class" position (that is, a community of workers rather than one of owners, managers, and professionals) especially militant in their political ideologies?

Interaction

Are there sizeable segments of the white, black, and Mexican-American populations for whom education, income or occupational similarity is more important in determining close friendships than is race? For example, do many whites feel that it is easier for them to have friendships with blacks or Mexican Americans of similar educations and incomes than with white persons of very different educations and incomes?

Data that allowed for some initial test of these questions were available from several Los Angeles surveys, Before moving to the specific results of these surveys, it will be helpful to note three empirical models of race-class interaction.

THREE EMPIRICAL PATTERNS

There are at least three ways in which race and class can combine empirically. The three patterns correspond roughly to the models presented in Chapter 4 (open market, minority subcommunity, and ethclass). *First,* class position may be more important than or override any racial effect (open market). Middle-class blacks and whites may have very similar child-rearing practices and aspirations for their children. *Second,* for some outcomes, race may be more important than class. Blacks may vote in a bloc to elect a particular black candidate, the differences between black and white voters being far more important than class differences within each race. *Third,* race and class are both important to the outcome and they combine to produce a result that is different from either taken singly. We shall call this blend of race and class factors an "ethclass effect."[1] A thesis throughout this volume is that "ethclass" is an underdeveloped concept that has great potential in explaining issues in contemporary racial stratification. For example, in the last chapter we observed that lower-class Chicanos, middle-class Chicanos, and middle-class blacks held very different views on the issue of police malpractice in the barrio, distinctions that would have been lost with a single-dimension race or class approach. How would these three examples look statistically? For example, how would an ethclass effect look in simple percentage tables? In the following hypothetical illustrations, race and class are viewed as variables that affect a person's distrust of the government. These examples are constructed to illustrate ideal types. Rarely do actual data turn out to be this clear-cut.

Case I — Class Overrides Race

	Black		White	
	middle class	*lower class*	*middle class*	*lower class*
%distrusting the city government	30%	50%	30%	50%

These hypothetical figures describe the case in which class but not race effects distrust. For both black persons and white persons, the lower class is more distrusting of the government than the middle class (50 percent minus 30 percent equals 20 percent difference by class). But the differences by race equal zero (30 percent minus 30 percent and 50 percent minus 50 percent equals zero percent difference by race). Such results would suggest that as blacks have or attain a middle-class position their level of distrust is reduced so that they resemble white middle-class persons on this attitude.

Case II — Race Overrides Class

	Black		White	
	middle class	*lower class*	*middle class*	*lower class*
% distrusting the government	50%	50%	30%	30%

It can be seen in this example that blacks are more distrusting of the government than whites with no class differences at all. Those arguing for black unity or a black perspective that cuts across class divisions would logically expect results such as these.

Case III — Ethclass Effects

There is not just one pattern but several that data could suggest an ethclass effect. The most important criterion to be kept in mind in the ethclass model is that race and class exert somewhat separate influences so that their combined effects are different from their individual effects. We have argued throughout this book that race and class hierarchies, though correlated, are separate, each affecting access to power, economic rewards, friendship choices, and status. Accordingly, combined effects should be a common occurrence. Two ways in which race and class unite could be labeled the "additive pattern" and the "interaction pattern." The following is an example of an additive pattern.

| | Black | | White | |
	Middle Class	Lower Class	Middle Class	Lower Class
% distrusting the government	30%	50%	10%	30%

It can be seen that class has an effect (differences between 10 percent and 30 percent or 30 percent and 50 percent) but so does race (middle-class blacks are different from middle-class whites and lower-class blacks are different from lower-class whites). What is especially interesting is that when race and class unite in the combination of "black lower class" one finds the highest proportion (50 percent) distrusting the government. The lower-class black percentage is the greatest because it represents the sum of race and class jointly operating. This is called an additive model. The reader can actually add up the effects of race and class in the following manner: viewing the white middle class as a baseline (the high end of the race and class hierarchies where one would expect the least distrust) one can assess the class effect by comparing middle-class and lower-class whites (20 percent difference) and the race effect by comparing middle-class whites and middle-class blacks (again, a 20 percent difference). Adding these two effects together gives us 40 percent, and when the 40 percent is added to the baseline of 10 we have the observed 50 percent black lower class combined effect.

Race and class can also combine in an interaction pattern as shown below:

| | Black | | White | |
	Middle Class	Lower Class	Middle Class	Lower Class
% distrusting government	30%	80%	10%	30%

In this model, the same combination of "lower-class black" has produced an extremely high percentage of persons distrusting the government. The simplest explanation of this statistical interaction is that something special happens when two independent variables get together in a particular combination, that is, something above and beyond what would be expected from their additive effects (50 percent). Blalock[2] discusses statistical interaction as somewhat analogous to what happens when hydrogen and oxygen are combined to produce water. The result is more than a simple sum of the parts. Though statistical interaction may seem somewhat rare, in the case of race-class combinations it may often occur. Poverty and race frequently combine to form communities of frustration and discontent. These ghettos and barrios usually involve a pile-up of deprivation and lack of redress channels that would result in exceptionally high, non-additive combinations. If urban renewal programs force low-income ghetto residents to move, create hostile police contacts, result in inadequate city services, and are accompanied by the presence of absentee landlords, these factors may combine to produce uniquely high feelings of distrust toward public officials and the city government.

There is still another ethclass possibility that should be mentioned. In the above combined-effect examples, race and class are separate but reinforcing factors. That is, they are seen as both salient and operating in the same direction to reduce life-chances. However, there are other instances in which race interests and class interests may *compete*. For example, a young black or Chicano person may constantly face the cross-pressures of unselfishly working for his brothers and sisters in a movement, but still have "class" interests in furthering his personal career through job mobility, and thus have aspirations of attaining a high income. In this case, the ethclass effect produces data which fall between pure race or pure class effects. In Chapter 6 we noted that many middle-class blacks may not be risk-taking revolutionaries (extreme of racial identification) but neither are they bourgeoisie "sellouts" interested only in their personal class advancement. Rather, many appear to have worked out a life-style between these cross pressures by supporting civil rights actions, participating in some forms of militant protest, and relating to the black experience through black theater, art, etc. In our very simple "distrust of the government" example one could find results such as these.

| | Black | | White | |
	Middle Class	Lower Class	Middle Class	Lower Class
% distrusting the government	30%	40%	15%	40%

Note that the black middle-class percentage (30 percent) falls between the white middle class (15 percent) and the lower class of each race (40 percent). The interpretation is that although the middle-class black may have slightly more confidence in the government as he has class resources to affect outcomes, he still may retain skepticism and distrust as a result of racial identification.*

*A distinction must be made between a two (or more) dimension ethclass effect and the single dimension form of ethclass that we have been discussing in this section. It was the two-dimension finding that signalled an ethclass effect in the Kahl-Goering study of stably employed black and white workers (chapter 6): middle-class blacks were found to be career oriented and materialistic on an economic dimension but more radical on politically oriented issues. Not only did this finding seem to be a logical mix of class and race interests, but it contrasted sharply with the middle-class white profile (materialistic and politically conservative). The point is that the full ethclass story could be told only by looking at both the economic and political dimensions. However, there are many instances in which race and class should unite to produce some special effect on a single diminsion such as distrust of the government. It is these single dimension (one dependent variable) cases that we are exploring in this chapter.

SUBJECTIVE POWERLESSNESS AND VALUES FOR CHILDREN: TWO EXPLORATIONS IN RACE AND CLASS FROM A LOS ANGELES SURVEY

The Los Angeles area provides a natural laboratory for the study of urban race relations, with sizeable numbers of blacks, Chicanos, and whites and smaller numbers of Indians and Orientals. The 1970 census data indicate that fairly sizeable proportions of Los Angeles black and

Spanish-surname persons are in skilled and white-collar positions and are earning incomes over $10,000. The data for this analysis comes from a Los Angeles metropolitan area survey (LAMAS II) conducted by the UCLA Survey Research Center in late 1969 and early 1970.[3] A number of attitudinal and behavioral questions were asked of a randomly selected goup of respondents. Three ethnic groups were sampled in sufficient numbers to provide a race-class analysis — 97 blacks, 251 Spanish-surname persons (mostly Mexican American) and 583 Anglos were interviewed by members of their respective races. The inclusion of Mexican Americans is considered one of the strong points of this analysis. As the nation's second largest racial minority, Mexican Americans have been grossly ignored in race and stratification models.

What is presented here is a secondary analysis of LAMAS data, an analysis begun with a spirit of exploration and discovery rather than with a carefully formulated theory developed prior to data collection. However, this is not to say that we are engaging in raw empiricism since rationales and logic do guide us to certain questions with the anticipation of certain results. Our basic design is to present the relationship between race and the dependent variables (perceived powerlessness and child rearing values) with controls for occupation, education, and income.

A white collar occupation, attainment of one or more years of college, and a family income of $10,000-25,000 will be considered "middle-class" socioeconomic level. Attainment of a skilled or semi-skilled blue collar job, high school graduation, and a family income of $5,000-10,000 will be called "working-class" level and an unskilled or service occupation, less education than high school graduation, and less than $5,000 family income is termed the "lower-class" level of socioeconomic status. One might consider combining these three measures into an overall index of socioeconomic status, but instead, an investigation of their separate effects might prove more valuable; perhaps attainment of "some college" has a different meaning in the black or Chicano community than for whites that would in turn lead to different results of the dependent variable in question. In the Chicano case, the high school dropout rates have approached a staggering 50 percent rate in some Los Angeles schools. If attainment of higher education among Chicanos is still rare, then those that have attended college may hold some unique outlooks. Such special educational effects would be averaged out or lost in an overall measure of SES.

There are certain shortcomings to the race-class analysis used here. Variables such as "family respectability" and participation in community organizations — variables that some have mentioned as important alternative channels of status recognition in the black community — are not included. Other relevant racial variables, such as living in, on the periphery of, or outside of the ghetto or barrio, have not been observed fully in this analysis. Practically all black respondents lived in predominantly black neighborhoods and most Chicano respondents lived in predominantly Mexican-American neighborhoods. Even with these limitations, this analysis may be viewed as a valuable step toward the development of more refined and more rigorously controlled race-class comparisons.

EXPLORATION NO. 1
SUBJECTIVE POWERLESSNESS
POWER HIERARCHIES IN INTERACTION

What is the joint effect of race and class on subjective feelings of control over one's own life and over the government? This first inquiry views race and class as power and life-chances hierarchies in interaction. From the LAMAS data, we can conceptualize a class hierarchy with middle, working, and lower-class levels and a race or ethnic hierarchy with Anglos at the top (Anglos having the greatest life-chances and ability to exert *power* due to their *racial* status), and Mexican-Americans in between Anglo and black but closer to black. Our rationale is that Mexican Americans, like blacks, are a conquered people and have faced a great deal of exploitation and oppression in their barrio communities, yet they have not generally faced the extreme color barrier and stigma that blacks have. Moreover, middle-class Chicanos in more open areas of the southwest, like Los Angeles, definitely face less social exclusion and have more assimilation options than blacks.

If feelings of powerlessness result from being low on both race and class hierarchies, then lower-class blacks (and, to a lesser extent, lower-class Chicanos) should be especially likely to express feelings of powerlessness. Further, if blacks and Chicanos advance in the class structure, their chances of personal influence and control should be improved, but perhaps not to the same extent as Anglos. The continued existence of segregated housing and other racial barriers may prolong a racial gap in perceived powerlessness. There should also be some difference between middle-class blacks and middle-class Chicanos. We have argued above that middle-class Chicanos can more easily assimilate and escape racial discrimination than middle-class blacks. Accordingly, we expect middle-class Chicanos to express less powerlessness than middle-class blacks.

To measure the respondent's feeling of control over outcomes, these (forced choice) questions were asked:

1. — When I make plans, I'm almost certain I can make them work.
   — It's not always wise to plan too far ahead because many things turn out to be a matter of good or bad fortune anyhow.
2. — What happens to me is my own doing.
   — Sometimes I feel that I don't have enough control over the direction my life is taking.
3. — Some people tell us there isn't much they can do to affect what the city government does. Other people say they can influence what gets decided in this city if they want to. How about you? Do you feel that you can affect what the city government does or not?

Note that questions one and two are measuring *personal* powerlessness or one's expectancy of control over personal goals or day-to-day affairs, whereas question three is a measure of *social* powerlessness, control expectancies in the broader community or society (for example, due to a lack of legal redress channels, bureaucratic red tape, or discrimination). The effects of race and class on personal and social powerlessness are presented in Table 7-1. Although there are fluctuations and minor reversals in the data that complicate attempts at summary statements, these patterns appear to break through:

Personal Powerlessness

1) We can see that an advance in socioeconomic position often reduces feelings of personal powerlessness, though different socioeconomic variables have different effects in the three racial groups; for blacks, only educational and income advancement are important in reducing feelings of personal powerlessness; for Chicanos, the educational effect is strong, the occupation effect weak, and income only has an effect on the "don't have enough control" item; for Anglos, all three socioeconomic variables have some effect on the measures of personal powerlessness.

2) In support of our "combined effects" hypothesis, unusually high proportions of blacks in the lowest income, occupational, and educa-

tional categories express personal powerlessness as compared with Chicanos and Anglos of the same low socioeconomic level. Morever, this pattern occurs for both of the two items. For example, 70 percent of the blacks in the $0-5,000 category choose the "can't plan ahead" alternative versus 49 percent of the Chicanos and 50 percent of the Anglos in the same income group. Similarly, 60 percent of blacks in lower blue-collar jobs feel they do not have enough control over their lives versus 31 percent of Chicanos and 19 percent of Anglos in the same occupational position. (In the first example, the lower-class black percentage of 70 represents an interaction effect of 10 percent above what would be expected from an additive model, while in the second example, the lower-class black percentage of 60 indicates a 22 percent interaction effect above the additive model.) The obvious interpretation is that of a unique "pile-up" of barriers and reduced life-chances for persons who are both lower class and black. That is, we are dealing with more than class constraints; race and class are interacting to produce an ethclass effect with uniquely high percentages with felt powerlessness. Moreover, blacks in white-collar jobs or with some college report noticeably higher feelings of powerlessness than comparable Chicanos and Anglos. It is only among blacks earning $10,000-25,000 that the differences between blacks and whites become minimal (8 percent difference and 10 percent difference, respectively). That is, middle-class income seems to be the only social fact that sweeps over racial barriers so that blacks feel about the same degree of personal power as Anglos.

3) Given the economic and power discrimination found in urban barrios such as the East Los Angeles barrio of this sample, we predicted that lower-class Chicanos would be similar to lower-class blacks on measures of powerlessness, whereas middle-class Chicanos would be closer to whites. However, the data show that Chicanos in lower SES positions are generally close to lower-class Anglos or in some instances (such as blue collar and under $5,000 on "don't have control") are intermediate between black and white. Among lower-class Chicanos, race and class do not combine to produce uniquely high proportions of personal powerlessness as is found with blacks. At the middle-class level, our assertions about Chicanos are clearly supported. In practically every instance, Mexican Americans at middle-class levels (white collar, $10,000-25,000, some college) are less likely to express power-

lessness than middle class black persons and are very similar to middle-class Anglos.

TABLE 7-1

Personal and Social Powerlessness
by Race and Class

	Personal Powerlessness				Social Powerlessness	
	Can't Plan Ahead		Don't Have Enough Control		Cannot Affect What Happens in City Government	
Less Than High School	%	N	%	N	%	N
Black	73	(37)	51	(37)	52	(31)
Chicano	51	(185)	32	(182)	43	(116)
Anglo	56	(146)	31	(147)	50	(125)
High School Graduate						
Black	47	(30)	30	(30)	44	(27)
Chicano	53	(38)	26	(38)	32	(28)
Anglo	41	(198)	22	(197)	40	(179)
Some College						
Black	43	(28)	43	(28)	23	(22)
Chicano	19	(26)	19	(26)	35	(26)
Anglo	23	(230)	20	(229)	24	(213)
Lower Blue Collar						
Black	56	(25)	60	(25)	46	(24)
Chicano	42	(43)	31	(42)	52	(27)
Anglo	46	(40)	19	(42)	41	(37)
Stable Blue Collar						
Black	54	(28)	36	(28)	37	(19)
Chicano	54	(111)	28	(109)	38	(74)
Anglo	45	(150)	30	(150)	40	(127)
White Collar						
Black	50	(24)	37	(24)	25	(20)
Chicano	33	(33)	25	(32)	19	(26)
Anglo	32	(108)	18	(306)	32	(285)
Less than $5,000*						
Black	70	(33)	49	(33)	41	(27)
Chicano	49	(100)	38	(97)	45	(62)
Anglo	52	(108)	26	(105)	45	(87)
$5-10,000						
Black	52	(27)	44	(27)	44	(25)
Chicano	51	(69)	22	(67)	38	(47)
Anglo	39	(122)	27	(123)	37	(109)
$10-25,000						
Black	43	(30)	30	(30)	36	(25)
Chicano	46	(44)	20	(44)	33	(33)
Anglo	35	(245)	20	(246)	33	(233)

* Respondents with family incomes over $25,000 (mostly whites) were omitted from the analysis to insure greater socioeconomic homogeneity among the three races at the higher end of the income scale.

Social Powerlessness

Turning to social powerlessness ("I can't affect the city government") we find results that are very different from those for personal powerlessness. Class almost completely overrides race. That is, the two hierarchies do not combine so that their joint effect produces the highest or lowest percentages of powerlessness. Lower-class respondents of all three races feel less efficacious in affecting the government than those higher in class but the differences between the races at any socioeconomic level are so negligible or inconsistent that they are not worth mentioning. In the case of *social power*, one's class position is the crucial fact. It is likely that lower-class Anglo, black, and Chicano persons perceive that demonstrations are useless and that they do not have the money, fluency in communication skills or entree that is necessary to play politics.

What emerges from all these data is quite fascinating. When it comes to one's feelings of personal control over day to day life patterns and plans for the future both race and class position are salient so that lower-class blacks (ethclass combination) express the highest feelings of personal powerlessness. It is likely that this measure of powerlessness is broad enough to pick up many components of the separate and unequal ghetto institutions in which race and class are intertwined. For example, a lower-class black woman may face combinations such as the indignities of the welfare system, consumer exploitation by local merchants (and a lack of reliable transportation to do comparative shopping), and the fact that her children are not learning anything in local ghetto schools — all are likely to register in terms of personal powerlessness. Educational or occupational mobility sharply reduces such feelings for Chicanos and income advancement for blacks. But feelings of control over the local government is a more specific dimension and one more directly linked to class resources (money, connections, communication skills). Poorly educated, low income whites are just as disenchanted with their chances of affecting City Hall as lower-class blacks or Chicanos. A perceived lack of influence over local government decisions is more of a class than a race problem according to these data.

EXPLORATION NO. 2
VALUES

In the data above, race and class — viewed as two somewhat independent "life-chances" hierarchies — were believed to be relevant to the outcome (perceived powerlessness) so that their joint effects would produce special ethclass combinations. However, there are many instances in which either the race or class hierarchy per se relates more logically to the outcome in question. For example, there are instances in which the theoretical rationale between social class and a given outcome is stronger than between race and the outcome. In such cases, we expect class position to override or cut across race effects so that middle-class blacks, Chicanos, and Anglos should be similar in outlook as should the lower and working-class segments of each race.

Our subject is values that parents emphasize in the rearing of their children. A number of studies show a tendency for middle-class parents to emphasize autonomy, independence, and thinking for oneself, while lower and working-class parents place greater stress on obedience and conformity to external standards.[4] Kohn argues that the middle-class stress on autonomy is due to *occupational environments* (middle-class white-collar jobs allow for and encourage more independent thought and judgment) and *education* (high degrees of education encourage intellectual flexibility, curiosity, and the questioning of tradition).[5] Our conceptualization of class as a distribution of life-chances and power changes slightly in this formulation to class as an index of opportunity and encouragement to exercise independent thought, judgment, and initiative. In this model, race does not seem to offer the same clear independent force in the direction of parental stress on childhood autonomy that class does. With class accounted for, there is no particular reason why blacks should emphasize obedience for their children more than whites. However, in the Chicano case, some race effect may persist due to the especially strong ethnic tradition of cohesion and respect for authority in the family. Will middle-class Chicanos be as autonomy-oriented as middle-class Anglos or will the presumed greater familistic-obedience orientation of Chicanos persist into middle-class levels?

In the Los Angeles survey, the following forced-choice item was included:

— "The most important thing for my children to learn is to think for themselves."
— "Obedience and respect for authority are the most important things children should learn."

Table 7-2 presents the response to this question, cross tabulated by race and socioeconimic status. Overall, there is a rather striking pattern: in all three racial groups an increase in socioeconomic status is associated with an increased proportion choosing ". . . think for themselves" and a decreased proportion choosing ". . . respect for authority . . . ." (The only major exception to the pattern is that black high school graduates are more likely to stress ". . . think for themselves" than blacks with some college.) In other words, the middle-class segment of each racial group is more likely to stress autonomy for their children than the lower-class segment. However, there are some interesting racial oscillations in this pattern. Chicanos in middle-class occupaticns and income categories (white collar, $10,000-25,000) are far less likely to prefer autonomy for their children than comparable blacks and Anglos. In other words, middle-income and white-collar Chicanos continue to stress respect for authority as a more important value than thinking for self. It is only educational achievement that has a strong effect in the Chicano group with 21 percent of those with less than high school favoring autonomy versus 54 percent of those with college. Apparently, Mexican Americans do have a stronger tradition of family authority and only educational achievement strongly alters this preference.[6] The other interesting racial note (to an otherwise class pattern) is the especially high emphasis on autonomy for blacks in higher income and occupational levels. For example, 66 percent of blacks in the $10-25,000 category favor thinking for self versus 45 percent of whites with comparable incomes. Perhaps some middle-class blacks are especially concerned with their child's training for independence to compete better in white society or as a part of a vision of a new, strong, independent black middle class.

EXPLORATION NO. 3
STRATUM SOLIDARITY IN A PERIOD
SHORTLY AFTER THE WATTS RIOT

One of the oldest traditions in stratification theory and research is to study not only objective strata but stratum consciousness, that is, perceptions of a class order and feelings of belongingness or solidarity with persons of a similar position. Thus, Marx felt that the revolution of the proletariat would occur only when workers banded together into an organized political group that perceived a common enemy, shared

TABLE 7-2

Autonomy Versus Authority*

	Black		Chicano		Anglo	
	% think for self	% respect authority	% think for self	% respect authority	% think for self	% respect authority
*Income***						
$0-5,000	29	58 (31)	24	66 (100)	32	65 (107)
$5-10,000	33	59 (27)	32	55 (69)	47	47 (123)
$10-25,000	66	31 (29)	32	59 (44)	49	42 (247)
Education						
Less than High School	29	69 (35)	21	67 (187)	32	62 (148)
High school grad.	60	27 (30)	34	58 (38)	39	55 (201)
Some college or more	41	52 (27)	54	42 (26)	62	31 (229)
Occupation						
Lower blue collar	38	54 (24)	23	65 (43)	39	56 (41)
Stable Blue collar	37	59 (27)	23	61 (111)	33	59 (152)
White collar	61	30 (23)	39	54 (33)	54	40 (310)

* The percentages do not add up to 100 because a small group of people of each race-class category could not choose between the two alternatives (e.g., "it depends). Since [there was absolutely no pattern to such responses they were omitted.

** Respondents with family incomes over $25,000 (mostly whites) were omitted from the analysis to insure great socioeconomic homogeneity among the three races at the higher end of the income scale.

common frustrations, and had a vision of a common destiny. For Marx, objective class was not sufficient for predicting political action but, rather, the exploitative and alienating forces of industrial capitalism had to develop into subjective class consciousness (a "class in itself" becomes a "class for itself").[7]

Though there have been a number of studies of class consciousness, there is very little research that considers the dual sources of stratum consciousness and solidarity among racial minorities in America. For example, each of the two hierarchies — race and class — that have been discussed in this book, involves differing degrees of subjective identification and feelings of solidarity. A young black worker on an auto assembly line may feel high degrees of both class and race consciousness. He may feel underpaid and used as a commodity as he participates in boring, repetitive, alienating work. As a result, he may identify with the interests and action (strikes, walk-offs) of other workers. But, in addition, he may see himself as a part of a racial hierarchy — denied power, achievement, and status because of a powerful white stratum — and, accordingly, feel solidarity with a brotherhood of blacks who face common oppression. The results of being high in both race and class solidarity may lead to a special kind of ethclass militance. Although this general line of reasoning has a strong Marxian overtone, the specific prediction is quite different. Marx predicted that the exploitative and alienating forces of capitalism would unite workers of all ethnic backgrounds into a common solidary group ready to move against the common enemy. Instead, our prediction assumes that racial solidarity (especially in the 1960s and 1970s) is such a powerful source of allegiance that class interests are not likely to sweep over race, but rather that class and racial identification must merge, blend, and reinforce each other to produce a militant outcome. There are some signs of a growing black working-class militance. Recent auto and postal strikes and walk-offs often involve a disproportionate number of black workers uniting in common cause. One of the few studies on the blend of race and class consciousness as a source of militance is found in John Leggett's *Class, Race and Labor*. He notes that Negro blue-collar workers have faced special race-class barriers that have resulted in greater in-group cohesion.

> Working-class membership in a marginal racial (or ethnic) group is another source of class consciousness. A racial or ethnic group is margin-

al when the cultural values of an individual society and/or a dominant class move employers to engage in racial discrimination against marginal workmen both at work and elsewhere. Such discrimination contributes to their job insecurity, social isolation, subcultural homogeneity, intensive interaction within a proletarian-class minority sub-community, and organized protest and class or (class-racial) consciousness.[8]

Said another way, while there have been many forces to weaken and splinter class consciousness and militance among white workers, black workers face an unusual combination of factors that would heighten in-group cohesion and militance.

In the Leggett study, militance was a verbal measure — defined as the predisposition to engage in aggressive action to advance the interests of one's class. White workers were found to be considerably less militant than black workers, particularly than blacks who earned moderate incomes and belonged to unions. Further, racial awareness was shown to accompany class consciousness. This finding is not surprising since conflict frequently occurs along class and race lines simultaneously.

Conceptual Possibilities

Studies of race and class consciousness would most likely involve four variables: race, racial consciousness, objective class, and class consciousness. For example, a person could be black, one who identifies strongly with his race, in a managerial position with weak feelings of class consciousness. The following is a cross-tabulation of four variables in the case of blacks to indicate the possibilities. Strong racial (black) identification is indicated by a +; weak racial identification by a −.

	Blacks Objective Class: Middle			
	1	2	3	4
Subjective Class	working	middle	working	middle
Subjective Racial	+ Black	− Black	+ Black	− Black
Identification	Id	Id	Id	Id

Thus, group 1 represents blacks in an objective middle-class position (e.g., white-collar job) who subjectively identify with the working class and who identify with their race.

	Objective Class: Working			
	5	6	7	8
Subjective Class	working	middle	working	middle
Subjective Racial	+ Black	− Black	+ Black	− Black
Identification	Id	Id	Id	Id

Our discussion of race and class consciousness among blue-collar workers leading to a militant reaction can be formalized by noting that those in group 5 (persons in blue-collar jobs who feel themselves to be a part of the working-class and identify also with the black community) will express the most militant posture in terms of race or class change, while those in group 4 will be least militant in terms of class or race change.

A Test from Watts Data

In the Watts data, there was an opportunity to test one version of the race-class consciousness theme.* Roughly half of the Watts sample (1965-66) consisted of employed blue-collar workers. The other half were white-collar workers. The study included some questions to tap the newly emerging racial identification of the mid-60s as well as a forced-choice question of class identification. The aim of the study design was to note the separate and combined effects of race and class identification on two measures of racial militance — approval of the Watts riot, and action strategies that should be used to liberate black people.

A special ethclass militance effect is anticipated among those in working-class (blue-collar) positions who identify with both their race and their class. The measure of class identification asked respondents, "which of these four social groups would you say you belong to — middle class, upper class, lower class, working class?" Admittedly, this is a rather crude question. What does it mean when a blue-collar worker identifies himself as "working class" rather than "middle class"? It may simply mean that, when presented with forced choice alternatives, the blue-collar manual worker picks "working class" as the best descriptive label and that's all. We expect, however, that many who choose the working-class label are saying much more: that they

---

*See Chapter VI, note 15, for further details on the Watts sample. Only employee subjects were involved in this part of the analysis.

eel a greater sense of solidarity with other workers, or identify with
he frustrations and common interests of the working man as opposed
o owners, professionals, and managers. Almost all of the respondents
n the Watts sample identified themselves as either middle class or
working class. (The few who called themselves upper class were added
to those who identified themselves as middle class and the few who
called themselves lower class were added to those who identified
themselves as working class) Three items were included to tap black
identification: "I look at everything from a Negro* point of view," "I
feel a sense of pride when new African nations gain their independence," and "I feel a sense of kinship with Negroes in Africa." The last
two African items are tapping a little different dimension of black
identification than "Negro point of view." Accordingly, we examined
their effects separately.

We have anticipated greater militant attitudes and action among
blue-collar workers who identify both with their class and their race.
As a first test of this idea, Table 7-3 presents data on approval of the
Watts Riot cross-tablulated by subjective identifications for both blue-
collar and white-collar workers. For blue-collar workers, both the
"Negro point of view" and African identification versions of black
consciousness are shown; for white-collar workers only the African
version is presented (the white-collar case base was too small to claim
validity for "Negro point of view").

Focusing first on blue-collar workers (top two-thirds of the Table) we
see that race and class consciousness do indeed combine to produce
the highest proportion approving the riot — 73 percent with the
"Negro point of view" item, 56 percent with the African identification
item. It is difficult to say whether class or race consciousness is the
more powerful predictor of riot militance since racial identification is
clearly a stronger force with the "Negro point of view" item while for
the African item, class identification is the more important. Note also
that the strongest combined effect of race and class consciousness
occurs not so much at the high end of identification but at the low end
— blue-collar workers who identify themselves as "middle class" and
who also score low in racial consciousness are uniquely non-
supportive of the Watts rebellion (30 percent in both cases). What is

*The word "Negro" instead of black was used in this survey. "Black" in the mid-1960s
still had a rather negative connotation.

quite interesting is that the pattern is exactly the same for white-collar workers (except that they more consistently score less militant than blue-collar workers).

TABLE 7-3

Approval of the Watts Riot by Race and Class Identification Among Blue-Collar and White-Collar Workers

Blue-Collar Respondents

	working class	working class	middle class	middle class
% Approving Watts Riot	+ Black ID*	− Black ID	+ Black ID	− Black ID
	N	N	N	N
	73 (34)	44 (59)	67 (10)	30 (37)
	working + Black ID**	working − Black ID	middle + Black ID	middle − Black ID
% Approving Watts Riot	N	N	N	N
	56 (66)	52 (27)	42 (26)	30 (20)

White-Collar Respondents

	working class	working class	middle class	middle class
	+ Black ID**	− Black ID	+ Black ID	− Black ID
% Approving Watts Riot	N	N	N	N
	47 (15)	44 (10)	28 (36)	19 (32)

*   "I look at everthing from a Negro point of view"
** African Identification

Blacks in white-collar positions who identify with the working man are far more militant than those who call themselves middle class. Perhaps these are blacks who themselves have only recently moved up from blue-collar jobs and who retain a strong identification with the black working class.

Action Ideology

When our measure of militant outlook is expanded from riot approval to a more sensitive breakdown of action ideologies we find that the ethclass combination of working-class identification and black identification is only predictive of selective kinds of militant ideology. One of the questions in the Watts data asked respondents to choose among four action strategies to liberate black people. The alternatives ranged from the rather conservative "firm negotiation for equal rights" to the more militant "keep the pressure on with more demonstrations and sit-ins" to two extreme responses," forget integration and improve the Negro community" and "if whites keep up their discrimination, Negroes should be ready to use violence — non-violence won't do it." It should be recalled that the mid-1960s represented (for blacks) a period of peak support for participation in non-violent civil rights demonstrations. In such a normative milieu of non-violence, equal opportunity, and integration, those emphasizing the development of a separate black community or a readiness to use violence appear to be opting for more radical alternatives. Accordingly, we judge "demonstrate" to be a normative response and "community" and "violence" to be radical responses of this period. Table 7-4 shows the effects of race and class consciousness on these four action strategies. What is particularly striking in these data is that the working-class identification in combination with racial identification produces the least support for demonstrations (39 percent blue-collar and 48 percent white-collar) and the most support for violence and internal community change. The pattern is even more pronounced when the "violence" and "community" ideologies are combined into a single "radical group" shown in parenthesis. For example, among blue-collar workers high in race and working-class indentification, 58 percent score "radical" while only 23 percent of those low in black identification and who identify themselves as middle class do. However, when we look at other categories, it appears that "demonstrate" is the more preferred response for them. Especially among white-collar workers, one finds high support for demonstrations and sit-ins. What do all these data mean?

When this analysis is added to the riot approval discussion above, we do find support for the thesis that those identifying jointly with a community of workers and an oppressed racial stratum are likely to hold an especially militant outlook toward social change, an outlook characterized by positive responses to the Watts outbreak (e.g., "I'm glad it happened and I feel proud"), a readiness to use violence if white discrimination persists, and an interest in a strong black community rather than an integrated society.

---

*The pattern is exactly the same with the "Negro point of view" measure of race consciousness except that violence reaches an even higher 38 percent among blue-collar race-class identifiers.

TABLE 7-4

Four Action Strategies to Liberate Black People by Class and
Race Identification (Kinship With Negroes in Africa)
Among Blue-Collar and White-Collar Workers

Action Strategies

Subjective Class and Black ID	% Firm Negotiation For Change	% Keep Pressure On With Demon- strations & sit-ins	% Forget Integration And Change Negro Community		% If Discrimination Continues Violence Will Be Necessary
		Blue-Collar Workers			
Working + Black ID	3	39	29	(58)	29
Working − Black ID	3	65	16	(32)	16
Middle + Black ID	9	56	24	(36)	12
Middle − Black ID	5	73	14	(23)	9
		White-Collar Workers			
Working +l Black ID	5	48	33	(47)	14
Working − Black ID	18	73	9	(9)	0
Middle + Black ID	9	70	16	(21)	5
Middle − Black	17	76	7	(7)	0

NEW DIRECTIONS FOR RACE-CLASS CONSCIOUSNESS RESEARCH

The data in this analysis are crude and of another time period in the black struggle. More sensitive measures of race and class consciousness as well as more current measures of race and class action are needed. For example, the simple class identification question in these data should be greatly expanded to find out the *degree* to which persons feel solidarity with or share common interests with a race or class stratum. Morris and Murphy[9] have developed a breakdown of degrees of stratum consciousness. Their paradigm (reproduced on page 146) shows that persons may vary from a complete denial of a stratification order (box 1) to strong feelings of solidarity with a stratum (box 4) to a willingness to engage in action to advance the interests of this stratum (box 6). Minority persons may vary from very low to very high identification with both their race and their class strata. The Murphy-Morris paradigm adds a great deal of leverage to the topic of race and class consciousness. Both the sources and the consequences of such consciousness need to be studied. There is also need for refinement at the action-ideology end of our analysis. For example, the "change the community" alternative of these data appear to be a kind of precursor to the current "black control of black institutions" outlook. Are those high on race and working-class consciousness today especially supportive of this ideology? In these data, there were no measures of *class* action, such as propensity to participate in strikes or walk-offs for higher wages or improved working conditions. Are working-class blacks who score high in both race and class consciousness especially likely to engage in such militant class action? Another intriguing area of study would be the conditions under which race and class conscious conflict, so that black workers are under the stress of competing loyalties between union interests and racial interests.

In sum, the study of the interaction between race and class consciousness appears to be a neglected and extremely important area for future research.

EXPLORATION NO. 4
CASTE VERSUS CLASS IN FRIENDSHIP CHOICE

One of the long held propositions in the study of social stratification is that persons of the same stratum are more likely to interact with each other than with persons of different strata. For example, college graduates in upper white-collar occupations are likely to have in common certain occupational experiences, values, and life problems. Contact, friendship, and marriage are likely to occur within the boundaries of such class worlds.[10] However, one's race or ethnic stratum also has a great deal to do with interaction and friendship. From one's ethnic position comes a sense of peoplehood or shared destiny. The extreme geographical isolation that separate minority and majority groups members is often said to breed distrust and awkwardness across race lines such that one can only feel comfortable with a person of the same race. Further, with the ethnic identity movements of the 1960s, many minority persons have expressed a preference for friendship within their own groups and a concomitant feeling that Anglos cannot be trusted, are racist, are overly materialistic, lack soul, etc.

With the many recent publications on the topics of a racially divided

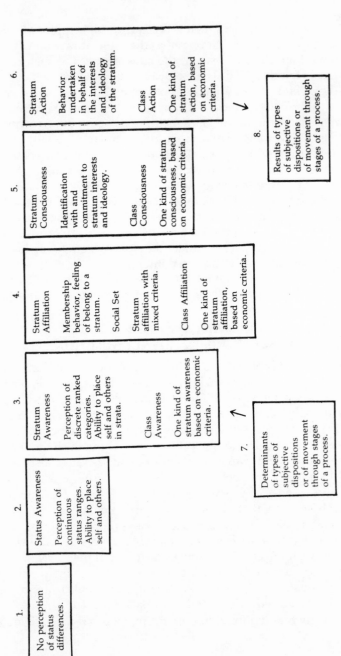

1.
No perception
of status
differences.

2.
Status Awareness

Perception of
continuous
status ranges.
Ability to place
self and others.

3.
Stratum
Awareness

Perception of
discrete ranked
categories.
Ability to place
self and others
in strata.

Class
Awareness

One kind of
stratum awareness
based on economic
criteria.

4.
Stratum
Affiliation

Membership
behavior, feeling
of belong to a
stratum.

Social Set

Stratum
affiliation with
mixed criteria.

Class Affiliation

One kind of
stratum
affiliation,
based on
economic criteria.

5.
Stratum
Consciousness

Identification
with and
commitment to
stratum interests
and ideology.

Class
Consciousness

One kind of stratum
consciousness, based
on economic criteria.

6.
Stratum
Action

Behavior
undertaken
in behalf of
the interests
and ideology
of the stratum.

Class
Action

One kind of
stratum
action, based
on economic
criteria.

7.
Determinants
of types of
subjective
dispositions
or of movement
through stages
of a process.

8.
Results of types
of subjective
dispositions or
of movement through
stages of a process.

Paradigm for the Study of Class Consciousness.

Source: Richard T. Morris and Raymond J. Murphy, "A Paradigm for the Study of Class
Consciousness," Sociology and Social Research, 50(April, 1966), 297-313.
Reproduced by permission of the authors and Sociology and Social Research.

nation, ethnic nationalism, and continuing white racism, one might assume that if social class propensity for interaction and race propensity for interaction were put into competition with each other, race would consistently be more important. That is, whites would prefer friendship with whites to friendship with blacks even if the white was of a very different social class and the black was of the same social class.

The question of race versus class as a determinant of friendship choice is more than sociological gymnastics. Stressed throughout this book is the trend of a rising black and Chicano skilled and white collar group employed in the dominant occupational structure. This trend suggests that Anglos, Chicanos and blacks employed by the same organization in skilled and white-collar jobs have greatly increased opportunities for equalitarian contact, some of which should lead to friendship or at least moderately close personal relations. This is not to suggest that large scale interracial friendship is at hand; for some time to come close, trusting friendship probably will be most likely to occur within an ethclass — choice of friends will be greatest for persons of the same race *and* same class. However, we are suggesting that there may be an increased *potential* for some interracial friendship among Anglos, blacks, and Chicanos of the same skilled and white-collar positions — that common class worlds may erode racial barriers enough to allow for moderately intimate friendship. What follows is an empirical exploration of this possibility.

In a large survey of attitudes of whites in fifteen cities,[11] a very interesting question was asked: "Who do you think you could more easily become friends with, a Negro with the same education and income as you or a white person with a different education and income than you?" Although there are serious problems with the question — it may be extremely hypothetical for whites who have no contact with blacks at the same socioeconomic level to make such a choice, and friendship can be interpreted in many ways from casual acquaintance at work to more intimate friendship — it is one of the first attempts to put race in competition with class as a determinant of friendship. About half of the white respondents chose the white person with a different education and income, approximately one-fourth chose "Negro same education and income," and the remaining fourth didn't know or felt that it would make no difference. The results of this survey show that race matters more than class in friendship choice.

I was sufficiently intrigued with the question used in this survey to try it out in slightly modified form with a number of ethnic groups in the Los Angeles area. In the Spring 1973 Los Angeles Metropolitan Area Survey,[12] the same question was asked of whites, blacks, and Spanish-surname persons matched by ethnic interviewers. The following refinements were made in the wording of the question, interviewing procedure, and analysis of results:

(1) "Different education and income" was changed to *"very* different education and income." The purpose of the question is to truly put race into competition with class. The original form may have been interpreted by many respondents to mean only a small or moderate difference in education or income (e.g., a college graduate versus one with a postgraduate degree or someone making $17,000 versus someone making $25,000). "Very different" implies that the person is considerably above or below the respondent in socioeconomic level.

(2) For black respondents, the question was rephrased: "White person of same education and income" versus "Black person of a very different education and income." Similarly, Spanish-surname persons were asked "Anglo same" or "Latino very different."

(3) A more systematic interview procedure was used to locate respondents who felt they could become friends with either person (person of the same class, different race or person of different race, same class). Only the race and class alternatives were presented by the interviewer. Persons who felt they could not choose between caste or class were probed: ". . . well, in general, which person would you choose?" If the respondent persisted that he could not choose and added that he could become friends with either person, he was coded "both." There are problems with this response. Some may be answering this way because they reject the entire premise that race and class determine friendship. (Similarly, studies have shown that some reject the idea that there are classes in American society.[13]) These respondents are expressing one version of the ideology of American individualism — friends are chosen for their personal qualities, not their income, education, or race. This denial that race and class are important may not carry over into their own behavior. On the other hand, some persons could be responding "both" because they genuinely believe they could become friends with persons of all classes and races. Because of the multiple interpretations for this response, less emphasis will be placed on it in the analysis.

(4) Controls for occupation, education, income, and age were introduced for each of the ethnic groups. Holding same level of socioeconomic status constant is an especially important procedure for this question in order to standardize a common reference group. For example, an upper middle-class white who responds "Negro same" is referring to a different reference group than the lower-class white making the same choice (the upper middle-class white is referring to a similarly situated black with high education and income, while the lower-class white is referring to a comparable low income, poorly educated black). Our general expectation is that class similarity will outweigh racial similarity in determining friendship but only at middle and higher SES levels where there is greater occupational proximity, less economic competition, and less of a tradition of prejudice.

Findings for Whites

Table 7-5 presents the white response with controls for occupation, education, and income. Several very interesting patterns stand out in these data. First, it can be seen that whites are most likely to pick "Negro of same education and income" at the higher (objective) levels of the occupation, education and income scales. For example, note that among college graduates and postgraduates, about two-thirds choose the "Negro same" response versus a very small proportion (14 to 15 percent) choosing "white different." The same pattern is apparent for those in professional and technical occupations and those in the highest income categories. Apparently, at the higher ends of the socioeconomic hierarchies class similarity (same education and income) is very important for friendship choice and such class similarity outweighs racial homogeneity for most respondents. (The one exception to this generalization is that managers are somewhat evenly split between the class and caste alternatives.) On the other hand, at lower levels of each hierarchy there is a "flipover" point with respondents choosing a white person of a different SES to a Negro person of the same SES. In the case of education, the flipover point is at high school graduation and lower; in the occupational hierarchy it is among blue collar operatives, and in the case of income, among those in the $5,000 or less category. In other words, at working and lower socioeconomic levels, white respondents report that they are more likely to choose friends within their own (white) racial group even if the white person is in a very different class position, above or below them. Whites in the

TABLE 7-5

Race versus Class: White Response with Occupation, Education, and Income Controlled

Friendship Easier With:

Control Variable: *Education*	*Negro Same SES*	*White Very Different SES*	*Both*	*N*
	%	%	%	%
Less Than High School	26	40	34	(111)
High School Grad	31	42	26	(205)
Some College	50	25	25	(173)
College Grad	66	14	20	(74)
Post Grad	69	15	16	(73)
Occupation				
Professional	58	18	24	(146)
Manager	41	39	19	(73)
Sales	44	32	24	(62)
Clerical	41	32	27	(145)
Crafts	47	29	24	(62)
Operatives	23	44	34	(62)
Income				
Under $5,000	29	33	38	(92)
$5-9,999	42	34	24	(136)
$10-14,999	46	33	21	(156)
$15-24,999	48	27	24	(147)
$25,000 or more	55	24	21	(82)

middle of the three hierarchies show a stronger class than race preference though generally not as strong as those at the top. For example,
forty-seven percent of the blue-collar craftsmen feel they could more
easily become friends with the Negro of the same income and education versus the twenty-nine percent of craftsmen choosing the white of
a different level.

These findings cannot be taken too far, based as they are on a single
question involving, for many, a rather hypothetical situation. Still, the
data encourage the interpretation that among whites, socioeconomic
equality is far more likely to break down racial barriers to friendship at
middle and upper-class levels than at working and lower-class levels.

Table 7-6 shows age is also an important factor in the caste-class
pattern. Younger whites are more likely to make a class choice (Negro
same), older whites a race choice (white different). Among eighteen to
twenty-nine year olds a full sixty percent choose the Negro of the same
education and income versus the twenty-one percent responding
white different. In contrast, among those over sixty, only twenty-four
percent picked Negro same as opposed to 41 percent choosing white
different.

TABLE 7-6
Race Versus Class: White Response With Age Controlled

Age		Friendship Easier With: % Negro Same SES	% White Very Different SES	% Both	N
18-29	1	60	22	18	(158)
30-39	3	49	24	27	(115)
40-49	4	47	29	25	(126)
50-59	5	36	39	25	(105)
60+	6	24	41	35	(123)

Before leaving the white data there is one other trend involving the
response "both" that needs to be pointed out. The proportion saying
"both" increases in the *lowest* level of each SES category — among
operatives, those earning under $5,000, and those with only a grade
school education. This is a surprising finding since these are groups
often depicted as the most prejudiced. Apparently, as one moves
down the socioeconomic hierarchies, two trends occur: (1) there is an
increased preference for the racial ingroup; and (2) there is an increase
in the proportion of persons rejecting both race and class as mean-

ingful criteria for choice of friends. Again, we are struck with the problem of interpreting the "both" response. Do such persons really mean that they are willing to interact with many persons of different races or classes or are they stating an ideology of American individualism in which race and class *should not* matter?

Findings for Blacks and Mexican Americans

We have found striking differences in the caste-class response among whites of different socioeconomic and age groups — notably, young whites and those whites in higher socioeconomic positions report that they could more easily become friends with a black person of the same education/income level than a white person of a very different level. But does this same trend apply to blacks and Mexican Americans? Are younger middle-class blacks more likely to choose a white person of the same SES level or does the "black pride" movement (prevalent especially among young college blacks) produce a preference for black friendship regardless of social class differences?

Before moving to such subgroup comparisons, it is important to note that higher proportions of blacks than whites give the "both" response (41 percent black versus 22 percent white for the total samples). This suggests that blacks, on the average, place less stress on race and class in choice of friends than do whites. Higher proportions of blacks may be saying, "I could become friends with either black or white, rich or poor, well educated or not, and it would depend on the individual person."

Table 7-7 presents the black response with controls for education and age. (The occupation and income control data are not presented as there were no consistent patterns worth noting.) Younger blacks are somewhat more likely than older blacks to feel they could more easily become friends with the *black* person of a very different education and income. There is a moderate trend for some young blacks to prefer race over class. Thus, twenty-nine percent of younger blacks versus only eleven percent of the older blacks respond "black different." However, this is not to say that *most* young blacks feel they can only relate to another black person as a friend since the young black group is almost evenly divided, across the three responses (about one-third each choose "white same," "black different," and "both"). Thus there is a group of blacks who are ethnically exclusive and they are more likely to be young but this is not the majority response for young blacks. The other side of the story in Table 7-3 is that older blacks overwhelmingly reject both race and class as important criteria for friendship, sixty-one percent choose "both."

TABLE 7-7

Race Versus Class: Black Response
With education and Age Controlled
Friendship
Easier With:

	% White Same SES	% Black Very Different SES	% Both	N
Control Variable:				
Education				
Less than				
high school	32	9	59	(34)
High school				
grad	34	28	38	(29)
Some College	25	38	38	(24)
Age				
18-29	32	29	38	(28)
30-39	29	29	42	(24)
49-49	35	18	47	(17)
50+	28	11	61	(18)

Turning to the education data in Table 7-3, we can see that there is an increased preference for black friendship as one moves up the education scale. Thus, only 9 percent of blacks with less than high school choose "black different" while a full 38 percent of those with college experience do. Conversely, black respondents with low degrees of education express the least degree of ethnic insularity with 59 percent responding "both" and 32 percent "white same." A racial in-group preference in friendship is more typical among blacks with college experience, however, this is not the majority response for college blacks since 38 percent of this group chooses "both" and another 25 percent "white same."

One consistent pattern emerges in the Spanish-surname data (Table 7-8). Mexican Americans in higher income and education positions (over $10,000, some college) feel friendship would be easier with an Anglo of the same class than a Latino of a different class. Conversely, an ethnic choice (Latino different) increases as one goes lower in the education and income categories. This rather strong preference among middle-class Mexican Americans for friendship with Anglos of the same class may reflect the fact of a more permeable color line and the fact that middle-class Mexican Americans have more opportunities for cross-ethnic friendshp (e.g., residential segregation in Los Angeles is far less for Chicanos than blacks). Occupation and age controls had no bearing on the Spanish-surname results. Note also that (as with the black sample) the proportion of Mexican Americans choosing "both" is much higher than the case for Anglos.

TABLE 7-8

Race Versus Class: Mexican American (Spanish Surname)
Response With Education and Income Controlled

Friendship Easier With:

Control Variable:	% Anglo Same SES	% Latino Very Different SES	% Both	N
Education				
Less than high school	24	28	48	(42)
High School grad	50	11	39	(28)
Some college	50	9	41	(22)
Income				
Under $5,000	31	25	44	(16)
$5-9,999	38	13	50	(32)
Over $10,000	51	12	37	(41)

Summary Statement

In the Los Angeles area we find that different age and socioeconomic subgroups of the Anglo, black, and Spanish-surname populations, respond very differently to the question of the race versus class as a determinant of friendship. Young whites and whites high or medium in the occupation, education, and income hierarchies report that class similarity is more important to them than racial similarity in the choice of friends. Similarly, higher SES Spanish-surname persons show a greater propensity to choose Anglos of the same (high) SES than Latinos of a very different SES. This, of course, does not mean that all of those who express a preference for a person of another race have behaviorally engaged in that kind of interaction. But it does express a readiness to interact across racial lines with persons likely to have similar tastes and life styles (class). However, among blacks, we find a moderate counter trend. It is among the young and college educated blacks that one finds a fairly high proportion choosing race over class.This does not mean that young middle-class whites and young middle-class blacks have no possibility of friendship contact since substantial proportions of young middle-class blacks also choose "both" or "white same." It does indicate, however, that the white response is somewhat out of alignment with the black response and that social class similarity does not in itself sweep over all racial factors.

NOTES TO CHAPTER 7

[1] See Milton M. Gordon, *Assimilation in American Life* (New York: Oxford University Press, 1964), p. 51 and Chapter 4 of this book.

[2] Hubert M. Blalock, Jr., *Social Statistics* (New York: McGraw-Hill, 1972), p. 337.

[3] See Chapter 6, note 45, for further details on the LAMAS surveys, I wish to thank the UCLA Survey Research Center for making these data available to me.

[4] See, for example, Melvin Kohn, *Class and Conformity* (Homewood, Ill.: Dorsey Press, 1969) and Melvin Kohn and C. Schooler, "Class, Occupation, and Orientation," *American Sociological Review 34* (October, 1969): 659-678.

[5] Kohn, op. cit.; Kohn and Schooler, op. cit.

[6] It is possible that religion rather than education is producing this difference. For example, Mexican-American Protestants may be more likely to finish high school and attend college than Mexican-American Catholics. It is also true that Catholicism stresses humility and obedience. Future studies on this topic (obedience vs. autonomy) should consider both religion and education.

[7] For an excellent review of this part of Marx's theory, see Reinhard Bendix and Seymour Martin Lipset, "Karl Marx's Theory of Social Class," in *Class, Status, and Power,* ed. Reinhard Bendix and Seymour Martin Lipset (New York: Free Press, 1966), pp. 6-11.

[8] John C. Leggett, *Class, Race, and Labor* (London and New York, Oxford University Press, 1968): 13.

[9] Richard T. Morris and Raymond J. Murphy, "A Paradigm for the Study of Class Consciousness," *Sociology and Social Research 50* (April, 1966): 297-313.

[10] See, for example, Joseph A. Kahl, *The American Class Structure* (New York: Holt, Rinehart & Winston, 1957), Ch. 6.

[11] Angus Campbell, *White Attitudes Toward Black People* (Ann Arbor, Mich: University of Michigan, Institute for Social Research, 1971), p.8.

[12] See note 45, Chapter 6 for further details on the LAMAS surveys. This is not a secondary analysis of data. That is, the author paid a fee to have the caste-class question included in the Spring 1973 survey with specifications of exact wording and interview procedure.

[13] Kahl, op. cit., pp. 167-171.

CHAPTER 8

CURRENT ISSUES AND POLICY: A SELECTED REVIEW OF RECENT RACE-CLASS STUDIES

. . . Black young persons have lower feelings of self esteem than white young persons.[1]

. . . Black women have more power and authority in household decisions than black men.[2]

. . . Even with social class controlled, black and Chicano children score lower on standardized IQ tests than white children.[3]

. . Tracking (dividing classes into college bound and non-college bound or high ability and low ability groups) is based solely on rational criteria such as grades and test scores (rather than race or class) and has positive effects for both the students and the school.[4]

In the last five years there has been a sharp increase in the number of studies that consider the interaction of race and class. We view this as an important trend both toward the more accurate explanation and prediction of human behavior (knowledge) as well as for improved social policy recommendations (action). This chapter focuses on examples of race-class research relating to social policy which challenge the four commonly heard assertions noted above. I would like to review some studies that force us to abandon, qualify, or at least question these four generalizations. My choice of studies is admittedly highly selective. My major criteria for inclusion were that the study be recent, methodologically sound, and have policy implications.

RACE, CLASS, AND SELF-IMAGE AMONG BLACK YOUNG PEOPLE

Many of the concepts and data about racial minorities — especially black Americans — developed during time periods when blacks faced extreme and rather uniform degrees of exploitation and oppression. A caste system with characteristics of non-mobility, ideologies of black inferiority, and rigid rules of interaction between white and black persons, was the milieu from which concepts such as "negative self-image" emerged. But with the beginning of minority group power movements, a moderate "opening" of the social structure and a substantial growth of stable working and middle-class segments, we are thrust into a very different context in which old generalizations need updating or at least ongoing empirical validation.

It makes good sense that members of racial minorities are likely to internalize at least some of the negative prejudice and discrimination that are built into our culture.[5] From this point of view, one of the most unfortunate effects of racial prejudice and discrimination is that many blacks, Indians, or Chicanos may come to believe what white people say about them. That is, a minority child growing up in a racist society may face a constant assault on his feelings of self worth.

> It is in the context of slights, rebuffs, forbidden opportunities, restraints and often violence that the minority group member shapes that fundamental aspect of personality — a sense of oneself and his place in the total scheme of things.[6]

Classic studies of black children in the 1940s and 1950s appear to substantiate the negative self-image thesis.[7]

Clark found that high proportions of black children rejected black dolls as the doll that "looks bad" and chose white dolls as the most desirable with which to play.[8] Moreover, under caste-like race relations the attainment of a higher class position did not seem to insulate the middle-class black from humiliating experiences that would reduce feelings of self worth. Consider the following account of a black doctor:

> Once last year as I was leaving my office in Jackson, Miss., with my Negro secretary, a white policeman yelled, "Hey, Boy! Come here!" Somewhat bothered, I retorted: "I'm no boy!" He then rushed at me, inflamed, and stood towering over me, snorting, "What d'ja say, boy?" Quickly he frisked me and demanded, "What's your name, boy?" Frightened, I replied, "Dr. Poussaint. I'm a physician." He angrily chuckled and hissed, "What's your first name, boy?" When I hesitated he assumed a threatening stance and clenched his fists. As my heart palpitated, I muttered in profound humiliation, "Alvin."[9]

However, recent evidence on race, class, and self-image challenge the assumption that blacks have lesser feelings of self worth. There are probably at least two factors operating in these data. First, with the "Black is Beautiful" and "Black Power" movements, there is a strong possibility that many black parents are no longer socializing their children for accommodation. Secondly, with a decline in the importance of racial caste and a concomitant increase in the importance of achieved ranks (see Chapters 2-4) middle-class blacks may face a very different set of factors affecting self-image than do lower-class blacks. To develop this point further, it would seem logical that a higher social class position would represent a cluster of resources that would aid a young black person in acquiring a positive image of himself. Coming from a middle-class household would typically mean that resources are not drained (as in the lower-class case) with economic problems; parents have more time and energy to support and praise the child's interests and ambitions, and white prejudice and stereotypes would be offset by the tangible accomplishments of one's parents. (It would be difficult for a young black person to accept the stereotype that blacks are lazy and less capable if his father was a hard-working foreman, engineer, or doctor.)

Two recent studies (data gathered in mid and late 1960s) clearly challenge the assumption of low self worth among young blacks. Each of the studies resulted in important race-class findings. In the first study by Chad Gordon,[10] class was the more salient variable. In a large sample of metropolitan Northeast ninth-graders, lower, working, and middle-class black and white students were compared on a measure of global self-esteem. This measure included the components of basic self-acceptance ("If I could change I would be someone different than myself"), self-rated brightness, sensed academic competence ("I sometimes feel that I just can't learn"), and sense of self-determination. Thus, the total score (global self-esteem) involved both academic and general measures of self worth. Within each race, social class (lower, working, middle) was somewhat important as a correlate of self-esteem while race was very weakly related to self-esteem. A middle-class white student was found to be almost three times as likely to rate high on self-esteem as a lower-class white student, and similarly, a middle-class black student was found to be over twice as likely to score high as a lower-class black student. Especially interesting is the finding that class overlaps with race considerably, so that *a middle-class black student is 2.6 times as likely to score high on self-esteem as a lower-class white student.* With Gordon's measure of self worth, it is clear that social class is a more important determinant of self-esteem than race. Middle-class white children have higher global self-esteem than lower-class white children and middle-class black children have higher self-esteem than lower-class black children, and at any given class level the difference between the two races is slight or nonexistent. (It is only at the working-class level that there is any racial difference to speak of, with 26 percent of the white students scoring high as opposed to 17 percent of the black students.)

Findings from the second study are even more at variance with the common assumptions about race and self-image. Rosenberg and Simmons[11] found that black children and teenagers consistently score higher on self-esteem than white children and teenagers.* Unfortunately, the two studies cited are not directly comparable since the authors used a different and more general measure of self-esteem that did not have the academic and "brightness" components of the Gordon measure. (Sample items: "A kid told me: 'There's a lot wrong with me.' Do you ever feel like this?" and "How happy are you with the kind of person you are.") In the Rosenberg-Simmons study, findings were especially surprising when race and class were jointly considered; socioeconomic status was found to have a bearing upon the self-concepts of white children, but no effect was observed on that of blacks. Thus, while 45 percent of the lowest-class whites (Hollingshead Class 5)[12] scored *low* in self-esteem compared to 25 percent of the highest socioeconomic group, the comparable percentages for blacks were 20 percent and 21 percent respectively. Moreover, in practically every race-class comparison blacks were less likely than whites to express low esteem. The authors carefully proceed through a series of steps to untangle this puzzle. The first logical possibility is that black children of low socioeconomic status do not evaluate their family's social position in the same way that the general society does. The children were asked, "How proud are you of your family's social position in the community?" (very proud, pretty proud, etc.), "How well do you think your parents have done in life?" and a five-step question asking where most people would rank their father's job (from best kind to worst kind of job). The results showed that black children are as likely as white to believe that their families have done well and are socially respected, despite the fact that the black children were

*The study involved at random sample of 2,625 third to twelfth grade pupils distributed in 26 schools in Baltimore city.

objectively far more likely to be in a lower-class family position than the white children. "This relative obliviousness to their objectively low position would appear to be a highly effective mechanism protecting their self-esteem." [13] Moreover, "both black and white children tend to elevate and exaggerate the respect accorded their families in the community or society but this inflation is substantially greater among blacks." [14] In Class 5, the lowest class assigned, black children were found to be more likely than Class 5 white children to be very proud of their family's social position. The authors argue that those at the lower end of the status hierarchy (lower-class blacks) have a special need to protect their self-esteem by inflation. Further, they posit that lower-class blacks have fewer challenges to their sense of worth due to greater social insulation from invidious comparisons. It was found that the lower-class black children attended schools in which the average social class level was similar to their own (a predominantly lower-class ghetto school) but this was not true for lower-class white children — all attended schools in which the SES level was higher than their own. "It is thus understandable that these black children would be less likely to have their actual low status forced upon their attention, thereby making it easier for them to inflate their social standing. Compared to the whites, the lower-class black children are in environments which are less offensive to their sense of personal worth." [15]

Two rigorous studies involving race, class, and self-esteem have produced findings which contradict the earlier generalization that minority persons in a racist society will have a negative self-image. In the first study by Gordon, race was a very weak determinant of self-esteem, while class did have some effect. When jointly considered, social class differences overwhelmed racial differences.The Rosenberg-Simmons study showed black children and teenagers to have greater feelings of self-worth than white children and teenagers, especially at the lowest class level. What may be overstressed in the latter study is the idea that societal evaluations (in the form of social class honor) are crucial to self-esteem. If a child both low on the race and class hierarchies persists in describing his family members as successful, the explanatory mechanism is "protective inflation" of his position. But psychological research emphasizes that the most important determinants of self worth are total acceptance of children by parents (or other adults) and clearly defined and enforced limits. [16] Black children and other minority children may be just as likely as white children to have a network of supportive interactions — that is, interactions with adults that involve well-defined limits, warmth, and respectful treatment — and this may be far more relevant to self-esteem than social honor or success in the broader society. "Inflation" may be an unnecessary explanation of the generally high self-esteem of lower-class blacks in the above study. It also quite possible that alternative models of acceptance and respect are found in ghettos and barrios, models that are not so dependent on white middle-class criteria of academic achievement. It is plausible that the Black Pride movement has had considerable effect on the self-images of young black persons in recent years. Perhaps this is one reason that the black respondents in the Rosenberg-Simmons study scored so high in self-esteem. How deep does "Black is Beautiful" go in determining positive self concepts? We need a great deal more research that takes into account jointly such factors as class environment, quality of interaction, the Black Pride movements, and healthy alternative forms of acceptance differing from traditional WASP (White Anglo-Saxon Protestant) criteria.

RACE, CLASS AND THE ALLEGED WEAK FATHER FIGURE

A great deal has been written on the pattern of female dominance in the black family. An exceptional degree of controversy and debate on the subject has taken place since the publication of the Moynihan Report.[17] Moynihan made very explicit connections between the "matriarchal" family structure and social pathology (poverty, crime, teenage pregnancy, etc.). For example, he states

> At the heart of the deterioration of the fabric of Negro society is the deterioration of the Negro family. . . . It was by destroying the Negro family under slavery that white America broke the will of the Negro people. Although that will has reasserted itself in our time, it is a resurgence that is doomed to frustration unless the viability of the Negro family is restored.[18]

Moynihan clearly mentions slavery and economic discrimination as causes of the matriarchy pattern. However, there is a subtle shift in emphasis later in the report: continued racial inequality is due more to this "pathological" family structure than to white racism and discrimination. The report seems to imply that until the black community gets its family life "together," there will be continued racial inequality.

More specifically, the Moynihan Report suggests that the matriarchy has been so institutionalized that is has become self-sustaining by its own internal dynamics — for example, there may have developed a "culture of distrust" in which young black women are socialized to doubt a man's ability to support a family.[19]

> To 'help' the black community, it may not be sufficient to directly assault institutional and informal racism in *white* society as it also seems necessary to intervene in the family in *black* society.[20]

Before any policy is enacted to "rehabilitate" the black family, much careful research is needed that involves both race and class. For one thing, there is considerable conceptual shagginess involved in the term *matriarchy*. Moynihan and many others are referring to the case of fatherless families in which the husband has left the household and the wife, by default, takes over authority. Comparative statistics do show that black families (especially lower-class blacks) have a higher proportion of female-headed households than white families. However, a substantial portion of the pattern appears to be due to class or economic poverty rather than race. For example, note the data in Table 8-1 drawn from the Kerner Commission Report.[21] The proportion of female headed households (1966) are shown for two income categories, a poverty group making $3,000 or less and a working/middle-class group making over $7,000. It can be seen that both white and black poverty families are more likely to be headed by a woman than white and black middle-class families. Thus, 23 percent of poor white families are headed by a female versus 4 percent of white middle-class families. However, the matriarchy pattern is especially pronounced among lower-class black families (42 percent). There is no way of knowing whether this very high percentage is due more to the twin barriers of race and class discrimination or to a special lower-class black subculture that encourages family break-ups (or both). However, if there is a black cultural factor, it should persist somewhat into the working and middle-class income group since many in this group are recently mobile from the lower class. Instead we find that the matriarchy pattern almost completely disappears in the black middle-class income group (8 percent) and is very close to the white rate (4 percent). Although far from conclusive, these data suggest that when there is greater economic stability, the matriarchy is strongly affected.

Apart from any cultural factors, reducing unemployment and economic discrimination would in all likelihood have a profound effect on the lower-class black family.

TABLE 8-1

Proportion of Female Headed Households (1966) by Income and Race

| Income | Race | |
	White	Black
Less than $3,000	23%	42%
Over $7,000	4%	8%

Source: Otto Kerner, *Report of the National Advisory Commission on Civil Disorders* (New York: Bantam Books, 1968), p. 261.

Besides the "fatherless family" definition of matriarchy, the term may be used to mean that both husband and wife are present but the wife is the more consistent breadwinner and, accordingly, seems to have more control over family decisions and socialization of children. Until very recently, there was no research assessing the separate effects of race and class on family authority in such "whole" families. Is the lower-class black male "emasculated" in such families? That is, is the husband submissive and the wife dominant in important household decision-making and does the father lack respect of and authority over his children? Since almost seven out of ten black households do have both husband and wife present (68 percent in 1968), the paucity of race-class research on this subject is remarkable. In a recent study by *TenHouten*,[22] conjugal (husband and wife) and parental (control over children) power in whole families were studied in four race-class categories — lower-class black, middle-class black, lower-class white, and middle-class white. The sample design involved simultaneous class controls for the status of the family and the status of the neighborhood. Further, only families with at least two children, fifteen to twenty-three years old, were included, so that teenage children could rate their parents in dominance and comment on parental control over teenage decisions. ("Who determines how late you stay out at night?"). When a number of measures of conjugal and parental power were employed there was either no evidence for a "matriarchal" pattern in the lower-class black group (compared with the other three ethclasses) or an extremely weak pattern. For example, when husband and wife were asked to respond to a male dominance scale (e.g., "Men should make the really important decisions in the family") lower-class black husbands and wives expressed the greatest acceptance of male dominance (opposite to the matriarchy expectation). However, lower-class black husbands may be especially sensitive on these kinds of questions. What is needed is more objective observation of household power and decision-making. Data from the perceptions of the teenage children may be particularly valuable since they were based on observations of parental *behavior* and, accordingly, should involve fewer statements of the traditional ideal culture in which the man is head of the household. From the questions: Does your mother boss your father? and Does your father boss your mother? (often, sometimes, seldom, and never) the following typology was constructed.

FIGURE 8-1

Typology of Parental Power

Frequency *Mother bossing* *Father*	*Frequency* *Father bossing* *Mother*	*Family type*
low	low	egalitarian
high	high	conflict
low	high	husband-dominated
high	low	wife-dominated

Adapted from Warren D. TenHouten, "The Black Family: Myth and Reality," *Psychiatry* 2 (May, 1970): 163. For the origins of this typology see also Murray A. Strauss, "Conjugal Power Structure and Adolescent Personality," *Marriage and Family Living*, 24 (1962): 17-25.

This next table shows the percentage of each family type by race and class.

TABLE 8-2

Percentages Of Family Types From Responses By Two Oldest Children

	Lower *Black*	*SES* *White*	*Middle* *Black*	*SES* *White*
Egalitarian	67	30	64	61
Conflict	12	9	20	12
Husband-dominant	19	56	12	24
Wife-dominant	2	4	4	3

Adapted from Warren D. TenHouten, "The Black Family: Myth and Reality," *Psychiatry*, 2 (May, 1970): 163.

It can be seen that the wife-dominated family is a very infrequent pattern in all four race-class categories. Certainly the lower-class black family does not stand out as more matriarchal. The most common family type is one of shared decision making or egalitarianism. It was found in lower-class black, middle-class white, and middle-class black families in over 60 percent of the cases. The only category that stands out as decidedly different is the lower-class white case with a much lower egalitarian proportion and a much higher husband-dominant proportion. In terms of conjugal power, there is not only an absence of female dominance in the lower-class black family but it occurs less frequently than in any other case.

In another part of the survey, questions to measure *parental* power were measured. First, parents were asked to respond to the statement: "Raising a child is more a mother's job than a father's." The percentage of parents who agreed are: lower-class black, 40; lower-class white, 40; middle-class black, 16; and middle-class white, 15. The data show a strong class effect but no race effect. In other words, for both races, lower-class parents are more likely to agree that mothers should dominate the parental role. This does not support a matriarchy prediction — one in which the woman would be uniquely powerful in the lower class black case.

Secondly, the teenaged children were asked power questions such as: "Who decides how late you can stay out?" and "Who decides what friends you go around with?" The most striking pattern is that teenagers of all four race-class groups report that both parents make the rules, though there is very slight tendency for mothers to have more power in the lower and middle-class black groups than the lower and middle-class white groups. The mean percentages of responses to five items are presented below.

TABLE 8-3

Parental Power by Race and Class

Lower SES

Father	Black Both	Mother	Father	White Both	Mother
6%	73%	21%	13%	73%	13%

Middle SES

Father	Black Both	Mother	Father	White Both	Mother
9%	73%	18%	7%	79%	13%

Adapted from Warren D. TenHouten, "The Black Family: Myth and Reality," *Psychiatry* 2 (May, 1970): 163.

In about three-fourths of all the groups, "both parents" made the rules with a slightly higher percentage of mothers having more power in black families than in white (21 percent versus 13 percent and 18 percent versus 13 percent) Other indices of parental and conjugal power were used involving interviews of the husband and wife. None indicated female dominance in the lower-class black category. The TenHouten study challenges the generalization that the black family often involves a pattern of female dominance.

THE PILE-UP OF RACE AND CLASS BARRIERS: POLICY RESEARCH ON EDUCATIONAL INSTITUTIONS

Lower-class black and Chicano children are far more likely to drop out of school and fall further behind at each grade level in their achievements than middle-class white, middle-class black, and middle-class Chicano children. Unfortunately, the most common explanation for failure has been the lower-class minority environment or the "cultural deprivation" or "culture of poverty" explanation. With slightly different variations for blacks and Chicanos, this explanation asserts that components of a depressed environment — apathy, low motivation, lack of cognitive interaction between parents and children, and a lack of books and magazines — cause failure. Writing about the education of Mexican-American children, Joan Moore notes "Federal financial assistance has encouraged southwestern educators to develop 'compensatory education' programs to help Mexican-American children compensate for certain inadequacies they display when compared to a 'standard' middle class child. The idea of 'cultural disadvantage' provides a rationale for action to overcome the minority group child's real or assumed deficiencies. It is designed not to change the school but to change the child."[23]

It is only recently that educational institutions themselves, their policies and their programs, have been studied in any critical, systematic way in this regard. For the first time, one finds articles on teacher expectations for failure, abuse in the use of IQ tests in classifying lower-class black and Chicano children, the negative consequences of tracking, and the class-ethnic composition of the student body as the determiner of "cooling out" mechanisms. The study of the patterns of racism and classism in educational institutions is an extremely important area with obvious implications for policy research. The failure to educate lower-class black and Chicano children is seen by many as not so much a function of a depressed environment as of an insensitive reaction of educational institutions to children produced from this environment — that is, the mechanical tendency to sort and classify students according to the degree to which they match the middle-class Anglo model. Schools are not so much deliberately attempting to exclude lower-class minority children as they are perpetuating an impersonal "conveyer belt" of failure for them by favoring an unmodified adherence to middle-class Anglo standards. There is often total insensitivity to the background of the lower-class child. For example, Mexican language and culture may often be tied to punishment and failure rather than being creatively integrated into the curriculum of the school.

The Misuse of IQ Tests

A provocative recent study by Jane R. Mercer[24] titled, "IQ, The Lethal Label," highlights the "overuse" of middle-class Anglo criteria for achievement in school. Mercer states:

> A large number of minority persons who can cope very well with the requirements of their daily lives are being labeled mentally retarded. They acquire these labels, not because they are unable to cope with the world, but because they have not had the opportunity to learn the cognitive skills necessary to pass Anglo-oriented intelligence tests. They do not conform to the typical Anglo, middle-class pattern; thus they appear "retarded" to the white middle-class clinician or teacher. Yet their behavior outside of the test situation belies their test scores.[25]

The research involved field samples of Chicano, black, and Anglo persons of all ages and a sample of 1,513 elementary school-aged children in Riverside, California (N = 598 Chicanos, 339 blacks and 576 Anglos). The study involved two important refinements not often found in race and IQ studies. First, both standardized IQ tests as well as a measure of *adaptive ability* were employed. The "adaptive ability" test was a measure of actual behavioral skill in the environment, the degree to which the person is able to function independently in the environment (e.g., independently shop in a store, choose certain items, and pay for them). The measure consisted of a series of twenty-eight age-graded scales. Second, many studies of IQ differences between the races have been controlled for SES measures such as occupation or income. However, Mercer's study is one of the first attempts to control for both ethnic culture and class factors simultaneously. For example, in comparing the IQ scores of Chicano and Anglo children, both class variables (such as "head of household in skilled occupation," and "mother expects children to have some college") and ethnic variables ("head grew up in U.S. rather than Mexico" and "family speaks English in the home") are controlled.

Similarly, for blacks, class as well as ethnic culture factors (e.g., mother reared in North, nuclear family intact) were controlled.

If it is true that IQ tests are Anglo-centric, then the more Anglicized a non-Anglo child is, the better he should do on the IQ test. That is, racial differences in IQ should wash out or be greatly reduced with these variables simultaneously controlled.

There are two findings in Mercer's study that are notably outstanding. First, the standard IQ test was far more predictive of behavioral skills (adaptive ability) for Anglos than for blacks or Chicanos: "Every Anglo who had an IQ below 70 was also in the lowest three percent on the behavior scales. But this was by no means true for minority groups. Fully 91 percent of the blacks and 60 percent of the Chicanos with IQs below 70 had *passed* the behavior test."[26] The implications are clear; a great many more Chicanos and blacks are likely to be mislabeled "retarded" than white children are by the sole reliance on a standard IQ test. In the second part of the article, black and Chicano children in the large elementary school sample were given a score from zero to five, depending on the number of ethnic and class characteristics that their families shared with the "average" Anglo family in Riverside. The mean IQ for each sub-group (e.g., Chicanos having one, two, three, four, and five characteristics) was then compared with the Anglo average IQ. The results (presented below) show that children whose families were *least* like the average Anglo family — that is, had none or only one characteristic like the average Anglo family — scored *lowest* in IQ (x IQ = 84.5 for Chicanos and 87.7 for blacks). However, with the addition of each Anglo middle-class characteristic the average IQ rose in a stair-step fashion. When all five characteristics were simultaneously controlled — that is, those who matched the Anglo pattern best — the differences between the races disappeared. "In short, when we controlled for the social backgrounds of the children, there were no differences in intelligence between the Anglos and the blacks or between the Anglos and the Chicanos."[27]

To prevent misclassification of minority children, Mercer calls for a pluralistic assessment of a child's ability based on four types of information. There should be a *sociocultural* index to classify a child's social and economic milieu. There should be a measure of *adaptive ability* that

TABLE 8-4

Comparisons of Chicano and Black I.Q. With Anglo I.Q.
As Cultural Factors are Controlled

Chicano-Anglo Comparison

Anglo Average IQ = 100

IQ = 90.4 N = 598 Chicano Average No Controls	IQ = 84.5 N = 127 0-1 Anglo Characteristics	IQ = 88.1 N = 146 2 Anglo Characteristics	IQ = 89 N = 126 3 Anglo Characteristics	IQ = 95.5 N = 174 4 Anglo Characteristics	IQ = 104.4 N = 25 5 Anglo Characteristics

Black-Anglo Comparison

Anglo Average IQ = 100

IQ = 90.5 N = 339 Black Average No Controls	IQ = 82.7 N = 47 0-1 Anglo Characteristics	IQ = 87.1 N = 101 2 Anglo Characteristics	IQ = 92.8 N = 106 3 Anglo Characteristics	IQ = 95.5 N = 68 4 Anglo Characteristics	IQ = 99.5 N = 17 5 Anglo Characteristics

Source: Jane R. Mercer, "IQ: The Lethal Label," reprinted from *Psychology Today* 6 (September, 1972): 95. Copyright © Ziff Davis Publishing Company.

would give us information about how the child functions in his home and neighborhood. An I.Q. test *interpreted against standard norms* could be used to determine whether the child can succeed in a regular public school without additional help. Finally, to determine the child's *potential* for learning, the same I.Q. could be used but this time interpreted within the child's ethnic norms. "Together these four measures will paint a far more accurate picture of a child's abilities than Anglo-oriented I.Q. tests can give. For example, if a Chicano child scores far above average for his ethnic group, then his intellectual ability is probably above normal, even if his actual I.Q. score is 100 — average for a group of Anglo middle-class students."

Race, Class and Tracking

It is widely believed that the American educational system is highly congruent with the ideal of an open class industrial society — one in which persons reach positions as a result of hard work, initiative, and ability rather than race, religion, or class. However, Mercer's findings (above discussion) on race and IQ suggest that lower-class black and Chicano children are often mislabeled as "retarded" or "low-normal ability." Unfortunately, such classifications are not neutral. The results of "objective" standardized test scores are used to separate children into high and low "ability" groups. Educators often justify tracking on the grounds that the more academically able college-bound students should not be slowed down in their progress by slower students. Further, there seems to be an assumption that the less bright will be more comfortable and have greater self-esteem in a group of other children with similar abilities. However, the critics of "tracking" note that the system produces failure. Those in a low track receive an inferior education and develop increasingly negative images of themselves and of the school system. More broadly, tracking is likely to be maintaining and solidifying existing social class lines. A diagram of this process might look like Figure 8-2.

Figure 8-2

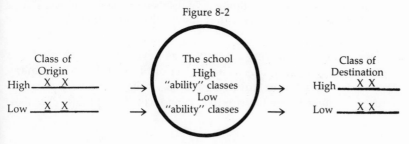

Working and lower-class young persons are less likely to be perceived by educators as having the requisite ability and motivation for college success and a challenging white-collar occupation. This results in low track assignment which in turn leads to a lower-class occupation. In short, the American educational institution is increasingly being criticized as maintaining inequality for lower-class segments of racial minorities and lower-class white children rather than facilitating academic growth and achievement.

Race and Track

To the knowledge of this author, there are no studies that note systematically the effects of race and class in low track placement. However, the following hypothesis seems plausible:

Lower and working-class persons of all races are likely to be placed in lower-ability tracks. However, misplacement of a normal child into a low track (or school) is especially likely among lower-class black, Chicano, and Indian children. This statement is based on several assumptions. First, there are strong historical definitions of these groups as intellectually less able so that the adjustment to middle-class criteria faced by any lower-class child is compounded. There is a ready-made backdrop of racial inferiority beliefs to which a minority child can easily be fitted. It probably takes an extremely clean-cut, middle-class, teacher-oriented minority child to break through these expectations. Secondly there has typically been a gross and insensitive reaction to black, Chicano, and Indian culture in Anglo institutions in general and in education in particular. Speaking Spanish or Navaho or Black English has been viewed by many teachers as a sign of nonconformity, resistance, or rebellion. Cahn observes among Indian children:

> The main achievement of the schools is to provide Indian children with an educational experience designed to root out all traces of their Indian heritage. . . . When an Eastern Oklahoma public school administrator was asked whether he thought English should be taught as a second language to Indian children, he blindly insisted that "only 'American' be taught in [the Indian] schools."[28]

Black English, until very recently, was never even considered as a legitimate second language. The dialect of black children that many Anglo educators found unintelligible was believed to be a substandard, extremely limited, primitive version of "acceptable" English.

Educational researchers have maintained that Black English is so deficient that different tenses cannot be expressed and that abstract-cognitive thinking cannot occur. Susan Houston[29] agrees that much of the language which educators elicit from black children is, indeed, inferior. However, she found that once black children learn that they can trust adults from the educational institutions, their language is far from inadequate. The language that black children use with their peers and adults they can trust is very different from the style, and the "register," that they use in school. Black English is often more creative, imaginative, and elaborate than standard English. There are significant differences between Black English and "White" English, neither of which is superior or more adaptive to their respective communities than the other. Houston reminds us that "An uninformed society has tended to obscure the differences, especially in classrooms that demand competitive and uniform performance irrespective of individual children's inclinations."[30]

Thirdly, lower-class black, Chicano,and Indian parents are least likely to have the bureaucratic expertise and influence to push very hard to be sure that their children are placed in a "high" or college-bound track class. Knowledge of the committees and people necessary to move the system is a resource found more often in middle-class white families.

"Programmed for Social Class"

"Programmed for Social Class" is a recent study by Schafer, Olexa, and Polk[31] that attempts to trace the influence of class on tracking and the subsequent effects of tracking on academic achievement. The authors estimate that about half of all the high schools in the United States use some form of tracking. The authors collected data from school transcripts of the recently graduated classes of two midwestern three-year high schools. One school was located in a middle-class academic community of 70,000 (graduating class that year = 753). A second, smaller school had a graduating class of 404 and was located in an industrial city of 20,000. Both schools had a two-track system: college preparatory and "general."

The first extremely important finding in the study is that both socioeconomic status and race affected which track a student took "quite apart from either his achievement in junior high or his ability as measured by IQ scores."[32] With the two schools combined into one total population, 83 percent of the students from white-collar homes were in the college preparatory track as opposed to 48 percent of the students from blue-collar homes. The relationship between race and track assignment is even stronger: 71 percent of the white students were in the college track as opposed to 30 percent of the black. Moreover, once students were placed in the "high" or "low" track at the end of the ninth grade, there was practically no mobility up or down. That is, there was a caste-like rigidity that followed assignment. "Only 7 percent of those who began on the college prep track moved down to the noncollege prep track, while only 7 percent of those assigned to the lower, noncollege track, moved up."[33] Even more important was the finding that track assignment was related to subsequent academic performance: those assigned to the college track made gains while the performance of those assigned to the lower track showed deterioration. This can best be illustrated by Figure 8-3 below.

FIGURE 8-3
G.P.A. Gap and Tracking

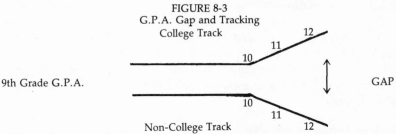

Note that at the ninth grade (before tracking) there was a small difference in mean GPA between the two groups; however, after tracking there was an increased gap with the college group rising and the non-college group falling in academic achievement. By graduation, after three years of tracking, the gap between the groups was very large. Not only was there a deterioration of academic performance in the low track group but less participation in extra-curricular activities, greater tendency to drop out, increased delinquency and more misbehavior in school. In other words, once placed in the lower track, many students showed an increased tendency to disengage from the high school as a source of meaning and self-respect.

These findings strongly suggest that tracking creates a certain amount of failure in the school. That is, tracking is an independent source of demotivation and failure apart from the ability or home environment of the student. However, believers in tracking can still argue that the observed differences between the college and non-college groups are due to individual ability; college preparatory students do better simply because they are brighter than the non-college group. It could further be argued that the less bright non-college group showed a deterioration of achievement because the work in the tenth, eleventh, and twelfth grades was increasingly more difficult. Similarly, the gains made in the college group could be explained on an individual motivation level — college-bound students worked harder and became more grade conscious as they got nearer to college. What is needed is a technique to sort out the deterioration effect of tracking with controls for home background, ability, and past achievement. Fortunately, in this study it was possible to get at the unique effects of tracking. Through the use of a technique known as test factor standardization the researchers were able to assess the effects of tracking on achievement with IQ, academic achievement before tracking (ninth grade GPA), and home environment (father's occupation) simultaneously controlled or ruled out. The argument is that if tracking persists in predicting achievement with the effects of these three factors eliminated, then tracking is a structural effect of the school that cannot be blamed on student ability. With the influence of the three factors eliminated, there was indeed a sizeable remaining relationship. Thirty percent of the college group as opposed to only 4 percent of the non-college group attained the top quarter of the class. At the low achievement end, only 12 percent of the college group were in the lowest quarter as compared with 35 percent of the non-college group. Tracking is carrying its own deleterious effects that are not explained away by the IQ or motivation of the student.

What, precisely, is happening in the low track group to produce a drastic decline in achievement? For one thing, there is likely to be an erosion of self-esteem. The lower track carries with it a strong stigma as illustrated by this interview of an ex-delinquent in Washington, D.C.

> It really don't have to be the tests, but after the tests there shouldn't be no separation in the classes. Because, as I say again, I felt good when I was with my class, but when they went and separated us — that changed us. That changed our ideas, our thinking, the way we thought about each other and turned us to enemies toward each other — because they said I was dumb and they were smart. . .
> *Did you think the other guys were smarter than you?* Not at first — I used to think I was just as smart as anybody in the school — I knew I was smart. I knew some people were smarter, and I *wanted* to go to school, I wanted to

get a diploma and go to college and help people and everything. I stepped into there in junior high — I felt like a fool going to school — I really felt like a fool.

Why?

Because I felt like I wasn't a part of that school. . .[34]

Teacher expectations are another major ingredient of the explanation. Teachers with low track classes are likely to underestimate the abilities of students, to define them as losers. Students easily pick up such definitions and perform at a lower level. This is not to say that most teachers in low track sections are *consciously* trying to produce failure. Rather, the teacher, by subtle forms of interaction (tone of voice) unconsciously sets in motion a negative self-fulfilling prophecy.[35]

Schafer, Olexa, and Polk also found evidence of peculiar grading policies in the two tracks. Interviews with teachers and other staff personnel in the schools pointed toward the existence of grade ceilings for the non-college group and grade floors for the college group. In other words, it was extremely difficult for lower track students to get a grade higher than a "C" even if objective performance was equal to a college track "B." Similarly, college track students seldom made a grade lower than a "B." "Several teachers explicitly called our attention to this practice, the rationale being that non-college prep students do not deserve the same objective grade rewards as college prep students, since they 'clearly' are less bright and perform less well." [36] No hard data were presented to assess the frequency with which this "ceilings and floors" policy was practiced. But if widely used in the two schools, it certainly explains why there was so little mobility between the two tracks and why there was a deterioration of performance in the low track. If students perceived that no matter how hard they tried they could not get higher than a grade of "C," demotivation and lowered commitment would logically follow.

NOTES TO CHAPTER 8

[1]See, for example, Kenneth B. Clark and Mamie P. Clark, "Racial Identification and Preference in Negro Children," in *Readings in Social Psychology*, ed. T. M. Newcomb and E. L. Hartley (New York: Holt, 1947); Kenneth B. Clark, *Dark Ghetto: Dilemmas of Social Power* (New York: Harper & Row, 1965), pp. 21 and 64; and Mary Ellen Goodman, *Race Awareness in Young Children* (Reading, Mass.: Addison-Wesley, 1952).

[2]See for example E. Franklin Frazier, *The Negro Family in the United States* (New York: Citadel, 1948); Hortense Powdermaker, *After Freedom: A Cultural Study in the Deep South*

(New York: Viking, 1939), and Daniel P. Moynihan, *The Negro Family: The Case for National Action* (Washington, D.C.: Government Printing Office, US Dept. of Labor, March, 1965).

[3]See A. M. Shuey, *The Testing of Negro Intelligence* (New York: Social Science Press, 1966); A. B. Wilson, "Educational Consequences of Segregation in a California Community," in *Racial Isolation in the Public Schools*, Appendices vol. 2 of a report by the U.S. Commission on Civil Rights (Washington D. C.: Government Printing Office, 1967); and R. Herber, R. Dever, and J. Conry, "The Influence of Environmental and Genetic Variables on Intellectual Development," in *Behavioral Research in Mental Retardation*, ed. H. J. Prehm, L. A. Hamerlynck, and J. E. Crosson (Eugene, Ore.: University of Oregon Press, 1968), pp. 1-23.

[4]For a review of some of the justifications of tracking (not the view of the authors), see Walter E. Schafer, Carol Olexa, and Kenneth Polk, "Programmed for Social Class: Tracking in High School," *Transaction* 7 (October, 1970): 39-46, 63.

[5]For a discussion of prejudice as a tradition built into our culture, see George Eaton Simpson and J. Milton Yinger, *Racial and Cultural Minorities* (New York: Harper & Row, 1965), ch. 5.

[6]Ibid., p. 147.

[7]Clark, 1947, op. cit. and Goodman, op. cit.

[8]Clark, 1947, op. cit.

[9]Alvin F. Poussaint, "A Negro Psychiatrist Explains the Negro Psyche," in Norman R. Yetman and C. Hoy Steele (eds.) *Majority and Minority: The Dynamics of Racial and Ethnic Relations* (Boston: Allyn and Bacon, 1971), p. 349.

[10]Chad Gordon, *Looking Ahead: Self-conceptions, Race and Family as Determinants of Adolescent Orientation to Achievement* (Washington, D.C.: American Sociological Association, Arnold and Caroline Rose Monograph Series in Sociology, 1972).

[11]Morris Rosenberg and Roberta G. Simmons, *Black and White Self Esteem: The Urban School Child* (Washington, D.C.: American Sociological Association, Arnold and Caroline Rose Monograph Series in Sociology, 1972).

[12]The Hollingshead Index of Social Position is made up of three components: occupation, education, and area of residence. Scale scores yield five classes from well-educated businessmen and professionals living in prestigeful areas (class 1) to marginally employed persons with less than high school education (class 5). See August B. Hollingshead, *Elmtown's Youth: The Impact of Social Classes on Adolescents* (New York: John Wiley & Sons, 1949), p. 37.

[13]Rosenberg and Simmons, op. cit., pp. 61-62.

[14]Ibid., p. 62.

[15]Ibid., p. 68.

[16]See, for example, Stanley Coopersmith, *The Antecedents of Self-esteem* (San Francisco: W. H. Freeman, 1967), p. 236.

[17]Moynihan, op. cit.

[18]Ibid., pp. 5, 30.

[19]Ibid., pp. 5, 47; see also, Lee Rainwater, "Crucible of Identity," *Daedalus* 95 (1966): 172-216.

[20]Warren D. TenHouten, "The Black Family: Myth and Reality," *Psychiatry* 2 (May, 1970): 147.

[21]Otto Kerner, *Report of the National Advisory Commission on Civil Disorders* (New York: Bantam Books, 1968), p. 261.

[22]TenHouten, op. cit.

[23]Joan W. Moore, *Mexican Americans* (Englewood, N.J.: Prentice-Hall, 1970), p. 81.

²⁴Jane R. Mercer, "IQ: The Lethal Label," *Psychology Today* 6 (September, 1972): 95.

²⁵Ibid., p. 44.

²⁶Ibid., p. 47

²⁷Ibid., p. 96.

²⁸Edgar S. Cahn, *Our Brother's Keeper: The Indian in White America* (New York: World Publishing Co., 1969), p. 37.

²⁹Susan H. Houston, "Black English," *Psychology Today* 7 (March, 1973): 45-48.

³⁰Ibid., p. 48.

³¹Schafer, Olexa, and Polk, op. cit.

³²Ibid., p. 40.

³³Ibid., p. 41.

³⁴Ibid., p. 43.

³⁵For a classic study of teacher expectations and the self-fulfilling prophecy, see Robert Rosenthal and Lenore Jacobson, *Pygmalion in the Classroom: Teacher Expectations and Pupils Intellectual Development* (New York: Holt, Rinehart & Winston, 1968).

³⁶Schafer, Olexa, and Polk, op. cit., p. 44.

Chapter 9

THE WHITE WORKING CLASS

Much has been written on the plight of blacks, Chicanos, and Indians in American society. Numerous accounts have made white poverty visible to the average American. However, it is only very recently that the white working-class stratum has been seriously discussed sociologically as another American minority group. In the last several years, social science literature abounds with articles on the frustrations and grievances of blue-collar workers.[1] The terms "blue-collar" and "working class" are loosely used. However, they seem to refer especially to semi-skilled and skilled manual workers in the "$5,000 to $15,000 a year" category. A collective social profile of the white working-class person emerges from these recent studies: he faces work situations that stifle initiative and creativity (the extreme of work alienation being an assembly line job), he has made little if any economic advancement when his small wage increases are corrected for inflation and taxes, he perceives a debasement of the American Dream exemplified by blacks receiving special privileges and opportunities and college students rejecting the work ethic and burning their draft cards, and he feels a sense of alienation from a distant political system that he cannot affect.[2] One might argue that many other Americans share such outlooks and that this is not a special feature of blue-collar life.

The thesis advanced here is that the protest methods and demands of student and black militants grate especially hard on the values, outlooks, and economic fears of the white working-class person. That is, the white working-class environment is another special combination of race and class that involves unique tensions and constraints. The purpose of this chapter is to make clearer the nature of the grievances of the white working class and to make sense out of them, to question the validity of various explanations for blue-collar anger.

179

It is interesting to relate the white working class to the paternalistic competitive trend in race relations discussed in Chapter 2. There it was noted that blacks, Chicanos, and American Indians are conquered minorities that have gone through different versions of paternalistic relations and are currently involved (in a competitive industrial society) in building an independent power base, establishing an identity, and competing with members of the majority group for certain resources such as white-collar and skilled jobs, political representation, and a college education for their children. The working-class segment of the white majority group may feel similarly engaged in tough competition for these scarce items. In industrialized, multi-racial societies, when the caste-paternalistic lid is lifted, the white working class is most likely to feel threatened by the new stance of racial minorities.

Working-class persons have small, but often hard-earned amounts of power, privilege, and prestige that they are anxious to protect. Recent studies indicate that it is not so much that white workers are opposed to blacks' getting their civil rights [3] (i.e., an equal chance for good housing, jobs, and education); it is rather that they are opposed to black gains that mean heavy losses to them. It is this zero sum problem ("your gain is my loss") that is at the heart of working-class anger. Black militant demands have upset many blue-collar persons and campus activism has also received a cool response, to say the least. Working-class persons are not likely to be sympathetic to student demands for special quotas for minority students, the establishment of black and Chicano studies programs, and more generally increased student power in running universities. Open-ended conversations, found in a recent study by Sexton and Sexton, clearly express some of these feelings:

> . . . Of course, my son's willing to do his duty to his country if he has to. And I feel the same way. But we can't understand how all those rich kids — the kids with the beads from the fancy suburbs — how they get off when my son has to go over there and maybe get his head shot off. They get off scot-free . . . and when they see they're going to graduate from college, and maybe get drafted, they raise such a stink. How come these privileged kids get away with messing up the colleges that we're paying to support? I'd give my right arm to get my son into one of those colleges and all these kids seem to do is parade around and denounce the government. What the hell have they got to complain about? If they

don't like it there, let them go out and get a job or get drafted like mine —
see how much they like that!

I've lived in this neighborhood all my life, and my father lived here
too. I worked all my life to buy this house, and now it's almost mine —
not much, but the only thing of much value besides my car that I own. I
built a lot of what's in it with my own hands. We liked this neighborhood
and decided to settle here in the first place because the neighbors were
like us. Now the black people have moved in. They've got a right to, I
guess, just like anybody else. They want a better life. But they're poor
people and they don't keep things up the way *we* used to. Most of my
friends and my brother were afraid when the blacks started moving in —
afraid that everything would go to hell and they wouldn't be able to sell
their houses — so they moved. Now they're gone. And the schools have
gone down. What have I got left? I guess I'll have to move . . . but, damn
it, this is my home. It takes a whole lifetime to make good friends, and
now they've all moved out. I'll be a stranger wherever I move. If more of
the blacks moved out into those fancy suburbs, where all those whites
who say they're so hot for civil rights live, then maybe there wouldn't be
ghettos in the neighborhoods like this. But the people out in the rich
suburbs won't let them in . . . unless, of course, they're from Harvard or
Yale.

We're carrying everyone on our backs. The rich don't work. They just
clip coupons and order us around. All those people on welfare and those
unwed mothers. They won't work. You couldn't *make* them work. They
just sit around and collect their checks, and *we* pay for it. Let those
women have as many children as they want, each one with a different
boyfriend. I don't care. Just don't ask me to pay for bringing them up. I
can just barely bring up my own kids.

The hippies and the college kids. They don't work. They just collect on
all the things we struggle to pay for. And they all think that we're dopes
and drones for doing it.[4]

There are valid points made in these statements. For example, it is not
just black demands and advancement that are producing anger, but, in
addition, considerable hostility toward the stereotyped white upper-
middle and upper classes (such as highly visible "privileged kids who
escape the Vietnam draft"). One can also see running through many of
the foregoing statements that the working man is angry because he
perceives he is being asked to pay the bulk of the price for justice for
blacks and for the Vietnam war. There is a certain degree of rationality
behind these responses. That is, the anger expressed can be seen as a

predictable, understandable response to tangible strains rather than totally as a case of personal bigotry. How typical are these attitudes? If a randomly selected group of blue-collar workers was compared to those higher in the occupational structure, would blue-collar persons stand out as more antagonistic toward students and black protestors than others?

"Blue Collar Anger," A Recent Study of the White Working Class*

In the latter part of 1969 and the first months of 1970, data were gathered by Jeffries and Ransford in a large, white section of Los Angeles (the San Fernando Valley) to test several hypotheses about the white backlash.[5] Not only was this a period of extreme campus unrest nationally but on two campuses in or near the sample area, student demonstrators briefly took control of campus offices. It was also shortly after the bitterly divisive Yorty-Bradley mayoral election. Thomas Bradley, a black candidate, was defeated after being charged by his opponent, Sam Yorty, with being controlled and manipulated by black extremists. Of particular interest to us were the reactions of the blue-collar workers to the black and student power movements.

Is the white working class uniquely antagonistic toward student and black demands? If so, why? Four hundred and seventy-seven Caucasian adults responded to an interview schedule dealing with reactions to student and black protest. The sample involved approximately equal numbers of blue-collar, business white-collar (managerial, sales, and clerical), and professional white-collar persons. Education was used as a second measure of socioeconomic status. Three measures of antagonism toward demonstrators were developed. "Student demonstrator hostility" is a three-item measure (an example of one of the items is "Even if they don't break the law, college students who are involved in demonstrations should be expelled"); "student power" is a one-item index ("Students should be given more say in running the college"); and "black demands unjustified" is a three-item measure (example, "Negroes are asking for special treatment from whites to which they are not entitled"). It is this latter measure dealing with black demands that we are mainly concerned with here. Note that this is not a measure of civil rights libertarianism but refers rather to the perceived legitimacy of black demands.

---

* An earlier version of this study appeared in *The American Sociological Review* 37 (June, 1972): 333-346.

There is an important difference between supporting equal opportunity for blacks in acquiring a good job or housing and supporting
black demands for quotas or reparations that may result in losses to the
white working class. Our purpose, then, was to find out if there was a
substantial correlation between SES (occupation and education) and
the above measures of antagonism toward demonstrators. In addition,
I was interested in assessing the importance of three explanations for
blue-collar anger. A brief statement of each of these explanations
follows:

1) The "Conformity-Idealization of Authority" Explanation

A number of studies indicate that the blue-collar environment stresses
the value of respect for authority. In the socialization of children, for
example, a recent study (Kohn, 1969) shows that blue-collar parents
are more likely to emphasize obedience and neatness in contrast to
middle-class parents who emphasize internal dynamics such as curiosity and self-realization. The stress on conformity and obedience is due
in part to occupational environments. Blue-collar persons typically are
in occupations which demand repetition, conformity and adherence to
rules. Thus Kohn and Schooler [6] find that men's opportunities to
exercise occupational self-direction — that is, to use initiative,
thought, and independent judgment at work — account for much of
the relationship between social class and authoritarian orientations.
Other studies indicate that working-class persons are less sophisticated in cognitive thinking. Being less well-read and less educated, as
well as more isolated from people with views different from their own,
thinking tends to be about concrete situations; that is, blue-collar
persons emphasize attributes of individuals rather than attributes of
abstract systems in their conversations. They usually hold to simple
moral and ethical perceptions of the world, rather than perceptions
involving relativity of judgment or competing values.[7] The lesser degree of abstract thinking feeds into the same point, that working-class
people are more likely to value conformity to basic institutions than to
question the existing system. From this perspective, it follows that
working-class persons will be more outraged by campus protest and
black demands than those higher in the class structure. Student protest and black protest symbolize a classic flaunting of authority and a
down-grading of institutions. The "four-letter words," the styles of
dress, and the direct confrontation methods all suggest disrespect for
authority.

2) Belief in the American Dream — Neglect of the Workingman's Needs

This revised class-conflict model, as opposed to a Marxian model in which the white working class is a revolutionary force for change, sees the blue-collar worker as reaffirming traditional beliefs in the openness of the American system. Hostility is directed toward the black lower class as undeserving of special opportunity as well as toward white liberal persons in power who seek to remake traditional America at the workingman's expense. Working-class people see themselves as having made modest economic gains through union victories and through their own hard work and sacrifices. They are far from economically secure, however. They tend to believe poor people and black people are at the bottom of the class structure because of their own laziness, not because of racism or other institutional barriers.[8]

Given their belief in hard work and in the openness of the American structure, working class persons are hostile toward ghetto rioters and black demands for quotas and preferential job treatment. It is not simply that they feel blacks do not deserve special opportunity. They are angry because it seems to them that they are being asked to pay the biggest price for "social justice." [9] If they yield to demands for special opportunities and super-seniority for black workers, they, not the secure upper-middle-class people, face the greatest threat of being laid off.

From the workingman's point of view, far too much attention is being paid to the poor, and especially the black poor. In a recent survey,[10] 65 percent of white middle Americans felt that blacks have a better chance than whites to get financial help from the government when they're out of work. Increasingly, white workers perceive that it is easier for an unemployed black to get aid and sympathy than a hard working white. Further, working-class people are angry because they perceive that they are taxed heavily to support welfare budgets for the poor, and they have fewer mechanisms like business expense accounts, to escape taxation. In short, they feel they are paying for the special opportunities given minority persons — compensations they believe to be unnecessary in a free and open society.

Although this second explanation for blue-collar anger (the American Dream and neglect of the working man's needs) is more clearly related to antagonism toward black militance, it also ties in with antagonism toward campus activism. A perception of the American system as open and just is antithetical to the student activist view that the American system is racist, elitist, exploitative, and excessively authoritarian. Further, the quintessence of the American Dream is sending one's children to college so they can advance in the social structure and have a better life. It is only with great sacrifice, however, that the working-class family can send their children to college. The shouting of affluent youth, "On Strike — Shut It Down!" is a multiple outrage to blue-collar people. Activist students are not only attacking American values, but threatening to close an only recently opened channel of mobility for working class children.

3) The Powerlessness Explanation

From this point of view, a critical dimension of the disaffection of white working-class people is their sense of powerlessness over "radical" changes occurring in the country, and over political decisions directly affecting their lives. Working-class people may perceive that they have few means to affect political change. Their occupational roles do not evoke respect and power in the larger society. Even in their own union the rank and file often have no real voice in making policy.

Recent student and black protest has, no doubt, heightened these feelings of political powerlessness. The worker may perceive that black and student militants have reached power centers and are forcing institutional changes that seem to him a distributive injustice or direct threat (for example, preferential hiring for blacks, relaxed entrance requirements and special aid for minority college students, and plans for increased school and residential integration that may affect him especially as an inner city resident living close to the ghetto). Of the "power structure's" various components, blue-collar workers may view the government as especially hard to move and preoccupied with the problems of blacks.

The powerlessness explanation would predict that white working-class people who feel politically powerless, i.e., who expect public officials to be unresponsive to their needs, will be especially antagonistic toward student and black activists. Each gain in power for militant students or blacks may be perceived as a reciprocal loss in power, status, or a way of life for the working-class person.

Note that the concept of powerlessness used in this study denotes a perception of the social system and does not necessarily refer to personal apathy or fatalism. Indeed, the more militant white action responses to black and student protest (such as "hard hat" demonstrations or the Tony Imperiale Armed Citizens Committee) suggest a high degree of personal confidence and efficacy combined with a low expectancy of being able to move a large impersonal system through normative action.

Findings

Is the working-class person more hostile toward student and black demands than those higher in the socioeconomic structure? Table 9-1 shows that this is indeed the case, with occupation moderately correlated with each dependent variable and education showing a stronger relationship. Seventy percent of the blue-collar workers interviewed scored high on "black demands unjustified" (agreeing with two or all three of the items) versus 40 percent of the white-collar professionals. The relationship is even more striking in the case of education, with a spread from 77 percent (less than high school) to 31 percent (college graduate). Similar results are found for the "student hostility" and

TABLE 9-1

Independent Variables (Occupation and Education) by Student Demonstrator Hostility, Student Power, and Black Demands Unjustified

	Student Demonstrator Hostility %				Opposition to Student Power %			Black Demands Unjustified %		
Occupation	Low	Med.	High	N	Low	High	N	Low	Med.	High
Blue collar	12	37	50	(163)	34	66	(164)	12	18	70
Business white collar*	26	44	30	(159)	52	48	(162)	21	33	46
Professional white collar	34	41	25	(137)	50	50	(139)	29	31	40
		Gamma = -.32			Gamma = -.21			Gamma = -.3		
		p < .001			p < .01			p < .001		
Education										
Less than high school	3	47	50	(60)	27	73	(63)	8	15	77
High school graduate	15	40	45	(149)	42	58	(149)	17	24	59
Some college	35	36	29	(152)	49	51	(153)	22	31	47
College graduate	36	46	18	(104)	60	40	(106)	37	32	31
		Gamma = -.37			Gamma = -.30			Gamma = -.3		
		p < .001			p < .001			p < .001		

*refers to clerical, managerial and sales.
Note: Statistical significance determined by chi square.
Source: H. Edward Ransford, "Blue Collar Anger: Reactions To Student and Black Protest," *American Sociological Review* (June, 1972): 339

"student power" items (though the correlation is noticeably weaker in the case of occupation and student power). People in blue-collar jobs and those with less than a high school education are clearly more antagonistic, but are the theoretical reasons advanced for blue-collar anger valid? To what extent do respect for authority, belief in the American Dream, and belief that worker needs are neglected interpret the relationship between SES and student-black antagonism? The following diagram may help to state the case:

FIGURE 9-1

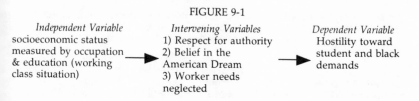

| *Independent Variable* | *Intervening Variables* | *Dependent Variable* |
| socioeconomic status measured by occupation & education (working class situation) | 1) Respect for authority 2) Belief in the American Dream 3) Worker needs neglected | Hostility toward student and black demands |

Strains inherent in the working-class situation lead to certain outlooks (intervening variables) and these in turn feed into hostility toward student and black demands. Statistical support for this model requires that when the three intervening variables are controlled the size of the correlation between socioeconomic status and student-black antagonism will diminish considerably. That is, by holding the intervening variables constant we should be sapping away much of the effect of SES on antagonism. Table 9-2 shows that the combined effect of the three intervening variables accounts for a sizeable fraction of the relationship between the independent and dependent variables. That is, in all instances the original zero-order correlation drops appreciably when all three variables are controlled. For example, the original Pearson r between education and student demonstrator hostility is moderate -.31 but drops to -.12 with the three intervening variables simultaneously controlled. Table 9-2 also reveals that control for "respect for authority" reduces the zero order correlation slightly more than the other intervening variables. However, the intervening variables were not standardized: respect for authority had three items in the scale while worker neglect had only one. As a result, one cannot conclude that "respect for authority" is a more important intervening link than "openness of the American system" or "worker needs neglected." One measure could simply be a better index of its respective concept than another. It is also interesting to note that the only surviving relationships are those between education and black antagonism (partial r = -.16p < .01) and occupation and black antagonism (partial r = -.16 p < .01). In other words, the three explanations account for about half of the relationship between blue-collar position and antagonism toward blacks. Apparently, there are other reasons for hostility that we have not fully measured, possibly perceived threats from black economic progress, or simple race prejudice.

TABLE 9-2

Partial Correlations Between Independent Variables (Occupation and Education) and th Dependent Variables with Respect for Authority, Belief in American Dream, and Neglect Workingman, Controlled Singly and Jointly.

Correlation Between Occupation and:	Zero Order	(1) Respect for Authority Controlled	(2) American Dream Controlled	(3) Worker Neglected Controlled	Simultaneou Control 1, 2, and 3
Student demonstrator hostility	−.20*	−.09	−.17*	−.14*	−.07
Opposed to student power	−.14*	−.06	−.12*	−.09	−.04*
Black demands unjustified	−.25*	−.18*	−.23*	−.19*	−.16*
Correlation Between Education and:					
Student demontrator hostility	−.31*	−.16*	−.25*-	−.24*	−.12*
Opposed to student power	−.24*	−.12*	−.18*	−.18*	−.09*
Black demands unjustified	−.32*	−.20*	−.24*	−.23*	−.16*

* p < .01

Note: Statistical significance determined by student's T (one-tailed test).

Source: H. Edward Ransford, "Blue Collar Anger: Reactions to Student and Black Protest," *American Sociological Review* 37 (June, 1972), p. 343.

SPECIFICATION FOR POWERLESSNESS

We have predicted that working-class persons who feel politically powerless will be especially antagonistic toward the student and black movements. The data (not shown) indicate definite support for this logic especially in the case of hostility toward student demonstrators. Thus, while 43 percent of the blue-collar workers who score low in political powerlessness are very hostile toward student demonstrators, 60 percent of the blue-collar workers who score high in power-lessness express hostility. Viewing education as the independent variable, the difference between the low and high powerlessness groups is even more striking, ranging from 36 percent to 59 percent. As an overview, it can be said that the blue-collar group and the less-than-high-school group who score high in powerlessness are more antagonistic toward students and blacks than anyone else in the sample.

CONCLUSIONS

The Ransford study shows that white working-class persons are more likely to be antagonistic toward students and blacks demanding massive changes in our society than are those higher in the socioeconomic structure. However, the size of the correlation is a moderate one. That is, although blue-collar workers tend on the average to be more hostile, some blue-collar workers are more supportive of student and black demands than some white-collar workers. Secondly, there was some confirmation for each of the theoretical explanations advanced. "Respect for authority," "the American Dream," "worker needs are neglected," and "political powerlessness" all figure into the explanation for blue-collar anger.

The mass media have tended to stereotype the white working man as a narrow-minded, intolerant bigot. His angry responses to students and blacks are often viewed as the effect of a prejudiced personality. In contrast, our model shows blue-collar anger to be rooted in the perceived social situation. From this perspective, much of the workingman's anger is a rational response to tangible strains, independent of personal bigotry. Lack of decision-making power on the job, the feeling that his hard-earned dollars are going for tax programs to aid blacks with no comparable programs for working-class whites, a power structure unresponsive to the needs of the workingman — these stresses probably affect working-class anger as much as a basic antipathy toward blacks per se.

White working-class people who feel politically powerless are especially antagonistic toward student and black protestors. Research in the black community conducted shortly after the Watts Riot [11] suggests a parallel finding: blacks who scored high in social powerlessness (low expectancy of gaining redress through institutional channels) were were more willing to use violence to get their rights. Similarly, a violence commission report [12] notes that militant white reactions to protest (armed citizen's groups) are found especially among those who are angered by excessive concern for minorities and who feel ignored by the polity. Apparently the potential exists for white as well as black militant action when individuals perceive a distributive injustice and, in addition, feel blocked in gaining redress through institutional channels.

WHITE ETHNICITY AND THE BLUE COLLAR SITUATION

The recent assertion of ethnic consciousness among blacks, Chicanos, and American Indians has made more and more untenable the assimilation-melting pot ideology. Pluralism of one sort or another is increasingly voiced as desirable and healthy (and likely) in the coming decade. What is surprising to many is that white ethnics (non-WASPS) are also asserting their cultural distinctiveness. Andrew Greeley feels that there is a direct relationship between black militance and the resurgence of ethnic identification among whites. "The new consciousness of ethnicity is in part based on the fact that the blacks have legitimated cultural pluralism as it has perhaps never been legitimated before. Other Americans, observing that now it is all right to be proud of being black, wonder, quite reasonably, why it is not all right to be proud of being Italian or Polish."[13] There are several important qualifications that need to be made concerning this ethnic consciousness. First, a great deal of it is not new at all. Ethnic ties, loyalties, voluntary associations, communities, and bloc voting have always been there but have been often ignored by social scientists. Secondly, certain white ethnic groups are more assimilated than others. Ethnic consciousness is most likely among white groups that were (and continue to be) excluded from WASP society. For example, Michael Novak sarcastically refers to the most-excluded white ethnics as PIGS: Poles, Italians, Greeks, and Slavs. "They were, in a word, 'peasants' — looked down upon not only by the WASPS, who saw them as socially, religiously and, yes, racially inferior, but by intellectuals (of varying backgrounds themselves) who saw them as unwashed, uneducated, and uncouth, as culturally inferior."[14]

Poles, Italians, Greeks, and Slavs are more likely to assert ethnic identity than the more assimilated Germans and Scandinavians (the Irish are, perhaps, midway between the PIGS and the most assimilated). Thirdly, ethnic awareness and identification may vary greatly by the area of the country. For example, in the San Fernando Valley section of Los Angeles (sample area for "Blue Collar Anger" study) one finds a large sprawling suburban region without the white ethnic communities of Newark, Chicago, Wisconsin, or New York. One would expect far more ethnic consciousness among white ethnics who live in or near communities established by first-generation immigrants. That is, common frustrations and interpretations of political events may be more easily identified and more readily shared in such communities.

We can speak legitimately of ethclass effects for white persons as well as for blacks, Chicanos, and Indians. Working-class Italians or Poles may have a unique political stance that is only understood by considering class and ethnicity together. Returning to the "blue collar anger" discussion, it is quite likely that certain ethnic outlooks and blue-collar outlooks reinforce each other.

Not all white ethnics are in blue-collar positions, but many are; when the two statuses occur together one expects an especially well-articulated view toward minority demands. It seems logical that working-class ethnics would especially feel a sense of distributive injustice when the rising minorities (blacks, Chicanos, Indians) are given reparations, special opportunities, and quotas. Working-class white ethnics who are close to the immigration experience and have struggled for a piece of the American Dream are not likely to support minority quotas, regardless of the minority group. Greeley writes:

> We must remember that these groups are only a generation or two removed from the old world. To be told that they are responsible or ought to feel guilty for the plight of blacks puzzles them. It was not their ancestors who brought black slaves to this country. . . . It was not their ancestors who enacted the Jim Crow Laws. . . . Furthermore, the white ethnics are close enough to their own immigrant poverty to realize that reform groups were not particularly concerned about them. No one ever worried about the Polish poor or the Irish poor, and no one seems to worry much now about the residual poverty groups in both these populations.[15]

It should be made clear that we predict that blue-collar ethnics are likely to feel especially high degrees of distributive injustice, not that they are more racist in outlook. There is no particular reason that a working-class Italian should be more racist in outlook than a working-class Anglo-Saxon. Indeed, Greeley reports from recent research at the

National Opinion Research Center[16] that Italian and Irish blue-collar ethnics are more liberal on matters of race and peace than their Anglo blue-collar counterparts. Even more interesting is the finding that the more involved an ethnic person is in explicitly ethnic behavior (involvement in an ethnic organization, for example) the more liberal are his outlooks on race and peace. That is, high ethnic involvement seems to be inversely related to racism and bigotry (Greeley, 1972).

It should finally be noted, that with increased ethnic pluralism, one no longer has a race relations model in which a uniform white majority group is juxtaposed against visible minorities who are asserting their separate identities. Rather, there is considerable cultural diversity and separate ethnic consciousness within the so-called "white majority" group. To understand such phenomena as political participation and voting blocs, we need to take into account more than social class. Ethnicity and class must be considered conjointly.

NOTES TO CHAPTER 9

[1] See, for example, Arthur B. Shostak, *Blue-Collar World* (Englewood, N.J. Prentice-Hall, 1964); Irving Howe, *The World of the Blue Collar Worker* (New York: Quadrangle Books, 1972); and Robert E. Lane and Michael Lerner, "Why Hard-Hats Hate Hairs," *Psychology Today* 6 (November, 1970): 45.

[2] See Michael M. Schneider, "Middle America," *The Center Magazine* (Nov./Dec., 1970), pp. 2-9.

[3] Richard F. Hamilton, "Liberal Intelligentsia and White Backlash," in Howe, op. cit., pp. 227-238.

[4] Patricia Sexton and Brendan Sexton, *Blue Collars and Hard-Hats: The Working Class and the Future of Politics* (New York: Random House, 1971), pp. 51-58.

[5] The "white backlash" studies that emerged from these data are Vincent Jeffries and H. Edward Ransford, "Ideology, Social Structure, and the Yorty-Bradley Mayoral Election," *Social Problems* 19 (Winter, 1972): 358-372 and H. Edward Ransford, "Blue Collar Anger: Reactions to Student and Black Protest," *American Sociological Review:* 37 (June, 1972): 333-346.

[6] Melvin Kohn and C. Schooler, "Class, Occupation, and Orientation," *American Sociological Review* 34 (October, 1960): 659-678.

[7] Lane and Lerner, op. cit., p. 105.

[8] Ibid., p. 46.

[9] Schneider, op. cit.

[10] "The Troubled American: A Special Report on the White Majority," *Newsweek* 71 (October 6, 1969): 28-73.

[11] H. Edward Ransford, "Isolation, Powerlessness, and Violence: A Study of Attitudes and Participation in the Watts Riot," *American Journal of Sociology* 73 (March, 1968): 581-591.

[12] Jerome H. Skolnick, *The Politics of Protest: Report to the National Commission on the Causes and Prevention of Violence* (New York: Ballantine Books, 1969).

[13] Andrew M. Greeley, "The New Ethnicity and Blue Collars," in Howe, op. cit., p. 291.

[14] Peter I. Rose, Review Essay of "The Rise of the Unmeltable Ethnics," *Contemporary Sociology: A Journal of Reviews* 2 (January, 1973): 14-15.

[15] Andrew M. Greeley, "America's Not So Silent Minority," *Los Angeles Times,* Opinion Section, December 7, 1969, pp. 1-2.

[16] Greeley, "The New Ethnicity and Blue Collars," op. cit., p. 295.

SELECTED BIBLIOGRAPHY

Allen, Robert L. *Black Awakening in Capitalist America*. New York: Doubleday, 1969

Banfield, Edward C. *The Unheavenly City*. Boston: Little, Brown and Co., 1968.

Bennett, Lerone Jr. "Black Bourgeoisie Revisited," *Ebony* 28 (August, 1973): 50-55.

Billingsley, Andrew. *Black Families in White America*. Englewood Cliffs: Prentice-Hall, 1968.

Blalock, Hubert M. Jr. *Toward A Theory of Minority-Group Relations*. New York: Wiley, 1967.

Blau, Peter M. and Otis Dudley Duncan. *The American Occupational Structure*. New York: Wiley, 1967.

Blauner, Robert. "Internal Colonialism and Ghetto Revolt," *Social Problems* 16 (Spring, 1969): 393-408.

_____. *Racial Oppression in America*. New York: Harper and Row, 1972.

Bloom, Richard, Martin Whiteman and Martin Deutsch, "Race and Social Class as Separate Factors Related To Social Environment," *American Journal of Sociology* 70 (January, 1965): 471-476.

Broom, Leonard and Norval Glenn. *Transformation of the Negro American*. New York: Harper and Row, 1965.

Brown, Dee. *Bury My Heart at Wounded Knee*. New York: Holt, Rinehart and Winston, 1970.

Blumer, Herbert. *Industrialisation and Race Relations. A Symposium*. London and New York: Oxford University Press, 1965.

Cahn, Edgar S. *Our Brother's Keeper*. New York: World Publishing Co., 1969.

Cohen, Elizabeth G. and Susan S. Roper. "Modification of Interracial Interaction Disability: An Application of Status Characteristic Theory," *American Sociological Review* 37 (December, 1972): 643-657.

Cruse, Harold. *The Crisis of the Negro Intellectual*. New York: William Morrow, 1967.

Cox, Oliver Cromwell. *Caste Class and Race*. Garden City: Doubleday, 1948.

Davidson, Chandler and Charles M. Gaitz. "Ethnic Attitudes as a Basis for Minority Cooperation in a Southwestern Metropolis," *Social Science Quarterly* 53 (March, 1973): 738-748.

Davis, Allison, Burleigh R. Gardner and Mary R. Gardner. *Deep South*. Chicago: University of Chicago Press, 1941.

Drake, St. Clair and Horace R. Cayton. *Black Metropolis: A Study of Negro Life in a Northern City*. New York: Harcourt, Brace, 1945.

Duncan, Otis Dudley and Beverly Duncan. "Minorities and the Process of Stratification," *American Sociological Review* 33 (June, 1968): 365-382.

Ebony. Special Issue on the Black Middle Class. 28 (August, 1973).

Edwards, G. Franklin. *The Negro Professional Class*. Glencoe, Illinois: Free Press, 1959.

Felice, Lawrence G. "Mexican American Self Concept and Educational Achievement: The Effects of Ethnic Isolation and Socioeconomic Deprivation," *Social Science Quarterly* 53 (March, 1973): 716-726.

Frazier, E. Franklin. *Black Bourgeoisie: The Rise of a New Middle Class.* New York: Free Press, 1957.

Glenn, Norvel D. "Negro Prestige Criteria: A Class Study in the Bases of Prestige," *American Journal of Sociology* 68 (May, 1963): 645-657.

Gordon, Chad. *Looking Ahead: Self-conceptions, Race, and Family as Determinants of Adolescent Orientation to Achievement.* Washington, D.C.: American Sociological Association. Arnold and Caroline Rose Monograph Series in Sociology, 1972.

Gordon, Milton. *Assimilation in American Life.* New York: Oxford University Press, 1964, pp. 19-83.

Grebler, Leo, Joan Moore, and Ralph Guzman. *The Mexican American People.* New York: Free Press, 1970.

Greeley, Andrew M. "The New Ethnicity and Blue Collars," in Irving Howe (ed.) *The World of the Blue Collar Worker.* New York: Quadrangle Books, 1972.

Gutierrez, Armando and Herbert Hirsch. "The Militant Challenge to the American Ethos: 'Chicanos' and 'Mexican Americans'," *Social Science Quarterly* 53 (March, 1973): 830-845.

Hannerz, Ulf. *Soulside.* New York: Columbia University Press, 1969.

Howard, John R. *Awakening Minorities.* Trans-action Books: Aldine Publishing Company, 1970.

Howe, Irving. *The World of the Blue Collar Worker.* New York: Quadrangle Books, 1972.

Kerckhoff, Alan C. and Thomas C. McCormick. "Marginal Status and Marginal Personality," *Social Forces* 34: 48-55.

Kerner, Otto. *Report of the National Advisory Commission on Civil Disorders.* New York: Bantam Books, 1968.

Kitano, Harry L. *Japanese Americans: The Evolution of a Subculture.* New York: Prentice-Hall, Inc., 1969.

Kronus, Sidney. *The Black Middle Class.* Columbus: Charles E. Merrill, 1970.

Lee, Alfred McClung. *Multivalent Man.* New York: Braziller, 1964.

Leggett, John C. *Class, Race and Labor.* London and New York: Oxford University Press, 1968.

Lenski, Gerhard E. "Status Crystalization: A Non-Vertical Dimension of Social Status," *American Sociological Review* 19 (August, 1954): 405-413.

_____. *Power and Privilege.* New York: McGraw Hill, 1966. Chapter 12.

Lieberson, Stanley. "Stratification and Ethnic Groups," in Edward O. Laumann (ed.) *Social Stratification: Research and Theory for the 1970s.* Indianapolis: Bobbs-Merrill Company, 1970. pp. 172-181.

Lewin, Kurt. "Leaders From the Periphery," in Kurt Lewin. *Resolving Social Conflicts.* New York: Harper, 1948.

Marx, Gary T. *Protest and Prejudice.* New York: Harper and Row, 1967.

Melemore, Dale S. "The Origins of Mexican American Subordination in Texas," *Social Science Quarterly* 53 (March, 1973): 656-670.

Mercer, Jane R. "IQ: The Lethal Label," *Psychology Today* 6 (September, 1972): 44-47 and 95-97.

Mittlebach, Frank G. and Joan W. Moore. "Ethnic Endogamy: The Case of Mexican Americans," *American Journal of Sociology* 74 (July, 1968): 50-62.

Moore, Joan W. "Colonialism: The Case of the Mexican Americans," *Social Problems* 17 (Spring, 1970): 463-472.

Moore, Joan W. *Mexican Americans.* New Jersey: Prentice-Hall, 1970.

Morris, Richard T. and Raymond J. Murphy. "A Paradigm for the Study of Class Consciousness," *Sociology and Social Research* 50 (April, 1966): 297-313.

Moynihan, Daniel P. "The Schism in Black America," *The Public Interest* 27 (Spring, 1972): 3-24.

Murphy, Raymond J. and James M. Watson. *The Structure of Discontent: The Relationship Between Social Structure, Grievance and Support for the Los Angeles Riot.* University of California at Los Angeles: Institute of Government and Public Affairs, 1967 (MR-92).

Noel, Donald. "A Theory of the Origins of Ethnic Stratification," *Social Problems* 16 (Fall, 1968): 157-172.

Olsen, Marvin E. "Power Perspectives on Stratification and Race Relations," in Marvin E. Olsen (ed.) *Power in Societies.* New York: Macmillan, 1970.

Parker, Seymour and Robert J. Kleiner. *Mental Illness in the Urban Negro Cummunity.* New York: Free Press, 1966.

Penalosa, Fernando. "The Changing Mexican-American in Southern California," *Sociology and Social Research* 51 (July, 1967): 405-417.

Purcell, Theodore V. "The Hopes of Negro Workers for their Children," in Arthur B. Shostak and William Gomberg (eds.). *Blue Collar World: Studies of the American Worker.* Englewood Cliffs, New Jersey: Printice-Hall, 1964.

Rainwater, Lee. "Crucible of Identity," *Daedulus* 95 (1966): 172-216.

Ransford, H. Edward. *Negro Participation in Civil Rights Activity and Violence.* University of California at Los Angeles Doctoral Dissertation. Ann Arbor, Michigan: University Microfilms, Inc., 1966.

Ransford, H. Edward. "Skin Color, Life Chances and Anti-White Attitudes," *Social Problems* 18 (Fall, 1970): 164-178.

Ransford, H. Edward. "Blue Collar Anger: Reactions to Student and Black Protest," *American Sociological Review* 37 (June, 1972): 333-346.

Rosenberg, Morris and Roberta G. Simmons. *Black and White Self Esteem: The Urban School Child.* Washington, D.C.: American Sociological Association. Arnold and Caroline Rose Monograph Series in Sociology, 1972.

Rodman, Hyman. *Lower Class Families: The Culture of Poverty in Negro Trinidad.* New York: Oxford University Press, 1971.

Rose, Arnold M. "Race and Ethnic Relations," chapter in Robert K. Merton and Robert A. Nisbet (eds.) *Contemporary Social Problems.* New York: Harcourt, Brace, 1961.

Scanzoni, John H. *The Black Family in Modern Society*. Boston: Allyn and Bacon, 1971.

Schafer, Walter E., Carol Olexa and Kenneth Polk. "Programmed for Social Class: Tracking in the High School," *Transaction* 7 (October, 1970): 39-46 and 63.

Sexton, Patricia and Brendan Sexton. *Blue Collars and Hard-Hats: The Working Class and the Future of Politics*. New York: Vintage, 1971.

Shibutani, Tamotsu and Kian M. Kawn. *Ethnic Stratification*. New York: Macmillan, 1965.

Siegel, Paul M. "Occuaptional Prestige in the Negro Subculture," in Edward O. Laumann (ed.) *Social Stratification: Research and Theory for the 1970s*. Indianapolis and New York: The Bobbs-Merrill Co., 1970.

Sorokin, Pitirim A. *Society, Culture and Personality*. New York: Harper and Row, 1947. Pp. 276-310.

Steiner, Stan. *La Raza: The Mexican Americans*. New York: Harper and Row, 1969.

TenHouten, Warren D. "The Black Family: Myth and Reality," *Psychiatry* 2 (May, 1970).

Tumin, Melvin M. *Comparative Perspectives on Race Relations*. Boston: Little, Brown and Company, 1969.

U.S. Bureau of the Census. *Current Population Reports*. Series P-23, No. 39, "Differences Between Incomes of White and Negro Families by Work Experience of Wife and Region: 1970, 1969, and 1959," Washington, D.C.: U.S. Government Printing Office, 1971.

U.S. Bureau of the Census. *Current Population Reports*. Series P-23, No. 42, "The Social and Economic Status of the Black Population in the United States, 1971," Washington, D.C.:U.S. Government Printing Office, 1972.

U.S. Bureau of the Census. *Current Population Reports*. Series P-20, No. 238, "Selected Characteristics of Persons and Families of Mexican, Puerto Rican, and Other Spanish Origin: March, 1972," Washington, D.C.: U.S. Government Printing Office, 1972.

U.S. Bureau of the Census. *Current Population Reports*. Series P-23, No. 46, "The Social and Economic Status of the Black Population in the United States, 1972," Washington, D.C.: U.S. Government Printing Office, 1973.

Warren, Donald I. and Patrick C. Easto. "White Stratification Theory and Black Reality: A Neglected Problem of American Sociology," paper presented at the 67th Annual Meeting of the American Sociological Association, August 28-31, 1972.

Williams, Jay R. *Social Stratification and the Negro American: An Exploration of Some Problems in Social Class Measurement*. Unpublished Doctoral Dissertation, Duke University, 1968.

Wrong, Dennis H. "How Important is Social Class?", in Irving Howe (ed.) *The World of the Blue Collar Worker*. New York: Quadrangle Books, 1972.

van den Berghe, Pierre L. *Race and Racism*. New York: Wiley, 1967.